Language, Society and Power

Language, Society and Power is the essential introductory text to studying language in a variety of social contexts.

This book examines the ways language functions, how it influences thought and how it varies according to age, ethnicity, class and gender. It considers whether representations of people and their language matter, explores how identity is constructed and performed, and considers the creative potential of language in the media, politics and everyday talk.

This fourth edition has been completely revised to include recent developments in theory and research and offers the following features:

- a range of new and engaging international examples drawn from everyday life — including material from social media and newspapers, cartoons, YouTube and television
- two new chapters which cover Linguistic Landscapes, including signs, graffiti and the internet; and Global Englishes, exploring variation in and attitudes to English around the world
- updated and expanded student research projects and further reading sections for each chapter
- a brand new companion website that includes video and audio clips, links to articles and further reading for students and professors.

Language, Society and Power is a must-read for students of English language and linguistics, media, communication, cultural studies, sociology and psychology.

Annabelle Mooney is a Reader in the Department of Media, Culture and Language at the University of Roehampton, UK.

Betsy Evans is an Associate Professor of Linguistics at the University of Washington, USA.

Praise for this edition:

'*Language Society and Power* stands out as the most exciting and unique introductory textbook available, primarily because it engages students where they live – this is language in the real world! The latest fourth edition offers a terrific range of recent case studies from around the globe. Each chapter leads students directly into theoretical ideas and analytic strategies applicable to their own research projects. The new addition of a companion multi-media website offers both students and professors a wide range of materials for lively and interactive classroom use.'

Brenda Farnell, *University of Illinois, USA*

'Since it was first published, this book has been the clearest and most student-friendly introduction to sociolinguistics I know of. This new edition brings the discussion up to date, including the role of the internet and social media, and the place of English in the world. I strongly recommend it to any teacher of sociolinguistics.'

Jonathan White, *Dalarna University, Sweden*

'The latest edition of Language, Society and Power offers an accessible, up-to-date and entertaining introduction to key concepts in sociolinguistics. It is sure – like its predecessors – to become an instant reading-list favourite.'

Mike Pearce, *University of Sunderland, UK*

'This new edition of Language, Society and Power is a great read and a fact-filled foundation for study. The story of the social lives of language is described with skill, humor, and artistry. In this new edition the story is brought up to date and expanded to cover Englishes around the world. It's a fascinating look at a twenty-first-century phenomenon.'

Richard F. Young, *University of Wisconsin-Madison, USA*

Language, Society and Power

An Introduction

Fourth Edition

Annabelle Mooney and Betsy Evans

Routledge
Taylor & Francis Group

LONDON AND NEW YORK

First published 1999
Second edition published 2004
Third edition published 2011

This fourth edition published 2015
by Routledge
2 Park Square, Milton Park, Abingdon, Oxon OX14 4RN

and by Routledge
711 Third Avenue, New York, NY 10017

Routledge is an imprint of the Taylor & Francis Group, an informa business

British Library Cataloguing-in-Publication Data
A catalogue record for this book is available from the British Library

Library of Congress Cataloging-in-Publication Data
Language, society and power : an introduction / edited by Annabelle Mooney and Betsy Evans. -- Fourth edition.

pages cm

1. Language and languages. 2. Sociolinguistics. I. Mooney, Annabelle, 1974- II. Evans, Betsy, 1966-

P40.L29987 2015

306.44--dc23

2014028169

ISBN: 978-0-415-73999-3 (hbk)
ISBN: 978-0-415-74000-5 (pbk)
ISBN: 978-1-315-73352-4 (ebk)

Typeset in Akzidenz Grotesk
by Saxon Graphics Ltd, Derby
Printed in Great Britain by Ashford Colour Press Ltd, Gosport, Hants

For Debbie and Jen

Contents

List of figures   xii
List of images   xiii
List of tables   xiv
List of newspapers, magazines and news outlets   xv
Transcription conventions   xvi
Preface to the fourth edition   xvii
Preface to the third edition   xix
Preface to the second edition   xxi
Preface to the first edition   xxiii
Acknowledgements   xxv

1   Language?   **1**
   1.1   Introduction   1
   1.2   Why study language?   2
   1.3   What is language?   3
      1.3.1   Language: a system   3
      1.3.2   Language: a system with variation   5
      1.3.3   The potential to create new meanings   6
   1.4   The 'rules' of language: prescription vs description   7
   1.5   Language: multiple functions   11
   1.6   Power   13
      1.6.1   Ideology   16
      1.6.2   Interpellation   17
   1.7   Powerful language?   18
   1.8   Summary   18
   Further reading   19

2   Language thought and representation   **20**
   2.1   Introduction   20
   2.2   Language as a system of representation   21
      2.2.1   Different kinds of language   22
      2.2.2   Signs and structure   24
   2.3   The Sapir-Whorf hypothesis   26
      2.3.1   Linguistic diversity   26
      2.3.2   Dyirbal   27
      2.3.3   Linguistic relativism and determinism   28
      2.3.4   Colour   30

2.4	One language many worlds	31
2.5	A model for analysing language	35
	2.5.1 Transitivity	36
2.6	'Political correctness'	38
2.7	Summary	40
	Further reading	40

3 Language and politics — **42**

3.1	Introduction	42
3.2	What is 'politics'?	43
3.3	Politics and ideology	43
3.4	Three persuasive strategies	45
3.5	Grass roots politics: introducing more linguistic tools	45
	3.5.1 Contrasts	46
	3.5.2 Three part lists and parallelism	46
	3.5.3 Pronouns	49
	3.5.4 Presupposition	49
	3.5.5 Metaphor and intertextuality	50
3.6	Words and weapons: the politics of war	51
	3.6.1 Toys and ideology	54
3.7	Extending metaphor	55
	3.7.1 Student as customer	57
3.8	Silly citizenship	59
	3.8.1 'That's just my opinion!'	60
3.9	Summary	62
	Further reading	62

4 Language and the media — **63**

4.1	Introduction	63
4.2	Mass media	64
4.3	Manufacture of consent	64
	4.3.1 Filtering the facts	65
4.4	Semantic unity	69
	4.4.1 Strategic communication	70
4.5	News values	72
	4.5.1 Actors and events	72
4.6	Experts and the news	74
4.7	News online	77
	4.7.1 Presenting news on the internet	79
4.8	New ways of 'doing' news: Twitter and the citizen journalist	82
4.9	Summary	85
	Further reading	85

5 Linguistic landscapes — **86**

5.1	Introduction	86
5.2	Defining the linguistic landscape	86
	5.2.1 Space and meaning	90

	5.2.2 Different kinds of signs	92
	5.2.3 Top down and bottom up as a continuum	93
5.3	Signs and multilingualism and power	96
	5.3.1 Invisible language	97
5.4	Signs and ideology	99
5.5	Transgressive signs: graffiti	101
5.6	Online landscapes	102
	5.6.1 YouTube	102
	5.6.2 Twitter	104
	5.6.3 Memes	105
5.7	Summary	107
	Further reading	107
6	**Language and gender**	**108**
6.1	Introduction	108
6.2	What is gender?	108
6.3	Inequality at the lexical level	110
	6.3.1 Marked terms	110
	6.3.2 'Generic' he	111
	6.3.3 Sexism in word order	112
	6.3.4 Semantic derogation	115
6.4	Differences in language use: doing being a woman or a man	116
	6.4.1 Tag questions	117
6.5	Gossip	118
	6.5.1 Gossip and men	120
	6.5.2 Features of men's talk	122
6.6	Gender and power	123
	6.6.1 Do women talk more than men?	124
	6.6.2 Silence is golden	126
6.7	Gendered talk: performing identity	126
	6.7.1 'Dude'	126
	6.7.2 Local ideologies: gender and sexuality	128
6.8	Summary	130
	Further reading	130
7	**Language and ethnicity**	**132**
7.1	Introduction	132
7.2	What do we mean by 'ethnicity'?	133
7.3	Ethnicity, the nation state and multilingualism	134
7.4	Racism and representations of ethnicity	135
	7.4.1 Reclaiming terms	136
7.5	Ethnolect	137
	7.5.1 'Wogspeak'	137
	7.5.2 African American English	139
7.6	Ethnicity and identity	141
	7.6.1 Lumbee English	141
	7.6.2 Gang identity	143

7.7		Discourses of authenticity	146
	7.7.1	Mexican ethnicity	146
	7.7.2	African American ethnicity	148
	7.7.3	Welsh turfing	149
7.8		Consequences for ethnolects	149
	7.8.1	Caribbean English	150
	7.8.2	Australian Aboriginal English	151
7.9		Crossing	153
7.10		Summary	155
		Further reading	155
8		**Language and age**	**157**
8.1		Introduction	157
8.2		What do we mean by age?	158
8.3		Early life stage	159
	8.3.1	Language used to talk to children	159
8.4		Adolescent life stage	160
	8.4.1	What teenagers do	161
	8.4.2	Multiple negation	161
	8.4.3	'Like' as a discourse marker	162
	8.4.4	Computer-mediated communication	164
8.5		Middle life stage	166
8.6		Later life stage	167
	8.6.1	Representations of older people	168
	8.6.2	Self-representation of older people	169
	8.6.3	Language used to talk to older people	171
	8.6.4	Construction of age in a travel agency	173
8.7		The creep of ageism	175
8.8		Summary	176
		Further reading	176
9		**Language, class and symbolic capital**	**177**
9.1		Introduction	177
9.2		What is social class?	177
9.3		Attitudes to class	179
	9.3.1	Class as other	180
	9.3.2	'Chavspeak'	181
	9.3.3	Pittsburghese	182
9.4		Linguistic variation	183
	9.4.1	New York City	183
	9.4.2	Norwich	184
	9.4.3	Glasgow	187
	9.4.5	London	188
9.5		Social networks	190
9.6		Communities of practice	191
9.7		Symbolic capital	193
9.8		Revising the British social class model	194
	9.8.1	Power and access to symbolic capital	196

9.9   Summary   196
Further reading   197

10 Global Englishes   **198**
10.1   Introduction   198
10.2   What does global English mean?   199
10.3   Learning English   202
        10.3.1 Two models   202
        10.3.2 'Lingua franca core'   206
10.4   Inside the inner circle   207
10.5   'Singlish'   208
10.6   Indian English   210
10.7   Pidgins and creoles   211
10.8   Linguistic marketplace   213
        10.8.1 Call centres and English   214
10.9   Linguistic imperialism   214
10.10   What do language varieties mean in the global
        context?   217
        10.10.1 Discourse in advertising and linguistic
                landscapes   218
10.11   Summary   219
Further reading   219

11 Projects   **220**
11.1   Introduction   220
11.2   Things to bear in mind with data collection   221
        11.2.1 What is data?   221
        11.2.2 Transcribing   221
        11.2.3 Data analysis   222
11.3   Projects   223
11.4   Research resources   230
        11.4.1 Where to find published research   230
        11.4.2 Other resources   230
Further reading   231

Glossary   233
References   241
Index   258

Figures

1.1	Factors involved in communication, Jakobson	11
1.2	Six functions of communication, Jakobson	12
2.1	Saussure's model of the sign	21
2.2	Syntagmatic and paradigmatic axes	35
7.1	Vowel length by ethnicity and HRT (Kiesling 2005)	138
7.2	Vowel length by speaker	138
7.3	Percentage of rhoticity for each speaker according to topic of discussion	142
8.1	Usage of 'like' as a discourse marker among Canadian youth	163
9.1	Percentage of use of 'r' by clerks in three department stores (Saks, Macy's and S. Klein)	184
9.2	Percentage use of non-standard (ng) by Norwich speakers according to social class	185
9.3	Jocks' and burnouts' use of negative concord	192
9.4	Percent use of negative concord by six subcategories of jocks and burnouts	192
10.1	Kachru's Circles of English	199
10.2	McArthur's Circle of World English	202

Images

2.1	'Eskimo'	27
3.1	Degree Mart	58
5.1	Bilingual Welsh sign	88
5.2	Official no smoking sign	88
5.3	Hand-drawn no smoking sign	89
5.4	No parking sign	91
5.5	Woof Woof, Staffordshire Wildlife Trust	94
5.6	Ladies' bathroom sign	94
5.7	Stop sign	95
5.8	High fives, Ryan Laughlin	96
5.9	Mondo macho	98
5.10	Doge graffiti	106
8.1	Plastic surgery advertisement	175
10.1	Learning English	203

Tables

1.1	Prescriptive and descriptive activity	10
3.1	Examples of Nukespeak	52
4.1	Media characteristics	78
4.2	Comparison of two news stories	80
6.1	Gendered order preference in personal binomials	113
6.2	Order of personal cojuncts in relation to power	114
7.1	Features of AAE	140
7.2	Semiotic resources for indicating group membership in Norteñas and Sureñas	145
7.3	Lexical items in CAE and SE	150
8.1	Percent of multiple negation, according to gender and age in Sydney	161
8.2	Lexical collocates of elderly with the highest joint frequencies among the top 50 collocates	168
9.1	Percentage use of non-standard (ng) by Norwich speakers according to social class	185
9.2	Percentage of use of non-standard (ng) by female and male Norwich speakers in four contexts	186
9.3	Question categories for Great British Class Survey	194
9.4	Summary of social classes	195
10.1	'To be' in the negative with contraction options	207
10.2	Examples of Indian English	211
10.3	Some features of Hawai'i Creole English (HCE)	212
10.4	Language most frequently spoken at home among Chinese resident population in Singapore aged five and over	216

Newspapers, magazines and news outlets

ABC News	The Australian Broadcasting Commission (publicly funded) or the American Broadcasting Commission (private company)
The Atlantic	A monthly US magazine with a website
BBC News	The British Broadcasting Commission (publicly funded)
Daily Mail	A UK daily newspaper
Faking News	An Indian satirical news site
Fiji Times	A daily English language newspaper from Fiji
The Guardian	A UK daily newspaper
Huffington Post	An American-based news website
The Independent	A UK daily newspaper
London Evening standard	A free London daily newspaper
The Mirror	A UK daily newspaper
Montreal Gazette	A daily English language newspaper from Montreal, Canada
MSNBC	American news and current events television channel with a website
The Occupied Times	An online publication
Slate	A US online magazine
The Straits Times	A daily English language newspaper from Singapore
The Telegraph	A UK daily newspaper
The Times of India	An Indian English language newspaper
Washington Post	A US daily newspaper from Washington DC

Transcription conventions

Detailed transcription conventions are as follows:

{laughter}	non verbal information
xxxxxx*{laughing}*	paralinguistic information qualifying underlined utterance
[.....]	beginning/end of simultaneous speech
(xxxxxxxx)	inaudible material
(......)	doubt about accuracy of transcription
'......'	speaker quotes/uses words of others
CAPITALS	increased volume
%......%	decreased volume
bold print	speaker emphasis
>...<	faster speed of utterance deliver
/	rising intonation
yeah:::::	lengthened sound
-	incomplete word or utterance
=	latching on (no gap between speakers' utterances)
(.)	micropause
(-)	pause shorter than one second
(1); (2)	timed pauses (longer than one second)

Preface to the fourth edition

In this fourth edition, we have sought to maintain the structure and focus of previous editions while making some revisions in response to the changing nature of linguistic research and feedback from our students and readers. We have added a new chapter on Linguistic Landscapes, focusing on the language and semiotics found in both the physical and virtual worlds. We have also included a chapter on Global Englishes, to highlight the variation in meaning, use and perceived values of Englishes used around the world.

This book introduces readers to some of the key concepts and issues in the exploration of language, society and power. We have maintained some of the analytic tools used in previous editions as these approaches are applicable to a range of texts, utterances and linguistic use despite constant changes to the way language is used in the world. The issues related to language, society and power are so complex and extensive it's difficult to give every issue comprehensive treatment. As such there is much more that could be covered in each chapter. We have chosen examples from scholars in the field that we hope are both accessible and illuminating. It is impossible to do justice to this research in the space available, however, and we encourage the consultation of the original work where possible. We have also maintained the tradition of including classic texts and studies while also using more recent research and approaches to show continuity and change in the field. Ongoing debates about standard language, sexism and discrimination on the basis of age or ethnicity all show that while a great deal of research has identified the key issues and questions, and provided solutions, some ideological views are extremely firmly entrenched. Ideology, the construction and maintenance of power and the performance of identity remain central in this edition. These topics recur throughout the book as they underpin our central concerns.

Chapters 1 and 2 introduce ideology and representation as well as some tools for analysing linguistic meaning at the level of the sign and sentence. We focus on the difference between description and prescription in Chapter 1 to make clear the connection between power and language ideologies. The attitudes that people hold about language use are intensely ideological and this can be seen in this and later chapters. Chapter 3 examines language and politics. While we touch on issues that are associated with routine meanings of 'politics' the emphasis in this edition is on the notion that a wide range of issues are, in fact, political. Thus, we employ a broad understanding of politics and cover topics such as the ideologies suggested by children's toys and the politics inherent in the relationship between students and higher education providers.

Chapter 4 focuses on mass news media. While this might seem to be a narrow focus, given changes in technology, especially in relation to social media and the World Wide Web, taking this approach allows us to explore various dimensions of representation, ideology and the construction and reception of news. Chapter 5 is a new chapter exploring linguistic landscapes. This has become an important area of research in sociolinguistics and because it examines our everyday environment it forces us to consider important aspects of ideology and how we are positioned by it through the use of signs, language and other semiotics.

The following chapters deal with the classic sociolinguistic variables of gender, ethnicity, age and class. We have tried to balance coverage of classic work in these fields with new issues and research in order to show that while identity is always performed it is nevertheless understood through ideologies that expect identity to be essential and fixed. Chapter 10 deals with Global Englishes. As with all other linguistic variation, the effect of language ideology, power and politics are significant here. While linguists are clear that all varieties of English are equal as languages, the political, social and ideological structure of the world means that not all varieties are treated equally.

Chapter 11 contains some resources for further exploration, including suggestions for student projects and lists of texts and websites that may assist in seeking out and analysing language in relation to power and ideology.

In keeping with the last edition, a book symbol 📖 is included against texts that appear in the companion Reader to this text. We have also included 🌐 to indicate where material is included on the website. In addition, suggestions for further reading are included at the end of each chapter and we encourage consultation of works cited in the chapters as well. We hope readers find these resources, and the issues covered in the text, interesting, illuminating and challenging.

Preface to the third edition

In this third edition, we have sought to continue the traditions so well established in the first and second editions. The course, out of which this book grew, is still running as required for students on the English Language and Linguistics programme at Roehampton University. While we have kept the structure and tone of previous editions, there have been some changes. The previous editions were authored by academics who had at some time taught at Roehampton. We have kept to this in as much as all of the authors of the present edition have either worked or studied at Roehampton. Indeed, some have done both. What we all have in common is an enthusiasm for the course.

As previously, authors come from all over the world. While we have continued to include material about global Englishes, in this edition we have sought to include examples from other languages. We have also tried to include material from internet sources. The internet is indeed a global phenomenon; we hope you will be able to find your own 'local' examples of the kind of material which we have indicated.

This book introduces students to the central concepts around the topics of language, society and power. Since the previous edition, things have changed in the world of sociolinguistics, and we have tried to capture some of these changes as well as indicating where the field has come from. It is our belief that it is impossible to understand some of the current issues in the field of sociolinguistics without having a sense of how the various topics developed. Certainly the material is only indicative of these changes; we have tried to keep material accessible to students without a background in linguistics, while also wanting to whet the appetite of students and encourage them to take forward their studies in the area.

The importance of language is something that will never go away. The increasingly mediated nature of contemporary society means that it is important to be aware of issues related to representation and ideology. This critical stance is common in many disciplines; we understand it as crucial for meaningful engagement with the world in all areas. Because of this, in the first four chapters, we spend time on the concepts of ideology and representation.

The first two chapters set out our approach to language, society and power. The tools and concepts introduced in these chapters recur throughout the book. While we have indicated, by way of cross-referencing, particular topic links between chapters, the core ideas of ideology and discourse are relevant throughout the text. We have kept to the structure of the book from previous editions with some minor changes. In the chapters on politics (Chapter 3) and media (Chapter 4) we have worked with a broad understanding of these concepts, in order to highlight the importance of power and the ideological choices that are made with any representation. We hope that such a broad focus will assist in developing critical skills and the 'making strange' of the familiar. The other topics we cover were chosen as we understand them to be the 'classic' sociolinguistic variables. We start with gender (Chapter 5), moving on to ethnicity (Chapter 6), age (Chapter 7), and class (Chapter 8). While each of these are areas of change in terms of the questions they ask, they have all, to some degree, also become implicated in a more general discussion of identity. We cover this in Chapter 9 and hope that the topics and issues from previous chapters will be borne in mind when thinking about identity. The final chapter has been altered slightly to address the issue of standard languages and attitudes towards language. While standard English is still an important area, and is included in this section, we thought it important to highlight the work conducted in the area of language attitudes. Further, we see this discussion as bringing the discussion back to where we start, that is, the question of what 'language' means and what ideas we already have about language.

A new addition is the projects chapter. We have sought to provide ideas for investigation of real language, building on the areas covered in the chapters. Included in this chapter is material to encourage students to think about research, issues around gathering and analysing data, as well as information about ongoing research and resources that may be useful in exploring some of the concepts introduced in this book.

As there is a companion Reader for the textbook (*Language, Society and Power: A Reader*, Routledge, 2011), we have indicated in the Further Reading sections any texts which are included in the Reader. The book icon is placed next to these readings.

Many of the changes have come about as a result of teaching the course. We would like to thank the students we have taught for their engagement, the sharing of their own thoughts and language, and their questions. The latter especially have helped us enormously in the writing of this book. Part of the reason for continuing to address our readers as 'you' is to try to capture the dialogue that we experience when teaching the course. Thinking about language is, for us, something which benefits from conversation, discussion and debate. We all have our own biases (something you should bear in mind when reading the book); reflecting on these in the company of others is, for us, an essential part of learning. In this spirit, as authors, we have benefited from the input of a number of people. Thus, alterations, at various stages, were prompted by incredibly helpful suggestions from current users of the second edition as well as reviewers of the draft of this edition. This detailed and constructive advice has been very useful and we are grateful for it.

We hope you enjoy thinking about language. While it can be challenging to develop the critical skills we believe are central to working with language, there is also a great deal of fun to be had.

Preface to the second edition

The first edition of *Language, Society and Power* was published in 1999, when the majority of the contributing authors were lecturers at Roehampton University of Surrey (then Roehampton Institute London). The book had evolved out of an identically titled course on which we had all taught, and which is still running as a required course for students on the English Language and Linguistics programme, and as a popular option for students in other departments. Since that first edition, several of us have moved to other universities and colleges, but we have all maintained an interest in studying language as a social entity. Thus, even though producing this second edition has required a great deal more co-ordination than the last time, we were all willing to be involved in revising and updating a project which has not only been enjoyable for us but which has also had a favourable reception from its intended audience.

The second edition has remained faithful to the first in many ways. We have maintained a focus on English (primarily British and American varieties). The first edition's glossary of terms potentially new to the reader (printed in bold in each chapter) has been retained but also updated. We have continued to make use of personal reference (something not typically found in academic texts), addressing the reader as *you*, and referring to ourselves as *I* or *we* as appropriate. We have also continued to assume that our readers are generally not, or not yet, specialists in the areas of language study and linguistics, and therefore need an introduction to the kinds of topics which feed into a broader examination of language and society. As such, the book does not offer comprehensive coverage of every possible issue within this vast subject area but, instead, provides a stepping-stone to exploring and thinking about at least some of them. Thus, each of the chapters deals with a topic that has been the subject of academic sociolinguistic investigation, and is supplemented with references to useful reading and other sources of material. There are substantial Activities throughout the text to help the reader engage more actively with the ideas being presented.

We have maintained the distinctive authorial 'voices' of the first edition, since they make for a more varied and interesting approach to analysis and discussion. One of the things that the majority of the chapters do have in common, though, is that they seek to interpret the ways in which language and language issues can be deconstructed to reveal underlying ideologies, or beliefs. While all of the chapters have a solid academic grounding, it is important to bear in mind that any interpretation of what people do and say is necessarily going to contain a certain measure of bias. Thus, while we can justifiably analyse a newspaper headline about immigration, for example, and state that its 'slant' reveals an affiliation to politically left- or right-wing principles, it must be remembered that any such approach is in itself ideologically determined: it reveals the analyst's belief that language is not a neutral tool of communication but instead a channel for how we see and construct the world around us. This tenet will become clearer as you read through the text.

Each chapter of this book deals with a different area of language, although there are connections between many of the chapter topics. We have designed the book so that it can be read from cover to cover as a continuous text, but also so that individual chapters can stand alone and be read in their own right. We have divided chapters into subsections, partly to indicate the structure clearly with subtitles and partly to help you find the sections you need to read if you don't need to read the whole chapter.

Chapter 1 interrogates the notion of 'language', and raises some of the underlying questions and ideas that will be relevant as you move into the other chapters. Chapters 2–4 all concentrate on the ideological properties of language, and on how it can be used to influence the ways in which people think and behave. Chapter 2 is concerned with the connections between language, thought and representation, and considers the extent to which language can be said to shape and perpetuate our worldviews. Chapter 3 moves on from the conclusions of Chapter 2 to consider whether, and how, language can be used in politics, and in other fields, to persuade people of particular points of view. Chapter 4 considers how language is used, and to what effects, in media such as newspapers and television with particular reference to news reporting and advertising. Chapters 5–7 deal with language use in connection with particular subgroups within a population. The terms or 'labels' that can be or are applied to members of those groups, and the effect of those labels, are considered. The chapters also look at the kinds of language choices members of those groups sometimes make. Chapter 5 focuses on language and gender, Chapter 6 deals with language and ethnicity and Chapter 7 with language and age. Chapter 8 considers how a further set of subgroup divisions, namely those which go into the construction of social class, affect language use. The last three chapters, 9–11, are concerned with attitudes towards language, and the relationship between language and identity. Chapter 9 deals with language and social identity, and Chapter 10 with the debates that surround the use of standard English. Chapter 11 provides a conclusion to the whole book with an overview of attitudes towards language.

Finally, we hope that you will enjoy reading and using this second edition, and that it will add another dimension to how you think about language and language use. We have certainly enjoyed putting it together, and we hope that at least some measure of our passion and interest in this everyday but extraordinary faculty will prove infectious!

Preface to the first edition

This book is based on a course of the same name that runs in the English Language and Linguistics Programme at Roehampton Institute London, and on which all the authors have taught. It began life as Language, Power, Politics and Sexuality, a short (five-week) introduction to language issues for students studying literature. Over the years the course has grown as interest in language study has grown, and it is now an introductory course for students studying language and linguistics, while continuing in popularity with students of literature. Many of the students taking the course are combining their studies with subjects such as sociology, media studies, women's studies, education and history, where they find that the issues raised are also relevant.

In preparing this book, we have assumed no prior knowledge of linguistics. We hope that students taking courses on the social and political dimensions of language use will find this a useful foundation text. Students of disciplines that include the study of language use, discourse and ideology, power relations, education, the rights of minority groups and equal opportunities should also find this a helpful text. Learners of English may find this a useful route to a better understanding of language use. Since we see language use as being central to many, or most, human activities, we hope that students studying apparently unrelated disciplines may also find it helpful to have a book which covers the range of issues we deal with here. And we have tried to make the text appropriate and interesting for the general reader.

The ideas covered in this book have been explored and developed with groups of students since the early 1980s. They are presented here as eleven topics, currently covered in a modular course on a week-by-week basis. Although they may look it, the topics are not discrete, but have overlapping themes and common threads which we have tried to bring out. Nor are they exclusive. As you read, you may well think of other areas of language use which are worthy of investigation or consideration, such as the relationship between language and health, or language and the law. Issues such as these are not omitted because we think that they are unimportant but because in a book of this length there is not space to cover everything. We hope what we have covered will assist your thinking about the relationship between language and the different dimensions of the societies in which we live.

The authors have taught as a team the course from which this book was generated. We felt that as a group we shared common values both about the topics we taught and our approach to teaching, and that this provided us with a solid foundation for writing this book also as a team. We distributed the topics amongst the six of us, according to our areas of special interest, and met regularly to review the drafts of our chapters and to discuss revisions. Our aim was to produce a coherent text that still reflected the ideas and writing styles of individual team members. To some extent, the different 'voices' of the authors should still be apparent.

Amongst other decisions we had to make as a team of authors, we had to decide on how we would use pronouns such as *I, we* and *you*. We could, for example, have decided to write impersonally, and avoid using personal pronouns as much as possible, which is quite common in academic writing. We had to decide whether we should refer to ourselves in the chapters as *I* (the individual writing the chapter) or *we* (the team of writers). We also had to decide whether we should use *you* to address our readers. The conventional, impersonal academic style is often criticised by people with an interest in the social and political functions of language because, as is discussed in Chapter 3, it can be used to make ideas seem less accessible than they need be, and to increase the apparent status of the writers by making them seem 'cleverer' than the readers. In the end, we felt the most honest and sensible thing to do would be to use *we* to refer to the team of authors, to acknowledge the input we have all had in each other's thinking and writing, but to use *I* if we write about our personal experiences. We have addressed you the readers as *you*.

Throughout the book we concentrate on the English language, although we occasionally use another language to illustrate a particular point. The main varieties of English looked at are British and American English.

There is a glossary of terms with brief explanations at the back of the book. Words which appear in the glossary are printed in bold the first time they occur in a chapter. You will also find at the end of each chapter recommended further reading which you can follow up if you want to learn more about a topic. If you want to check whether a topic is covered in this book, and where, the index at the back gives page numbers.

We have included Activities throughout the text. Some ask you to reflect on your own use of, or feelings about, language. Some ask you to talk to other people, to elicit their language use or thoughts on certain issues. Some require you to collect data from other sources around you, such as the newspapers or television. Some you will be able to do alone, and some need group discussion. One of the main reasons we have included Activities is that we believe that the ideas we are discussing in this book really come alive when you begin to look for them in the language which goes on around you. We have seen students' attitudes change from mild interest, or even a lack of interest, to absolute fascination when they have started to investigate language use for themselves.

If the ideas we have presented here are ones you have come across before, we hope we have presented them in such a way as to provoke further thought, or make connections you hadn't previously made. If you haven't thought about some of the ideas we raise here before, we hope that you also find them exciting and spend the rest of your life listening to what people say, reading newspapers and watching television commercials differently.

Acknowledgements

As this book is now in its fourth edition, the number of people involved in reaching this point is extensive. We would like to thank Deborah Cameron and Jennifer Coates who designed the course that led to this book. We retain the dedication to them as a tribute to their extensive work in establishing the programme and the course. We hope to have continued the traditions they established in a way that would please them.

Our students on all our courses have also provided invaluable feedback and information about particular issues and also in terms of giving us a clearer idea of our audience. We'd like to thank readers who have provided reports and reviews as well as those who contacted us about the book. While it hasn't always been possible to cover what was requested, this input has been very useful in honing our ideas about content, structure and focus. Our editor at Routledge, Nadia Seemungal, has been unstinting in her enthusiasm, support and patience.

Both of us have benefited from support from our colleagues, family, friends and readers. They have our heartfelt thanks. We have also looked to previous editions for material, ideas and sensibility; this has been of great importance and we would like to thank our colleagues who worked on these texts. Particular thanks to Dr Christopher Marlow for giving us a home and providing inspiration and support at a critical stage.

The authors and publishers would like to thank the following for permission to reproduce copyright material:

Image 2.1 on p. 27 is reproduced with the kind permission of Russell Hugo © 2014 russ@portnw.com.

Image 3.1 on p. 58 is reproduced with the kind permission of Russell Hugo © 2014 russ@portnw.com.

Images 5.1 and 5.2 on p. 88 are reproduced under terms of the Open Government Licence v1.0.

Image 5.5 on p. 94 is reproduced with the kind permission of the Staffordshire Wildlife Trust http://www.staffs-wildlife.org.uk/

Image 5.6 on p. 94 is reproduced with the permission of the Orpheum Theatre and Vancouver Civic Theatres.

Image 5.8 on p. 96 is reproduced with the kind permission of Ryan Laughlin © http://rofreg.com

Image 5.10 on p. 106 is reproduced with the kind permission of James Scott.

Example 7.8 on p. 154 is reproduced with the kind permission of Professor Shalini Shankar and the American Anthropological Association. Shankar, S. (2008). 'Speaking like a model minority: "FOB" styles, gender, and racial meanings among Desi teens in Silicon Valley', *Journal of Linguistic Anthropology*, 18 (2): 268–289 at page 274.

Image 10.1 on p. 203 is reproduced with the kind permission of Russell Hugo © 2014 russ@portnw.com.

Figure 10.2 on p. 202 is reproduced with the permission of Cambridge University Press. McArthur, Tom (1987) 'The English languages?' *English Today*, 3 (11): 9–13.

While every effort has been made to trace and contact copyright holders of material used in this volume, the publishers would be grateful to hear from any they were unable to contact.

CHAPTER 1

Language?

1.1	**INTRODUCTION**	**1**
1.2	**WHY STUDY LANGUAGE?**	**2**
1.3	**WHAT IS LANGUAGE?**	**3**
1.4	**THE 'RULES' OF LANGUAGE: PRESCRIPTION VS DESCRIPTION**	**7**
1.5	**LANGUAGE: MULTIPLE FUNCTIONS**	**11**
1.6	**POWER**	**13**
1.7	**POWERFUL LANGUAGE?**	**18**
1.8	**SUMMARY**	**18**

1.1 INTRODUCTION

Even though we use language constantly, we usually take it for granted. When we pay attention to it, it's usually because something has gone wrong, or because we're passionate about the topic or speaker. While we will consider cases where things go wrong, in this book we focus more often on how language works successfully, in common situations, in different ways, for different people. We also consider the effects that language can have, especially in relation to power, representations and control. Before we do this, we need to think about what 'language' is. This is not an easy task. What counts as a language is a political, cultural and technical question. As will be discussed, there are well-established languages that are often not considered to be 'proper' languages by people in general. To make matters even more complicated, individuals don't always use language in the same way. The language we use when we talk to our friends is not the same as the language we use to write a letter of complaint. Language varies depending on the people using it, the task at hand, and the society in which it all takes place. Linguists study language for many different reasons, with various questions that they want to answer. Whatever path this research takes, it always treats language as a system. Studying systems might sound tedious, but linguists do more than that – they describe the systems. Linguists describe the construction of these complex and changing systems, working with examples of language from the everyday world. And this is not just any set of rules for construction – language is a system that enables people to tell jokes, write poetry, make an arrest, sell you washing powder, pay a compliment and wish you good night.

1.2 WHY STUDY LANGUAGE?

It's important to study language because *language matters*. For example, the choice of words to describe a person or event can reveal the attitude of the person writing or speaking. One such example concerns US CIA contractor Edward Snowden, who, in 2013, released classified material relating to British and American surveillance programmes. How he was described in the subsequent media coverage is instructive. Those who saw his actions as bravely exposing secret and harmful state actions call him a 'whistle-blower' or 'patriot'. Those who argue that he was bound to protect the confidentiality of this material label him a 'traitor'. This example shows how one word can serve as a shorthand for a whole argument about and position on Snowden's actions. Paying attention to these choices is part of having a critical awareness of language. This is a skill that this book will help you develop.

Norman Fairclough argues that a 'critical awareness of language ... arises within the normal ways people reflect on their lives as part of their lives' (1999: 73). Such reflection is well worth encouraging; Fairclough argues that the ability to understand how language functions, to think about it in different ways, is crucial to understanding society and other people. Critical awareness isn't important because it makes us more accomplished or more intelligent; there is much more at stake. Fairclough argues that to understand power, persuasion and how people live together, a conscious engagement with language is necessary. That is, critical thinking about language can assist in resisting oppression, protecting the powerless and building a good society. Ferdinand de Saussure, sometimes referred to as the founder of modern linguistics, puts it rather more starkly. He writes: 'in the lives of individuals and societies, speech is more important than anything else. That linguistics should continue to be the prerogative of a few specialists would be unthinkable – everyone is concerned with it in one way or another' (1966: 7). People often say that quibbling over word choice, such as in the Edward Snowden case, is 'just semantics'. But it is much more than this. It's about the meaning of the words used (semantics) but also the context in which the words are used.

Semantics is just one of the areas of linguistics that explores how we understand and construct meaning; there are many others. Some linguists work to describe the construction of word order (**syntax**) or the sounds that make up words (**phonetics**, **phonology** and **morphology**). Looking closely at language can tell us about:

- how our brains understand and process language (psycholinguistics)
- how we learn languages, and so how best to teach them (applied linguistics)
- how social factors (age, gender, class, ethnicity, etc.) affect the way people use language (sociolinguistics)
- how it might be possible to have a realistic conversation with a computer (artificial intelligence)
- what is distinctive about literature and poetry (stylistics)
- how people in different cultures use language to do things (anthropology)
- the relationship between words and meaning and the 'real' world (philosophy)
- whether someone is guilty of a criminal offence (forensic linguistics)
- the structure of non-verbal languages (e.g. sign languages).

This is far from a full account of the various kinds of linguistics. The subfields here are much richer and further reaching than the bullet points suggest. The important thing is to realise that language can be examined in a variety of ways with diverse and specific concerns in mind. It's also important to point out that these areas aren't completely separate. We may want to know something about how brains process language if we're interested in finding good teaching methods, for example. The ways linguists in these areas go about studying language may overlap. For example, the kind of analysis that is done in stylistics will be similar in some ways to the work done by forensic linguistics because there is a similar attention to the detail of language and some of the same tools of analysis are used. In this book, we'll be exploring what language can tell us about people as individuals, as members of groups, and about how people interact with other people. This is called sociolinguistics. The subject of our attention here is the way that language is used in normal life, by all kinds of people, to accomplish all manner of goals.

1.3 WHAT IS LANGUAGE?

As we noted previously, language matters and in this book we'll be exploring the way different groups of people are represented by and use language. To be able to do this, we need to understand how linguists study language and what it means to say that language is a system.

1.3.1 Language: a system

If we look closely at language, we find that it is in fact a rule-governed system. This may make it sound like language is *controlled* by rules that prevent it from changing. However, this is not what we mean by system; we need to be clear about what kind of rules we're talking about. These 'rules' are more like inherent 'building codes' that enable a speaker to use their language. The building codes in language tell users of the language how to combine different parts of that language. This includes inherent building codes about which sounds and words can be combined together. For example, we all know inherently, if English is our first language, that 'ngux' is not a word that is possible in English. The building codes of English sounds (**phonemes**) tell us that we can't have 'ng' at the start of a word. In the same way, if I tell you that I recently bought a 'mert', you would be able to form the question, 'What is a mert?' Even though you don't know what a 'mert' is, if I tell you I bought one this lets you know 'mert' is a noun. You would already know how to make its plural ('merts'). This is because of the building codes in English about where certain kinds of words go in sentences (**syntax**) and how to form plurals (**morphology**). Theoretical linguists work at discovering these building codes for particular languages, including signed languages. Although sign language uses a different **modality**, that is, manual, facial and body gestures, it is comprised of the same components we've described for spoken language. Linguists' research on spoken and signed language can be used to say something about language in general, that is, linguists can come to conclusions about all languages, grouping them according to certain structural criteria and even make arguments about how the language faculty itself works. Linguists don't decide on building codes and then try to make everyone follow them. Rather, linguists examine language to discover what the building codes are that make it work, that is, the things that make communication possible. This means that linguistics is **descriptive** (we'll come back to this important concept). As language changes, new building codes are discovered and described by linguists. Even the variation that sociolinguists examine is systematic: it appears to be amenable to description in terms of building codes.

The set of all the building codes that need to be followed in order to produce well-formed utterances in a language is referred to as 'the grammar' of a language. The theoretical linguist Noam Chomsky made an important distinction between competence in and performance of a grammar. To have **competence** in a language means to have knowledge of the grammar. **Performance** refers to the way individual speakers actually use language. It is possible, therefore, for a speaker to have grammatical competence of a language, but lack **communicative competence** of that same language because they are unaware of rules of social relationships, taboo or other cultural conventions. Knowing how to greet someone or what constitutes appropriate 'small talk' are examples of this competence. Communicative competence has also been called 'sociolinguistic competence' or 'pragmatic competence'.

However, it's not the case that only language has 'rules'. Other systems of communication have inherent 'rules' too. The traffic signal that tells us when it's safe to cross the road is green. Around the world, there are differences in the shape of the light. Some traffic signals include a word like 'walk' or a picture shape that suggests a person moving. The red light (in whatever shape it happens to be) tells pedestrians to stop. This signal varies from place to place. Some countries have a flashing red light, for example, indicating that you shouldn't start crossing the road. While there are differences in the way different countries configure their traffic signals, there is one thing that is the same: the traffic signals can't tell you to 'skip' or to 'watch out for the tiger'. They tell us only about whether or not we can proceed (either on foot or in our car). Even a new combination would not of itself provide a new message. For example, if both red and green lights were illuminated at the same time, you would probably conclude that the light was faulty, not that a new message was being communicated. Such lights are very limited in what they can communicate. The structure of spoken and written language means it is possible to invent new words, exploit existing structures and repurpose existing spoken and written texts. This is true in all manner of contexts, from interaction with friends and family to more public interactions in the realm of politics and media. This key component of human language is called recursivity. This is what makes human language different from other kinds of communication, such as traffic lights.

1.3.2 Language: a system with variation

We tend to talk about English as though it is the same everywhere; but even in one city, the English that people use varies widely. Of course this is true of any language. When we talk about 'a' language, we are referring to something that is rather abstract and elusive. Variation in language is a challenge, as it prompts us to think about how we can classify different varieties in relation to each other. How we choose to classify these varieties can vary according to linguistic and political considerations. We might think that a language variety can be identified geographically, such that everyone in England speaks English, while everyone in the United States speaks American English. But, if you listen to someone from Liverpool in England and then to someone from Brighton, it's clear that there are some important differences.

There are differences in the way that people pronounce words, which varies systematically and often on the basis of geography. Such differences can be dealt with in terms of **accent**. There are other differences between speakers of English in relation to the words they use for particular things (vocabulary) and even the order in which words are placed (syntax); we can talk about this collection of features in terms of **dialect** or **variety**. We will use the neutral term 'variety' because very often non-linguists use the term 'dialect' in a pejorative way. To say, for example, that Australian English is not a variety in its own right but merely a 'dialect' of British English, immediately places Australian English in a subordinate position to British English. Most speakers perceive that different varieties of a language exist on a hierarchy that awards a lot of prestige to those varieties at the top of the hierarchy and very little prestige or even stigmatization to those at the bottom. How decisions are taken about what is 'correct', 'standard' or even attractive and desirable for a language is very often related to power (there are many different kinds of power, a topic that we consider in later chapters). For example, research has shown that speakers of English in Western countries believe that British English is the most correct variety of English in the world (Evans 2005). The most likely reason is that speakers perceive British English to be the 'original' English and others varieties are 'spin-offs' of the original. In addition, the longstanding historical position of the United Kingdom as a powerful country plays a role in this perception. By contrast, Indian English, in spite of it being a first language for some (Sailaja 2009: 2), is not perceived as having the same status as Englishes spoken in the West (The issues of 'world Englishes' are taken up in Chapter 10). As we have described, linguists value all varieties equally regardless of their origins so this perception of a hierarchy of Englishes is not a descriptive one.

1.3.3 The potential to create new meanings

It's not only possible to create new words, it is essential. When new objects are made, for example, we need to know what to call them. In deciding this, we follow the building codes about how to construct an acceptable word in whatever language we're using. It's also possible to use existing words in a new way. For example, US scholars have noticed that the word 'because' has recently been used in a new way (Zimmer, Solomon & Carson 2014). This word has been used in the English language for hundreds of years as a conjunction (usually followed by 'of') as shown in Example 1.1.a.

Example 1.1
a.   The picnic was cancelled *because* of the rain.
b.   The picnic was cancelled because rain.
c.   Fido ate too many biscuits because delicious.

More recently, 'because' has been turning up in sentences as a sort of preposition, as in Examples 1.1.b. and 1.1.c. New uses for old words and changes to the kind of word it is (noun, verb, etc.) are far from unusual. The use of a conjunction as a word to serve new functions, as in the 'because' example, is unusual. This new use is particularly interesting to linguists and they are still studying this new usage in order to ascertain just what the additional linguistic role of 'because' might be.

Very new uses or unconventional uses of language aren't often found in dictionaries. Many people believe that because something cannot be found in 'the dictionary', it's not a legitimate use of the language. However, the lack of a dictionary entry is not evidence for the new word's legitimacy. It is important to understand that dictionaries are descriptive but they are also conservative in that they tend to include new meanings of words only when they have demonstrated some longevity. The Oxford English Dictionary won't amend their content every time you and your friends come up with a new use for a word.

The fact that the role of dictionaries is to describe language and not dictate use is often misunderstood. An online campaign called 'Geek is Good' argues that rather than 'geek' being a negative term for people it should be understood as a positive word. They claim that 'geek' has been mis-defined and that dictionaries are somehow responsible for the negative associations of the word.

> There are dictionaries out there that still look down on geeks and mis-define them as outcasts.
> We think that this is wrong. Where would we be without Geeks?
> They're heroes. Gods. Saviours. At Google, they're the new rock stars.
>
> (http://www.geekisgood.org/)

But the Geek is Good campaign's belief that dictionaries 'mis-define' geek is not quite right. Dictionaries describe how people use the term. It may well be that if the way 'geek' is used changes enough, and for long enough, this change in meaning will be documented. However, the Geek is Good campaign might be pleased to learn that the collocation 'geek chic' has already been recognised by the OED. They define it as:

> geek chic n. a glamorization of the culture and appearance of geeks; the style associated with geeks
>
> (www.oed.com)

The OED didn't change the definition because of someone lobbying them to do so. Dictionaries chart the way that language is used. It is possible, then, that campaigns such as Geek is Good may change the way people use the word 'geek' and so, ultimately, change the meaning described in the OED.

1.4 THE 'RULES' OF LANGUAGE: PRESCRIPTION VS DESCRIPTION

Linguists understand that language change such as new word formation is a fundamental part of language. However, linguists aren't the only people interested in language. Most people have opinions about language and language use. Looking at the letters pages in a newspaper, on blogs or even listening to the radio we notice that people have very strong ideas about language. There may be particular words or expressions that are commented on, perhaps because they cause offence, or because they are considered to be 'grammatically wrong'. For example, Prince Charles, at a British Council launch of a five-year program to preserve 'English English', said: 'People tend to invent all sorts of nouns and verbs and make words that shouldn't be' (*The Times*, 24 March 1995). This is a very common belief among speakers of all languages.

What do you think about these words in Example 1.2? Do you think they are useful additions to English? What do you suppose someone with Prince Charles' point of view would say about them?

Example 1.2
a. ginormous (adjective): bigger than gigantic and bigger than enormous
b. woot (interjection): an exclamation of joy or excitement
c. chillax (verb): chill out/relax, hang out with friends

For linguists, and for **lexicographers** who compile dictionaries, meaning is determined by use. That is, we don't judge a use of a word as 'correct' or 'incorrect' because our concern is mutual understanding. This can be captured more precisely by talking about the difference between **description** and **prescription**. Linguists are concerned with describing what people do with language (description) while people who want to say that a certain use is incorrect are setting down rules for proper language use (prescription), quite apart from what people actually do. Prescriptivists have very strong ideas about how language should be used. They have clear ideas about what is 'correct' and what isn't. Prescriptivists seem to think that if language changes, if 'rules' are broken, that the heart of language will be torn out. As we've pointed out, for linguists, these changes are an inherent feature of language and very interesting. As languages are used, they change naturally. Although language changes, it is always systematic; that is, language changes are always consistent with the building codes of that language. The difference between prescriptive and descriptive perspectives might take some getting used to; but it is fundamental for any study of language.

Many prescriptivist requests to respect the 'rules' also come with some kind of warning: breaking the rules will lead to breaking the language itself. 'The crisis is imminent', we are told; 'things have never been this bad, it's all the fault of young people, foreigners and poor schooling'. The themes of prescriptivist arguments remain consistent over time. Disapproval of the way some people use language, especially in relation to grammar and the meaning of words, has a very long history known as 'the complaint tradition' (Milroy & Milroy 1999). The idea that language is in decline and that this is someone's fault, dates back to at least the fourteenth century (Boletta 1992; see also Crowley 2003). You can find many contemporary examples of the complaint tradition in newspapers and on the internet.

The concept of correctness and 'Standard English' is a tricky one (Trudgill 1999). 'Standard English' (or 'standard' in any other language) is defined by speech communities and not linguists. Therefore 'standard' refers to many varieties that speakers believe to be correct. In this book, we use the expression 'standard English' to refer to this popular definition. This term is intended to acknowledge that non-linguists believe that there are varieties that are more correct than others, a belief predicated on prescriptivist ideas but one that we do not endorse.

In contrast, prescriptivists feel it's important to have guidelines or 'rules' for the best way of speaking. So they assert the importance of the 'rules' by recording them in books and teaching them to students. It's very important to consider who 'makes' these rules for language use and why they insist everyone follow them. Rules for language use (remember: we're *not* talking about the 'building codes' we described previously) are dictated and maintained by educated members of the higher social echelons of society. They are the members of society who have the power to sanction members of the speech community for not 'following the rules'. These sanctions might take the form of a poor mark in school, a failed job interview or lack of a promotion at work. So, knowing the prescriptive rules of language clearly has consequences. Because prescriptive ideas about language circulate in our culture, it is not uncommon to form judgements about other people because of their use of language. For example, OKCupid, an online dating site, gave advice to its users on how to use language in order to get more replies. They analysed half a million messages making first contact to see how successful they were in getting a reply and developed some 'rules' for the people using the website. Their first rule is:

> Be literate
> Netspeak, bad grammar, and bad spelling are huge turn-offs. Our negative correlation list is a fool's lexicon: ur, u, wat, wont, and so on. These all make a terrible first impression. In fact, if you count hit (and we do!) the worst 6 words you can use in a first message are all stupid slang.
>
> (Rudder 2009)

Thus OKCupid is suggesting that members who use 'Netspeak, bad grammar, and bad spelling' give the appearance that they are 'stupid'. We will think hard about this judgement and throughout this book dissect the ideologies behind this position.

Another example of the complaint tradition that prescriptivists make is that speakers use the word 'literally' incorrectly when they use it as an intensifier, because that is a different meaning from its 'original' one. For example, one blogger complained about Hollywood stylist Rachel Zoe using 'literally':

> Stylist Rachel Zoe, on the other hand, sure doesn't seem to know when to stop using the word 'literally.' Who doesn't want to see Rachel Zoe say literally literally 29 times in a minute in 29 seconds, beginning with, 'I literally want to cut myself in half'?
>
> (Triska 2012)

The complaint about the 'unconventional' use of literally is especially interesting because it is not clear that 'literally' has always enjoyed the 'literal'

meaning that is being claimed for it. The figurative meaning is attested from at least the eighteenth century, according to the Oxford English Dictionary (OED). This meaning is described as follows:

> *colloq.* Used to indicate that some (freq. conventional) metaphorical or hyperbolical expression is to be taken in the strongest admissible sense: 'virtually, as good as'; (also) 'completely, utterly, absolutely'.
>
> Now one of the most common uses, although often considered irregular in standard English since it reverses the original sense of *literally* ('not figuratively or metaphorically').

(www.oed.com)

The distinction made here is important. The OED lists this meaning as 'colloquial' and then notes that this is 'considered irregular in standard English'. This clearly demonstrates that not all speakers use the word in the same way. If there are many ways to say the same thing, how is it possible to know whether 'literally' is being used correctly or not? It all depends on whether we take a descriptive or prescriptive position.

Activity 1.2

Consider the example sentences in Table 1.1. Decide which ones would be considered 'correct' from a descriptive or prescriptive position. What features of the examples make you think so?

Table 1.1 **Prescriptive and descriptive activity**

	Prescriptivist	Descriptive
Example: *Mary don't usually be at church.*	*Not correct: it does not follow prescriptive rules for negation in English*	*Correct: it consists of a structure allowed by the building codes of English*
a. If I was you, I'd study harder for exams		
b. Sally wants out of the car		
c. Dog the up quickly ran road		
d. We should not have went to that party last night		
e. I book read yesterday have the		

Examples c. and e. are 'not correct' from either a prescriptivist or descriptivist perspective because they don't conform to the building codes of English and therefore don't communicate a clear message. That is, it's difficult to determine what they mean. Examples b. and d., on the other hand, communicate a clear message, and are 'correct' from the descriptive perspective.

From the prescriptive perspective, though, they are 'incorrect' because they don't follow prescriptive rules. In b.(i) and d.(i), slight modifications to the example sentences make them each prescriptively correct.

b.   Sally wants out of the car
b.(i) Sally wants *to get* out of the car
d.   We should not have *went* to that party last night
d.(i) We should not have *gone* to that party last night

You may feel like examples b. and d. don't conform to the building codes of English. In fact, there are varieties of English where examples c. and e. are used. There are so many different kinds of English that some constructions might actually sound impossible to you. We'll encounter this idea again in Chapter 10.

1.5 LANGUAGE: MULTIPLE FUNCTIONS

A single utterance can do more than one thing. Roman Jakobson, a twentieth-century linguist, argues that 'Language must be investigated in all the variety of its functions' (2000: 335). It's useful to look at Jakobson's schema of functions in a bit more detail as it helps to have a framework to describe and investigate the different functions of language. Without this, it can be difficult to think about the various ways that we use language.

	CONTEXT	
ADDRESSER	MESSAGE	ADDRESSEE
	CONTACT	
	CODE	

Figure 1.1 Factors involved in communication, Jakobson

He starts by describing the components of communication that one needs to take into consideration (see Figure 1.1). First, there is the Addresser (in the left side of the schema): the person who is speaking. Second, there is the Addressee, or the person being spoken to (on the right side of the schema). Third, to fully account for the message from the Addresser to the Addressee we need to examine four things (in the centre of the schema) that mediate the communication between the Addresser and the Addressee. For the message to be communicated there has to be a medium of communication, which may be verbal, written or even visual (*contact*). This will have some influence on how the *message*, the content, is encoded; whether through words or hand signals for example. Whatever *code* is chosen (words or hand signals), it must be one that both *addresser* and *addressee* mutually understand. The *message* will also be sent and received in a *context*, that is, there will be a social and linguistic environment that frames the message (e.g. at work, at a party, on the phone, etc.).

'Each of these six factors [in Figure 1.1] determines a different function of language' (Jakobson 2000: 335). We can see these functions set out in Figure 1.2 in the same format as the components just examined. The *emotive* (or expressive) function is in the position of the Addresser, as it 'aims a direct expression of the speaker's attitude towards what he is speaking about' (2000: 336). The **referential** function of language is what we might normally think of as information, or the **denotative** function of language, but also includes the ideas, objects and conventions which speakers share knowledge of. The referential function allows us to ask someone to pass the salt, and receive the salt (rather than the pepper). The **conative** function of language relates to the addressee (hence placed in the addressee/right hand side of the schema). This function helps us describe messages that are intended to have an effect on the audience. This might be anything from a command, an insult or an attempt at persuasion.

	REFERENTIAL	
EMOTIVE	POETIC	CONATIVE
	PHATIC	
	METALINGUAL	

Figure 1.2 Six functions of communication, Jakobson

People usually think primarily of the referential function of language. We need to consider all the functions to account for the way language works. If a person says 'it's cold in here', you may understand this as simply being a comment about the level of air conditioning. If you're sitting near an open window, however, it would be reasonable to interpret this as a request to close the window; thus, it's a message where the conative function (a request to shut the window) is highlighted. Common stereotypes about British speech describe a preoccupation with the weather. So, in a conversation among British people, 'it's cold in here' may well be understood as small talk, or making conversation. This is the **phatic** function. The purpose is not so much to communicate information (anyone in the room can tell what the temperature is), but rather to be polite to make 'small talk'. One way to do this in British culture is to talk about something that is socially acceptable and not terribly significant. Knowing this is an example of communicative competence that we described earlier.

It's important at this stage to note that the conative function is different from connotation. **Connotation** is the subjective or personal aspect of meaning, which can be contrasted with **denotation**, which is the literal definition. While denotation is related to the referential function of language, connotation is more likely to be related to the emotive function. To come back to Jakobson's schema of functions, remember that the conative function is about addressing someone, using **imperatives** or **vocatives**.

The poetic function was of great importance to Jakobson as he was looking specifically at language and literature. The poetic function is important in everyday language, though, and draws attention to the message for its own sake. The most obvious examples of messages with significant poetic function often also have an important conative (and indeed emotive) function. Advertising, whether spoken or written, often takes advantage of the poetic function of language (i.e. the form of the message). The same is true of political and other persuasive texts.

The final function that Jakobson draws our attention to is the **metalingual**. This is language that refers to language and communication while communicating. This function is vital for successful communication to continue to take place. When we ask someone to repeat or rephrase or explain again what their message is, we are exploiting the metalingual function of language. In short, we are able to talk about talking.

All these functions of language are always present. We can, for example, look at the poetic function of any piece of language, whether it's literature, advertising or a mathematics textbook. Generally, however, we only notice functions when they're **foregrounded**. For example, we tend to notice the poetic function of language when a message is particularly nicely phrased. These functions are also central in understanding how people use language to do things, whether it is to get a window closed or to be elected to government. In the same way, the functions of language are the means by which power can be exercised over people.

Try to identify texts or speech situations that are good examples of each function Jacobson identifies. Do you think there are any functions of language he has not included?

Activity 1.3

Language performs a variety of functions. We use it to do a whole range of things, from talking to our friends to applying for jobs. This flexibility is important and not something we always think about. When we are confronted with a new use of language or have to use language in an unfamiliar way, we are likely to become aware of the choices available and the significance of the words we choose. In everyday language use, however, this usually goes unremarked.

1.6 POWER

Finding a full definition of power with respect to language is not straightforward. The many functions of language mean that there are different ways in which power can be exercised. While there are some examples of power being used to change language directly, the relationship is generally more subtle. We saw that speaking a particular variety of English (e.g. British

English) may make it possible to perform particular actions or influence particular groups of people. But even small variations in language use can bring benefits to speakers. People who speak the standard variety of British English, for example, will be thought to be more educated and more capable than others. This may give them access to better employment, institutions with power or even a better education. This is because of the attitudes that people have about language. While the speakers gain from being able to speak the standard language, and so have a degree of power, it is not the case that they − as individuals − are controlling others. Rather, having competence in a prestigious language is in itself beneficial.

We noted that language change is an inherent part of language, yet some people feel that language should stay the same. Some nations even have institutions that attempt to regulate the form of their language by stipulating which forms are 'correct' (the Académie Française in France for example). Although this is not terribly common, other examples can be found. The former president of Turkmenistan, Saparmurat Niyazov, exercised his power directly over language. In 2002 'He decreed that the month of January should be named after him and April after his mother' (Parfitt 2006). He also named a town after himself (or more correctly the title he insisted upon − Turkmenbashi − 'leader of all Turkmen') and decreed that 'bread' also be called by his mother's name (Paton Walsh 2006). This is an example of straightforward legal and political power being used to change language. Such action is generally only possible where there is absolute singular authority, as was the case with this dictator.

Activity 1.4

Do you think some kinds of language use should be regulated by law?

Many countries regulate what people can say and write, or at least punishments exist for certain kinds of linguistic activity. The most common areas of 'regulation' relate to threats, encouraging others to commit crimes, protection of intellectual property and damaging someone's reputation. But would it be permissible to regulate other kinds of speech? Should gossip be illegal for example? In September 2013, an Indian website announced that the government would require those spreading rumours to have licences.

> Upset with the fact that anyone with an internet connection and basic language skills can take part in rumor mongering, the government is thinking of issuing licenses for rumor mongers.
>
> (Patrakar 2013)

While this was a joke announced on a humorous fake news website, in the previous year there was some confusion about whether or not gossiping was, in fact, illegal in Fiji. Vosamana reports in the *Fiji Times*:

> In her formal address, police constable Mere Mocetoka told the women that anyone was liable to spend one year in prison if found gossiping or making bad remarks about another person.
>
> (Vosamana 2012)

While this was a real news report, it appears that the police officer had misinterpreted a law that stipulates insulting people is a crime (ABC 2012). While 'gossip' can refer to a number of different activities (see Chapter 6), it would be possible for certain kinds of malicious gossip to warrant legal penalties. Of course, this requires that the line between 'gossip' and 'slander' or 'libel' be well and truly crossed. That is, it would not be the case that gossip as such is illegal but rather that a person was making statements damaging to another person's reputation. This kind of offence is found in many countries.

Influence over language, and influence over people through language, is far more commonly achieved in less obvious and direct ways than passing a law. Of course there are situations where physical or institutional power has a direct influence on how language is understood. When a police officer asks you to stop your car, for example, the institutional power (and perhaps even their weapon) lends a particular force to the spoken request (Shon 2005). In fact, such a request would more likely be understood as a command, because of the context in which the speech takes place.

A person doesn't need to have an obvious position of power in order for this to be exploited linguistically. When a manager uses a particular form of language the power comes partially from her position (as your boss) but perhaps also from the kind of language that is used. We can think about this not as physical power, or even institutional power, but as 'symbolic power' (Bourdieu 1991). Calling it symbolic power draws our attention to the link between power and symbols, that is, between power and language. To call it 'symbolic power' is not to say that the power is ineffective (we'll come back to Bourdieu's notion of symbolic power in chapter 6). It is possible to insult, persuade, command, compliment, encourage or make a promise using language. While these can be seen as individual acts, when repeated over time, the culmination of such linguistic acts might change the way a person sees an issue.

Thus, while language is important in the exercise of power at particular moments, we also need to understand that language can have an influence across long stretches of time. I can be commanded to do something now, but I can also be influenced to think and behave in a certain way pretty much all the time. This certainly involves language, but we need something more. Fairclough puts it as follows:

> It is important to emphasize that I am not suggesting that power is *just* a matter of language. ... Power exists in various modalities, including the concrete and unmistakable modality of physical force ... It is perhaps helpful to make a broad distinction between the exercise of power through *coercion* of various sorts including physical violence, and the exercise of power through the manufacture of *consent* to or at least acquiescence towards it. Power relations depend on both, though in varying proportions. Ideology is the prime means of manufacturing consent.

> (2001: 3)

The concept of **ideology** is a difficult one to come to terms with and we'll keep coming back to it in this book. Like language, an ideology has a structure. This structure can be mapped and understood by paying attention to the way the choices are made in language. That is, language creates and represents ideological concerns. The general idea is that because language is connected to ideology in this way, we can be encouraged to do things, not because someone has commanded us at a particular point in time, but because we have internalised certain values that mean we *want* to do certain things. This internalising of values takes place over longer stretches of time. Language is crucial to the creation and maintenance of 'common sense' ideology. You can think about ideology as a way of structuring the manner in which language is used to communicate a more general message involving values and beliefs; in short, a worldview.

1.6.1 Ideology

Ideology may seem a long way from language change and 'incorrect' uses of language; but power, and especially symbolic power, is supported by ideologies. Looking at language closely allows us to pick out these ideologies. In the same way that we can deduce the structure of a language by studying the way people use it, we can also describe the structure and content of an ideology. Because scholars have many approaches to defining ideology, we can't describe them all here. We'll describe a few key ideas that will provide you with the tools you need to understand language and power.

The critical linguists Gunther Kress and Robert Hodge define ideology 'as a systematic body of ideas, organized from a particular point of view' (1993: 6). In everyday contexts, 'ideology' is something negative or at the very least, loaded. We think that only groups like terrorists have an ideology; but because ideology is simply a way of describing a set of beliefs and behaviours that are thought of as natural, we can see that everyone has ideologies. There are ideas we take for granted, values that we hold and ideas that we believe in that seem perfectly natural. It is this common sense, this seemingly natural and normal way of thinking and acting, that we can talk about in terms of the dominant ideology, or **hegemonic** ideology. So, ideology is a way of talking about a whole set of ways of thinking and acting.

The French sociologist Pierre Bourdieu points out that, in addition to individuals having their own ideologies, ideology also exists on the group level: 'ideologies serve particular interests which they tend to present as universal interests, shared by the group as a whole' (1991: 167).

Given that all groups have a particular point of view, everyone has ideologies. However, we tend to only talk about 'ideology' when we want to draw attention to the power or the particular interests ideologies have. To label another group's values as 'ideology' is common; to talk about one's own values in the same way is not common at all. A group's ideology will be unmarked for that group. However, thinking about our own 'taken for granted' values, as members of groups or as individuals, is an important task for critical thinking.

In summary, some key things to remember about ideology are that they are held by individuals *and* groups and they are often not recognised by the individual or group as a powerful influence on their own behaviour.

1.6.2 Interpellation

The way that language is used to describe and address people shows how language can position individuals. We noted that language has a number of different functions, one of these being the conative function, that is, oriented towards the addressee. This can have implications in terms of relations of power. Louis Althusser describes this as the audience being 'hailed' in a particular way (1971). This means that language is used to address people and thus position them in some way. Think of the police officer example we described previously. When an officer speaks to a person, that person is positioned in relation to the officer as an individual and also positioned in a relationship of power. Althusser calls this positioning **interpellation**. His point is that we are positioned by (or hailed by) an ideology.

We'll take language as an example again. You may think certain swear words aren't offensive, but the dominant view in society is that some words are taboo. Even if you want to use these words, it's impossible to ignore the way they are understood. Ideas about what is and what is not an obscenity don't go away simply because a person doesn't agree with them. While you're not compelled to follow these rules, you will nevertheless be held accountable to them. We are all interpellated by this ideology of language even if we don't agree with it. More specifically, Althusser calls societal institutions, which are not necessarily part of the state (that is, the government) but that nevertheless perpetuate the same ideological values, the Ideological State Apparatus (ISA). For example, educational institutions and the media are ISAs because they perpetuate many of the dominant ideologies of contemporary society. The idea that men and women are fundamentally different and that money is a measure of someone's worth are both dominant ideologies that are largely left unquestioned by the media.

For Althusser, the ISA communicates and confirms the dominant ideology, most notably in relation to political and economic structure.

Globally, we can argue that the dominant mode of political organisation is democracy and that of economic structure is a form of capitalism. Clearly there are alternatives to these, however in most parts of the world these are the common sense, taken for granted values that are sanctioned by education, the media and the government. We are hailed by the dominant ideologies of democracy and capitalism and it is very difficult to opt out or resist these systems. To understand this position, and perhaps to challenge it, we need to look closely at the messages that hail us. In the final section of this chapter, we're going to consider some ideologies connected to language; in particular, how it should be used.

1.7 POWERFUL LANGUAGE?

In this book we consider how language, ideology and power all come together. Sometimes the power that language has is difficult to observe. The notion that there is a correct form of English, discussed earlier, is an ideology that has substantial repercussions (Lippi-Green 1997) and those repercussions can be seen as the effects of the power of language. For example, scholars have shown that attitudes to accented language can prevent a person from getting hired for a job (e.g. Carlson & McHenry 2006), interfere with their education (e.g. Labov 1982) and prevent a person from finding housing (e.g. Purnell, Idsardi & Baugh 1999). Employment, education and housing are three essential aspects of life.

Using language in a particular way sends a message about the things you think are important and communicates something about who you are. We draw conclusions about people because of the language they use. For example, the language used by people with high status will generally garner more respect than language associated with marginalised people. While this may seem entirely unproblematic, it is also ideological. Whether a language variety reflects something positive or negative depends very much on what or who that variety is associated with.

1.8 SUMMARY

In this chapter, we've introduced some of the themes and issues that are taken up throughout this book. Understanding language as a system, with inherently understood structure, is important in exploring the kinds of variation that we find. Studying language allows us to understand the way people exercise power and, in turn, ways this can be resisted. The rules that we're interested in are those that explain what people actually do (descriptive), rather than being rules about what people should do (prescriptive). While some people are uncomfortable with language change, it is inescapable and unstoppable. It is also exciting, as such change is possible exactly because of the creative possibilities that language provides. This is an important language function, but there are others. We started thinking about the relationship between language, ideology and power. This relationship is one that we continue to explore in the following chapters as it can take some time for this complex interaction to make sense. Studying language allows us to think critically about power and helps us see that what we might think of as 'common sense' is nevertheless ideological. In the next chapter, we consider the tools we need to think about some of these questions in more depth.

FURTHER READING

Bauer, L. and Trudgill, P. (eds) (1998) *Language Myths*, Harmondsworth: Penguin.

Crystal, D. (2007a) *The Fight for English: How Language Pundits Ate, Shot, and Left*, Oxford: Oxford University Press.

Crystal, D. (2007b) *Words, Words, Words*, Oxford: Oxford University Press.

Fairclough, N. (1999) 'Global capitalism and critical awareness of language', *Language Awareness*, 8(2): 71–83.

Montgomery, M. (2008) *An Introduction to Language and Society*, 3rd edn, London: Routledge.

Trudgill, P. (1999) 'Standard English: What it isn't', in T. Bex and R. J. Watts (eds) *Standard English: The Widening Debate*, London: Routledge: 117–28.

CHAPTER 2

Language thought and representation

2.1	**INTRODUCTION**	20
2.2	**LANGUAGE AS A SYSTEM OF REPRESENTATION**	21
2.3	**THE SAPIR-WHORF HYPOTHESIS**	26
2.4	**ONE LANGUAGE MANY WORLDS**	31
2.5	**A MODEL FOR ANALYSING LANGUAGE**	35
2.6	**'POLITICAL CORRECTNESS'**	38
2.7	**SUMMARY**	40

2.1 INTRODUCTION

In order to examine in detail the functions of language discussed in the last chapter, we need to learn about the frameworks and terms for talking about the way language works. We began this in the last part of the previous chapter when we discussed Jakobson's schema and concepts such as ideology and interpellation. In this chapter, we explore Ferdinand de Saussure's theory of signs, which will provide a way of discussing how meaning is constructed at the level of the word, how this can change, how words fit together into larger structures (sentences) and what happens when we make choices in sentences. Thinking about words as signs may take a while to get used to; likewise, the use of 'sign' in the technical sense introduced in this chapter can also take some time to feel familiar. These models of meaning are important though, as they help articulate the way small changes can have significant consequences for the meaning communicated. When we understand this model it is possible to discuss what 'politically correct' means and how such a concept is used to maintain and resist power.

2.2 LANGUAGE AS A SYSTEM OF REPRESENTATION

Language is one way of representing reality. There are other signs that we can use to do this; you could take a photograph of something, paint a picture or even write a piece of music. In the definition that we're working with, all 'signs' have two parts: a concept and an object or marker that is connected to the concept. The pedestrian signals at a crosswalk that tell you when to walk or not are signs because of the connection between the red light (the object) and the concept of stopping. Without these two parts, the red light would just be a red light. When we know that red means 'stop', the red light becomes a sign.

Words in language, therefore, are signs. For Saussure, a sign is made up of two things: a **signifier** and **signified**. His definition of the sign makes a distinction between the sound we hear (the **signifier**) and the concept this makes us think of (the **signified**) (see Figure 2.1). So, for example, when you hear the sounds represented by the letters d-o-g, you think of the concept 'canine mammal'. Together, the word sound and the concept it invokes form a sign. It is important to note 'A linguistic sign is not a link between a thing and a name, but between a concept and a sound pattern' (1966: 66). These cannot be separated in the sign; to try and do so would be like trying to cut only one side of a piece of paper (de Saussure 1966: 113). A signifier needs at least one signified for there to be a sign. If there is no such signified, the alleged signifier is merely a sound that *could* be a signifier; it is not a sign by Saussure's definition.

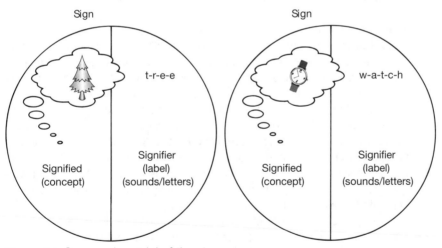

Figure 2.1 Saussure's model of the sign

The connection between words and their meaning is accidental: there is no reason why bread should be called 'bread'. The arbitrary connection between words and their meaning was one of Ferdinand de Saussure's great insights. Saying that the connection between the signifier and the signified is arbitrary doesn't suggest that words can mean whatever we like. 'The term [arbitrary] simply implies that the signal [signifier] is *unmotivated*: that is to say arbitrary in relation to its signification [signified], with which it has no natural connexion in relation' (de Saussure 1966: 69). You might be thinking that signifiers have a natural connection with their signifieds, for example, in the case of onomatopoeic words; those we use for the sounds animals make. However, while a bee in English will 'buzz', in Japanese its sound is represented by 'boon boon'. This shows that there is no straightforward connection between concepts and sounds. Even the sounds of the natural world that we might assume are heard in the same way by everybody are represented differently by different languages. At best, such examples of animal noises and the like are marginal cases of how language reflects meaning and depend on conventional associations (especially when written) or the speaker's ability to imitate the noise made by the animal.

There is more to Saussure's work than his work on signs. He is also usually credited with being the founder of **structuralism**, which had great influence on linguistics, literary criticism and the social sciences. We'll look at structuralism when we consider signs later in the chapter. In Chapter 1, we established that language is a system; systems have rules and these rules structure the language. The system of language allows us to talk about and represent the world around us. But just as the relationship between word and meaning is arbitrary, so too is the way that language divides up the world.

2.2.1 Different kinds of language

Saussure distinguishes three kinds of language. Recall in Chapter 1 we discussed the difficulties of knowing exactly what we mean when we talk about 'language'. The three aspects Saussure describes help with some of these difficulties. The first of these is '*langage*', which has been translated as 'human speech' including its psychological and physical aspects, belonging both to the individual and to societies. It is the most general category and is comprised of the following two aspects, which will be our focus here. These two parts of 'langage' are '**langue**' and '**parole**'. You can think of langue as competence and parole as performance (both in Chomsky's terms that we discussed in Chapter 1). The former is the overarching language system, the latter being individual use of language. While they are treated as separate by Saussure, they are also closely linked.

Langue is the system that makes parole possible. In so far as langue makes speech possible, it has a social element. As we'll see when we look more at definitions of signs, the social and conventional agreement on how signs are constructed is crucial. You can think of langue as the rules of the game, the entire system, including the building codes discussed in Chapter 1 together with communicative competence. Saussure provides a musical metaphor, comparing langue to a symphony; how good it is as a composition is not related to how a particular orchestra may perform it (1966: 18).

While individuals draw on langue every time they use language, they don't have direct access to langue. Langue is 'not complete in any speaker; it exists perfectly only within a collectivity' (de Saussure 1966: 12). We can only talk about langue sensibly if we have a community of speakers. You can't have a language all by yourself. This is why there is a social aspect to langue.

Every instance of language in the world, all actual utterances, is parole. As speakers, we perform parole acts. While as speakers of a language we rely on shared understanding (accounted for by langue), as individuals we can do things with language that haven't been done before. You can construct a sentence that is so odd that you can be pretty confident that no-one else has ever said or written it. For example, 'The surly clouds gathered their amusing faces and spat furiously on my new chartreuse coloured coat'. While this is a slightly poetic example (representing clouds as people, with faces and moods) because of langue, the system we all share, you should be able to understand this original parole act.

It is the relationship between langue and parole that is important. The system and rules of langue can change. These changes are very slow, and may take hundreds of years. Individuals start using a new word, or an existing word in a new way (all these usages are parole), and other language users understand and adopt this. When this new linguistic behaviour is well estab-lished, we can say that the new form has become part of langue, one that we all understand. The last part is important; the new behaviour has to become recognised and conventional, such that other people understand it. That is, acts of parole draw on *and* contribute to the abstract system of langue. As Saussure puts it, 'Language has an individual aspect and a social aspect. One is not conceivable without the other' (1966: 8). The distinction between langue and parole, however, allows us to think through their differ-ences, while understanding that they are linked. It allows us to understand how language use can be individual and original and yet still be communicative.

While this is only a model, it is a useful one as it helps us understand how language enables us to communicate and how language changes. It is parole that we are normally most concerned with in this book, at least as a starting point. There are a number of reasons for this. The first, and most important, is that we don't have direct access to langue. While it would be very convenient if it were the case, langue is not a big book somewhere with all the codes written down. The only access that we have to the codes of langue is through the particular uses of language, that is, parole. From this evidence, we can try and map what the code is.

The second reason we focus on parole is that as sociolinguists we're primarily interested in how people use language. The creative aspect of language means that speakers will always do things that are different, new and surprising. The concept of langue and its relationship with parole allows us to describe and account for this.

Because instances of parole both draw on and contribute to langue, as individual speakers we have some power over what langue contains. Were we all to decide to call 'bread' 'dice', for example, eventually that would become part of langue. Yet, while many speakers might not make conscious decisions to change linguistic signs, change nevertheless occurs.

2.2.2 Signs and structure

We have described how a sign needs both a signifier and a signified to be a sign. In this model of meaning, Saussure postulates that a sign needs other signs in order to have meaning. He suggests, 'Signs function, then, not through their intrinsic value but through their relative position' (de Saussure 1966: 118). That is, the meaning of a linguistic sign depends on its relation to other signs. It may be useful to think of this relation using a spatial metaphor, where the meaning of each sign is contained in a space. The space that signs occupy fits together, such that if a space is occupied by one sign, that same space can't be occupied by another. In the example of traffic signs, we could say that 'red' means 'stop' because 'green' means 'go' and amber means something else. In this context, the meaning of 'red' depends on what it does not mean ('go').

Consider, for example some linguistic signs that are related, that are in the same semantic field:

walk, march, stagger, amble, run, jog, dash, sprint

All of these linguistic signs say something about moving on one's feet. We might group the first four together, as we can say that they're all kinds of walking. In the same way, we might group the other four together as they're all kinds of running. If we were to take a semantic approach, we could look at the relationship between these words. We could argue that 'walk' and 'run' are more general than the others, in that marching, staggering and ambling can all be thought of as kinds of walking. We might want to represent this relationship as follows:

	Walk			**Run**	
march	stagger	amble	dash	jog	sprint

In any case, while 'ambling' is a kind of walking, it is slower than a 'walk'. 'Staggering' is also a kind of 'walking', but one less orderly and even than a 'walk'. What 'march', 'stagger' and 'amble' mean can be understood in relation to what they do *not* mean. The space that 'stagger' occupies is defined by the space that 'march' and 'amble' occupy. Given this metaphor of space, we can say that 'stagger' means what it does because it does *not* mean 'march', 'amble', 'run' or 'skip'. It also doesn't mean 'breakfast', 'butterfly', 'snore', 'kitten' and so on, but it may be easier to think of the structure of the system of signs in relation to concepts that are more similar to the word one is looking at. We can say that the space a sign occupies, what it means, is delineated by the spaces all other signs leave behind: 'In language … whatever distinguishes one sign from the others constitute it' (de Saussure 1966: 121).

In terms of new signs, this means the whole system of signs, the space they occupy, will be reconfigured when a new sign is introduced. If we imagine that only 'run' and 'walk' are the signs available, to describe someone moving in a rhythmic way, but not particularly fast, we would have to use the sign 'walk'. However, when we introduce 'march', some of the space that 'walk' occupied will be taken away by this new sign 'march'; 'walk' will no longer be the best way to describe this rhythmic way of moving. This semantic space is in the realm of langue. We can alter this space and the place of signs in it by what we do with language in the world, in parole.

The way we've been talking about langue may seem all encompassing and monolithic as if we're talking about the langue of the whole English language. If we included the whole English language, we'd be considering all the different varieties of English: British, American, Australian, Indian, Singaporean and so on. Depending on the kinds of questions we're asking this may make sense, but in thinking about how to use language in a particular context, it only really makes sense to include specific varieties. For example, in Indian English, 'wallah' refers to a tradesperson or worker, usually of a particular kind that is specified in the first part of a compound noun phrase. Thus, taxiwallah is a taxi driver. In the abstract langue that encompasses all English 'wallah' would jostle for semantic space with 'tradesperson' and other similar terms. In other parts of the English-speaking world it may not be relevant as a sign at all. It would simply be a sound, as there would be no conventional linking of this signifier ('wallah') to a signified. Thus, when considering the relationship between various signs, we need to know which signs and relationships are relevant in the communicative context we're concerned with.

We can talk about these changes over time with the following terms: **synchronic** and **diachronic**. The first, synchronic, refers to a particular point in time. The second, diachronic, allows us to talk about how language changes over time. For example, the term 'slut' is now generally understood as a negative term (*BBC News* 2013). This is the synchronic perspective. If we appeal to diachronic meanings, however, it is possible to observe that this was not always the case. This term used to mean a woman of untidy habits and appearance (OED). While some people still use 'slut' in this way it is nevertheless understood as offensive.

We need to appreciate both diachronic and synchronic aspects to understand language, as language 'always implies both an established system and an evolution; at every moment it is an existing institution and a product of the past' (de Saussure 1966: 8). We'll see in later chapters that changes over time and comparing variation in language at a particular time are crucial if we're to understand how people are using language and what the significance of any use may be.

Activity 2.1

Find an etymological dictionary (like the Oxford English Dictionary) and trace the history of the meanings of 'slut'.

Activity 2.2

Think back to words that you no longer use but that you once did. The words you used to positively evaluate something as a young teenager are good choices here. What did they mean? Do they mean the same now? Why did you stop using them? What would you think of someone who used them now?

2.3 THE SAPIR-WHORF HYPOTHESIS[1]

2.3.1 Linguistic diversity

Because of the arbitrary relationship between signifier and signified, and because signs take their meaning from their relationship to other signs, there is no single way for languages to describe reality. We can call this linguistic diversity, and it is the first part of the Sapir-Whorf hypothesis. The world can be described in any number of ways and languages differ in terms of the signs that comprise them. Sapir was an anthropological linguist and as such, encountered the different ways languages represent the world.

The familiar myth that 'Eskimos' have hundreds of words for snow is relevant here as this myth is based on the idea of linguistic diversity. In 'The Great Eskimo Vocabulary Hoax' Geoffrey Pullum traces the history of this myth and provides the necessary evidence to debunk it. Even if it were true, however, Pullum asks us to consider how interesting this would really be. 'Horsebreeders have various names for breeds, sizes and ages of horses; botanists have names for leaf shapes' (1991: 165). There appears to be a fascination with multiple terms for the same thing in other languages, but if we look at the variation in a single language, for example in specialist fields of English, we also find various names for some things and different ways of representing reality (see Image 2.1).

Image 2.1 'Eskimo'

Think of an area of your life where there are a lot of terms to make fine distinctions. This will probably be in an area in which you have expert knowledge, and you might not have noticed the variety of terms. You might refer to all contemporary music as 'pop music' or you might have a variety of words to designate differences. Discuss this with your colleagues; do you all have the same set of terms for different domains?

Activity 2.3

2.3.2 Dyirbal

Just as languages encode semantic differences in various ways, grammatical systems also vary. It is the obligatory aspects of grammar that are interesting, the details that a speaker has to specify to express a well-formed, grammatically acceptable utterance. It is worth looking at an example of this. In the indigenous Australian language Dyirbal, whenever a noun is used, it must be accompanied by a noun-marker that indicates which class of nouns it belongs to. Nouns, then, are divided into four groups and this must be indicated when the nouns are used in a sentence. Dixon, who described this language, was initially puzzled as to how these groupings were made. He

> noticed that children learning the language did not have to learn the class [467] of each noun separately, but appeared to operate with a

number of general principles. In addition, different speakers assigned noun class to new loan words in a consistent way.

(2002: 466–7)

Eventually, he was able to group these classes in the following way:

Class 1: human masculine; non-human animate
Class 2: human feminine; water; fire; fighting
Class 3: non-flesh food (including honey)
Class 4: everything else

(Dixon 2002: 467)

In addition to the groupings described by Dixon there are a number of other principles that help decide which noun class things belong to. Some of this is linked to Dyirbal mythology. The point here is twofold. First, the specification of noun class is compulsory in this language. A well-formed Dyirbal utterance needs this information (i.e. it is part of the building codes for Dyirbal). Second, the Dyirbal language divides the world up in a particular way, for example, it places special emphasis on things that can be consumed as food by putting all these objects in the same noun class.

The value of exploring this linguistic diversity, the way languages divide the world differently, is that it reminds us that linguistic signs are neither natural nor stable. While striking examples can be found in other languages' division of reality, we need to remember that our own division of reality is worth consideration. In a sense, we need to treat our own language as a foreign language, and examine the relationships between signs. In doing so, we can come to an appreciation of the representation of reality that language performs. In summary, the first part of the Sapir-Whorf hypothesis states that different languages construe the world differently and these differences are encoded in the language.

2.3.3 Linguistic relativism and determinism

The second part of the Sapir-Whorf hypothesis is somewhat more controversial, largely because scholars disagree on what Sapir and Whorf actually intended the hypothesis to mean. Because of this disagreement about what Sapir and Whorf were claiming, the hypothesis is variously labelled, depending on the strength of the arguments, as linguistic relativism or determinism. The hypothesis is that our language has a bearing on the way we think, that is, that the terms of our language have some kind of effect on the categories of thought available to us. The strong version of the hypothesis, linguistic determinism, is often called 'the prison house view of language'; that the limits of language are the limits of the world.[2] The implication is that if a linguistic sign is not available for a particular concept, that concept is difficult or impossible for the speaker to imagine. But, as we've seen, language allows us to create new meanings, whether these are words for new objects or items of specialist language. If the strong version of linguistic determinism were correct, it would simply not be possible to do this. As a result, linguistic determinism is not a widely held view.

The question then becomes, does language influence thought and behaviour in any way at all? Benjamin Whorf, who was an amateur linguist and fire inspector, argued that there was some connection between them. In his work, he noticed that people behave according to the way things are labelled rather than in terms of what they really are. The best-known example from his work as fire inspector is the way individuals threw cigarette butts into oil drums labelled 'empty'. Even though 'empty' may signal a benign absence, in the case of oil and other flammable materials, even a small amount of residual material in the functionally 'empty' container can be anything but benign. As Whorf puts it, 'the "empty" drums are perhaps the more dangerous, since they contain explosive vapour' (1954: 198). Despite the very real danger, the 'empty' sign appeared to encourage risky behaviour.

Linguistic relativism, the version of the Sapir-Whorf hypothesis that seems plausible, is much less confining than linguistic determinism. It suggests that language, as in the case of 'empty' in Whorf's example, influences the way we think. However, if the connection between language and thought is not absolute (as determinism would have it), then how far does it go? It might help to think of linguistic relativism as relating to how language *influences* the way we normally think; rather than language *determining* thought. The linguist John Lucy uses the phrase 'habitual cognition' (Lucy 2005: 303) to demonstrate that linguistic determinism is not the way to explain the connection between language and thought. That is,

> the broader view taken here is not that languages completely or permanently blind speakers to other aspects of reality. Rather they provide speakers with a systematic default bias in their habitual response tendencies.
>
> (Lucy 2005: 307)

Lucy argues that the signs and structure of language influence thought. This is a much more modest argument than that of linguistic determinism. It is also incredibly useful, not just in considering languages such as English and French, but also in paying attention to more localised and specialised language use, such as the language of botanists for example.

Habitual modes of thinking can be very important. Obviously habits can be changed, but to do so takes effort and will. Moreover, generally, we're not aware of our habits of thought. Have you ever considered it unusual that we describe space in terms of 'left' and 'right', 'ahead' and 'behind', in relation to a forward-facing body? You probably haven't, since this seems normal; it is habitual. In some languages space and location are described in relation to compass points, that is, whether something is 'north' or 'south'. This is certainly a habit that we all could learn; but it would take time before it was habitual. Until then, we would probably think in terms of 'left' and 'right' and then (with the aid of a mental compass) 'translate' into the new system. We explore the habitual connection between language and thought with the example of what you might consider a very basic quality: colour.

2.3.4 Colour

The issue of colour has occupied a number of linguists over the years (Berlin & Kay 1969). You might be surprised to learn that not all languages use colour in the same way. Indeed, some linguists argue that colour itself is not a category found in all languages (Wierzbicka 2005). Here, we take just one example of a difference between two languages that have colour terms: Russian and English. While English has one basic term for 'blue', Russian has two: 'goluboy' for lighter blues and 'siniy' for darker ones. Of course it is possible to make this distinction in English, but the point is that it is not an *obligatory* distinction. In Russian, a speaker has to decide whether something is 'goluboy' or 'siniy' as there is no less specific term for 'blue'. As Lera Boroditsky puts it, 'Languages force us to attend to certain aspects of our experience by making them grammatically obligatory. Therefore, speakers of different languages may be biased to attend to and encode different aspects of their experience while speaking' (2001: 2). With colour, we are dealing with a semantic rather than a grammatical category, but the argument is the same.

The researcher Jonathan Winawer and colleagues in psychology (Winawer, Witthoft, Frank, Wu, Wade & Boroditsky 2007) investigated the case of blue in Russian and English in order to determine whether the difference in language can be said to lead to a difference in thought. The researchers first asked subjects to divide a variety of shades of blue into light blue/goluboy and dark blue/siniy. This first established the boundary for each individual between the two categories. Despite the lack of basic terms for these two blues (English speakers have to qualify 'blue' in some way), the boundary for Russian and English speakers was about the same. The subjects were then given three squares of colour, two side by side and one square below these. They were asked which of the two squares was the same as the single square below. The time the answer took, and other information, was collected and analysed. Winawer and colleagues conclude:

> We found that Russian speakers were faster to discriminate two colors if they fell into different linguistic categories in Russian (one siniy and the other goluboy) than if the two colors were from the same category (both siniy or both goluboy).
>
> (2007: 7783)

Echoing the quotation from Boroditsky seen previously,

> The critical difference in this case is not that English speakers cannot distinguish between light and dark blues, but rather that Russian

speakers cannot avoid distinguishing them: they must do so to speak Russian in a conventional manner. This communicative requirement appears to cause Russian speakers to habitually make use of this distinction even when performing [7784] a perceptual task that does not require language.

(Winawer *et al.* 2007: 7783–4)

This provides some support for the influence of language on thought. Remember that this is not an absolute determinism, but rather that we form particular *habits* of thinking based on our language. We can certainly learn to recognise new categories of colour and new ways of conceptualising space, but the language that we speak means that we tend to use the categories provided by that language without thinking too much about it. These categories may seem self-evident, but if we think about it, we can see that there are other ways of dividing up the world.

2.4 ONE LANGUAGE MANY WORLDS

Even in a single language such as English there are many ways of representing the world. These representations are often the result of particular habitual ways of thinking, or worldviews. The example given of the botanist is worth recalling here. The way a botanist thinks and talks about plants depends on the botanical language available to them. Obviously if a new plant is discovered, that will have to be named. But when deciding how to classify this plant, the botanist will look at the kinds of features considered important in their discipline. The features that matter to botanists are directly connected to the aims of this science: to categorise and understand plants, trees and other flora. The features that the discipline gives importance to can be understood as being structured by the botanist's (world) view of plants. Colour probably would not be important, but how the plant reproduces will be. We can say, then, that a particular set of values underlie this structure because some things are important and some are less important. Finally, we can call this worldview the ideology of botany, that is, the values, ideas and features that define botany as a discipline; the things that are taken for granted in order to conduct the work of a botanist.

We don't tend to think of fields of science as having an 'ideology'. We tend to associate 'ideology' with beliefs that are somehow negative, subjective or simply other. But as we saw in Chapter 1, an ideology is a set of beliefs. The reason we tend only to identify the beliefs of other people is because we consider our own (individual and group) beliefs to be normal, natural and obvious. Fairclough calls this 'naturalization', which he defines as giving 'to particular ideological representations the status of common sense, and thereby mak[ing] them opaque, i.e. no longer visible as ideologies' (1995: 42, see also Bourdieu 1991).

Simpson writes:

> An ideology therefore derives from the taken-for-granted assumptions, beliefs and value systems which are shared collectively by social groups. And when an ideology is the ideology of a particularly powerful social group, it is said to be dominant.
>
> (1993: 5)

Here again we see how ideology links to power. We all have beliefs. Such beliefs become significant with respect to other people when the belief holders are in a position to get their point of view accepted as the norm.

We can see evidence of particular ideologies at work in language. As mentioned in the previous chapter, ideologies work like filters, changing the way things are represented according to the values of the ideology. For example, in many countries, there has been a change in the way recipients of government services are described when compared with a few decades ago (Mautner 2010). Rather than being referred to as 'people' or 'citizens', we are now 'customers', 'service users' and 'clients'. This signals an ideological shift towards government services framing (and speaking to and behaving towards) the public in the way a business or corporation would. The power of government means that it's very difficult to question or change this way of referring to members of the public. Further, particular ways of using language encourage certain kinds of behaviour.

Activity 2.4

Imagine what it would be like if you considered the relationships you have with friends as a 'customer/company' relationship. How would you talk about your friendships? What would you expect from your friends? How might this change the way you behave as a friend?

Thinking about friendships in the terms of Activity 2.4 would probably change both your behaviour and expectations. You might think about the time and money you have 'invested' in the friendship and whether you were getting 'good value' for this. You might expect your calls to be returned in a prompt manner, you would expect good 'service' from your friend and so on.

The idea that language influences the way we behave is perhaps most obvious in the case of certain metaphors. Lakoff and Johnson (1980) argue that our thought processes are structured along metaphorical lines. For example, when we describe a verbal argument, we are likely to use words such as 'attack', 'defend', 'won', 'lost' and so on. From evidence of the language we use to talk about arguments, Lakoff and Johnson suggest the existence of the metaphor ARGUMENT IS WAR. We use the language of war to describe arguments. They go further than this, and argue that this metaphor (ARGUMENT IS WAR) actually structures how we think about arguments. For Lakoff and Johnson (1980), the words we use are thus evidence of the way we think.

This way of speaking (and thinking) about arguments is probably so familiar that it doesn't seem particularly interesting. The familiarity of these expressions may hinder our attempts to explore any effect they may have. With some linguistic signs it can be easier to look with a critical eye. Imagine someone is being fired. Her boss has a number of choices.

Example 2.1
a.   You've been fired
b.   I'm making you redundant
c.   Your job has been outsourced
d.   All roles in your section have been demised
e.   We're providing you with new opportunities

Firing someone can be represented and communicated in various ways. Everyone understands what 'being fired' and being 'made redundant' mean. These days, the concept of outsourcing is probably also very familiar. But to 'demise' jobs is fairly opaque (*Guardian* 2013). Perhaps the stress of having to decode the message somehow displaces the disappointment of being fired or makes it easier for the manager to fire them.

War metaphors are common. Make a list of war terms and then where they are used other than to talk about real battles.

Activity 2.5

As we have seen, some languages place things into different 'classes'. For this activity, it might help to work with some colleagues. Choose some objects around you, and either gather them in one place or mark them in some way. Develop a classification system that sorts the objects into classes. Try and develop some reasons for the classes. You may have trouble allocating objects to just one! You'll need to think carefully about the objects and the features you use to construct your classes, and should give each a name. Then, tell some colleagues which class each belongs to, but not what the classes are or how they are defined. They will need to try and figure out your classification system.

This is exactly the kind of task that Dixon had to work through when describing the noun class system of Dyirbal (Section 2.3.2).

Activity 2.6

The police forces in the UK often use the radio to communicate with each other. Before 2009, there was no uniform way for police to speak over the radio. The lack of a common system meant that communication was not always efficient or clear. In emergency situations, it is very important that the right information is conveyed to the right people at the right time. Moreover, talk on the radio is expensive (Meyer 2007). It is therefore important to minimise the time spent on air while maximising the information conveyed. One way of ensuring clarity of communication at these times is to make sure a clear concise form of speaking is the norm. Two linguists, Edward Johnson and Mark Garner, together with police experts, developed a new way of communicating over the radio (NPIA 2007).

The system they developed, Airwave Speak, was created around the principles of 'Accuracy, Brevity, Clarity and Discipline' (British APCO 2007). Everyone has a call sign. If my call sign is 'Whisky Echo' and my recipient's call sign is 'Bravo 67' I would start with:

■ Bravo six-seven, Bravo six-seven from Whisky Echo Over.

This shows that when ending an utterance, 'over' is said. Other common phrases include:

■ Yes yes – for yes
■ Out – to signal that the conversation is finished
■ Received – to indicate the message has been heard.
■ Acknowledge – to check the other person is receiving
■ Read Back – to ask for information to be read back, in order to check correctness; responded to with 'Reading back'
■ Repeat – to ask someone to repeat what they said; responded to with 'Repeating' to indicate that the message is being repeated.

There are also protocols that set out the order in which information should be provided. For example, when describing a car, an officer would follow the order Colour, Make, Model, Type and Registration number. In giving this information, it would be marked, that is the officer would say 'Colour red, Make Toyota, Model not known, Type hatchback' and so on.

Using the conventions just outlined and the one added here, describe to a colleague the last time you got a lift from someone, whether it was a family member, friend or a taxi. For describing people use the information structure Name, Age, Sex, Height and mark this information in the same way as for cars. Does this start to feel 'natural'? How long does this take?

2.5 A MODEL FOR ANALYSING LANGUAGE

It's not necessary to create new words or expressions to convey ideological meanings. When speaking or writing, we constantly make choices, even if we are not aware that we are doing so. We decide which word to use from a number of possible alternatives, and we decide what kind of grammatical structure we'll use. Saussure's model of meaning that we encountered earlier, when looking at how the meaning of signs depends on their relationship with each other, also helps us to understand the significance of these grammatical choices.

Figure 2.2 is a visual representation of Saussure's model of the different relationships between the elements of an utterance. There are two axes we refer to in order to discuss the choices that are made when an utterance is created. The **syntagmatic** axis describes the order in which words are placed; the **paradigmatic** axis is used to refer to all the other words that could have been chosen for a particular slot. We can think of the syntagmatic axis as being horizontal and the paradigmatic as vertical, as shown in Figure 2.2.

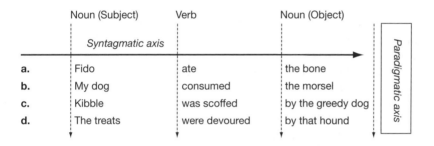

Figure 2.2 Syntagmatic and paradigmatic axes

If we consider simple sentences such as those in Figure 2.2, there are a number of choices available. As we can see from the form of the verb, the first two examples (a. and b.) are in the **active** voice (ate, consumed) and the second two (c. and d.) in the **passive** (was scoffed, were devoured). The active sentences **foreground**, that is, draw attention to, the dog that ate the food. The passive sentences, on the other hand, foreground the food. Thus, choosing between the active and the passive has an effect on what the reader's attention is drawn to. What the choice of the active means can only be understood in relation to all the other choices that could have been made, in relation to the passive, for example (Montgomery 2008).

The paradigmatic axis has been represented as running vertically. In each position a choice has to be made. Do we describe the dog's action as 'eating', 'consuming', 'scoffing' or 'devouring'? 'Eat' looks like the neutral choice; but it is still a choice. If 'scoffed' had been chosen, a negative attitude is immediately signalled. 'Scoffed' only has meaning because of the relationship it has to all other linguistic signs, and most importantly, in relation to the other signs (verbs) that could have been chosen in its place (see Section 2.2.2).

When these choices are made, we're making a decision not only about language and signs, but also about how we represent the world. By paying attention in our analyses to the choices made along these two axes, we can begin to reconstruct the values and beliefs that constitute a particular ideology. It's important to note that whether or not the choices are conscious, in a kind of premeditated way, they are still meaningful as choices. As we described in Chapter 1, one key insight about the relationship between language and ideology is that what may not seem like a choice to an individual speaker, can nevertheless be said to be chosen by their own ideological position rather than consciously.

2.5.1 Transitivity

To analyse these choices in more detail, we need a way of talking about different linguistic choices. There are a variety of theories that make this possible. What follows is a scaled-down version of Simpson's transitivity analysis (Simpson 1993). **Transitivity** usually relates to whether or not a verb needs to take a direct object; 'hit' requires a direct object (something being hit), while 'sit' does not. Thus, transitivity analysis is concerned with who does what to whom/what. The difference between this model and others is that it has a slightly different terminology. This is because rather than describing the rules for a well-formed sentence (which is what traditional grammars tend to do), this model includes information about the meaning of the clause.

Example 2.2 is a phrase that has two nouns and one verb. If we change the active form of the verb to the passive form, we have to change things around a bit to end up with a well-formed sentence. We have to change the form of the verb (from 'ate' to 'was eaten') and we have to include a preposition ('by') before Mary.

Example 2.2

a.	Fido	ate	the bone
b.	The bone	was eaten	by Fido

As discussed, Example 2.2b starts with, and so focuses on, the bone. If we described these sentences in terms of nouns and verbs or subjects and objects they would look the same, that is, both are structured Noun, Verb, Noun, or Subject, Verb, Object. We need the terminology provided by transitivity analysis that tells us which noun is doing the action to what. The doer is the Actor, and that which something is done to is the Goal. Verbs are always called Process.

Example 2.3

ACTOR	PROCESS	GOAL
Fido	ate	the bone

You shouldn't think of the term 'Goal' in the sense of something being aimed for. Dogs, broccoli and people can all occupy the goal position. The goal 'represents the person or entity affected by the process' (Simpson 1993: 89). Usually, sentences will have more than an Actor, Process and Goal. The detail that is often given can be labelled 'Circumstances'.

In more comprehensive versions of this **transitivity model**, there is specific terminology for different kinds of verbs. 'Thinking', for example, is a 'mental process'; while 'saying' is a 'verbal process'. In a similar way, the other roles have different terms in relation to these processes; for verbal processes, the 'actor' becomes the 'sayer' and the 'goal' the 'verbiage'.

The important thing is that even the stripped down terminology of Actor, Process, Goal and Circumstances allows us to describe the relevant difference between our two examples.

Example 2.4

	ACTOR	PROCESS	GOAL	CIRCUMSTANCES
a.	Fido	ate	the bone	in the doghouse

	GOAL	PROCESS	CIRCUMSTANCES	ACTOR
b.	The bone	was eaten	in the doghouse	by Fido

You probably know that in the passive form, the actor is not required for a well-formed sentence. If we take away the actor, we are left with:

Example 2.5

GOAL	PROCESS
The treats	were devoured

Because the Actor has been deleted, we call this choice 'Actor deletion' or 'Agent deletion'. Note that the 'circumstances' can be deleted too, but their removal is not quite the same as the deletion of the Actor because circumstances provide additional information. When we are told that treats were devoured, we know that someone must have devoured them; they can't have been eaten without some actor intervention. Thus, the deletion of the actor serves to foreground the goal and background the person responsible. Sometimes such deletion may be because of lack of information; we know that the treats were eaten, but we don't know who did it. In other cases, it can be to deflect blame from the actor. Consider the following headlines:

Miss Venezuela and British husband shot five times by robbers
(*Mirror*, January 8, 2014)

Briton and his beauty queen ex-wife killed in front of daughter
(*Telegraph* January 8, 2014)

These headlines are similar, in that both foreground the 'goal', the couple who were murdered.

Example 2.6

	GOAL	PROCESS	ACTOR
a.	Miss Venezuela and British husband shot five times by robbers		

	GOAL	PROCESS	CIRCUMSTANCE
b.	Briton and his beauty queen ex-wife killed		in front of daughter

In the second headline (Example 2.6b.), we see an example of agent deletion. Despite the surface similarities here, the transitivity analysis reveals an important difference. In the first headline (Example 2.6a.), the reader finds out who did the shooting. In the second, the actor has been deleted. Instead, other information is provided.

Activity 2.7

Compare the headlines about the same event below using the transitivity model and the syntagmatic and paradigmatic axes. What bias is present?

Venezuelan ex-beauty queen Monica Spear murdered
(*BBC News* 2014)

Teenagers among suspects arrested for murder of former Miss Venezuela Monica Spear and British ex-husband
(*Independent* 2014)

Family's anguish after beauty queen and British ex-husband shot dead in front of daughter, 5, in Venezuela
(*London Evening Standard* 2014)

Former Miss Venezuela Monica Spear is slain
(*Washington Post* 2014)

Venezuelan leaders scramble to discuss crime as outrage spreads over slaying of beauty queen
(*Montreal Gazette* 2014)

2.6 'POLITICAL CORRECTNESS'

For some, it seems reasonable to think that language can be used in a way that doesn't discriminate or demean. This position is often referred to as 'political correctness'. Linguists often refer to this as 'language reform' because it has at its heart a concern with what we could call representational justice. Here too, there are traces of linguistic determinism. Suppose there were a group that is discriminated against (let's call them 'martians') and suppose that the term 'martian' is pejorative. If a new term to refer to them were suggested, for example 'marsites', would martians cease to be a marginalised group? Would people think about martians differently if they were known as 'marsites'?

As we've already seen in Chapter 1, people tend to have strong views about their own language, and may strongly resist any changes made to it, especially if it means that they have to change their own linguistic behaviour. Cameron notes that people seem to object to their language choices being seen as political choices; 'Choice has altered the value of the terms and removed the option of political neutrality' (1995: 119). There are three main reasons people do not like language reform (Burridge 1996). The first is that people don't like linguistic change (see Chapter 1). The second is people resent being told what to do with their language. The third is that they are uncomfortable when told that a term they thought was neutral or inoffensive is actually laden with meanings they did not intend. When someone is told their language use is offensive, it feels very much like their character is under attack (they are a bigot, racist, misogynist and so on). This kind of language change is then resisted using the accusation that these changes are frivolous and about 'political correctness'. 'Political correctness' has come to be associated with trivial and pointless changes in language because of this resistance. Thus, 'political correctness' (PC) and what we understand it to mean is a direct result of more or less conscious effort directed at discrediting certain kinds of language reform and those who advocate it. At the same time, and related to people's views on their owner-ship of language, others argue that PC is an imposition of authority, a command to speak (and perhaps think) in a particular way. In this sense, they argue, it breaches rights to freedom of thought and speech.

Cameron notes that the circulating definitions of PC all come from people denouncing a particular 'politically correct' change or attacking the concept as a whole. This tends to be political too: 'the way right-wing commentators have established certain presuppositions about "political correctness" over the past few years is a triumph – as a sociolinguist I cannot help admiring it – of the politics of definition, or linguistic interven-tion' (1995: 123).

Definitions and representations are important. While we've looked at the choices that can be made along the syntagmatic axis in some detail with transitivity analysis, we need to see the link between choices along the paradigmatic axis (the other words we could decide to put in any particular slot) and these issues of representation. Issues of representation should not be seen in isolation. The choices that are available in a language have signif-icant consequences. Cameron points out that language reform 'changes the repertoire of social meanings and choices available to social actors' (Cameron 2014 [1990]: 90). This means that language reform provides social actors and people with particular ways of representing themselves and being represented by others. Language reform can provide people with positive terms in which to construct their identity. This is particularly impor-tant where no such positive terms previously existed.

Activity 2.8

The following are some examples of 'politically correct' language: some are actually in common use, some have been reported by the media, but are not actually used at all. Which ones are 'real' examples? What social meanings are being created by the new terms?

- Winterval
- Vertically challenged
- Ethnic minorities
- Coffee without milk
- Differently abled
- Comb free
- Senior
- Non-denominational holiday shrubbery
- Herstory

2.7 SUMMARY

In this chapter, we've seen that the way people represent the world matters. Every language choice, whether consciously intended or not, demonstrates an ideology. While we often consider ideology to be a bad thing, it's important to remember that we all have habitual ways of thinking about the world and this is reflected in the habitual choices we make in language. Because it's habitual, we don't think about the values expressed by the choices. To be able to think about these issues of representation we need tools such as transitivity analysis to describe these choices. We also have to be aware of the fact that arguments about language are very often ideological in the sense that they rely on certain assumptions about what is correct or standard. The way that correctness is defined is itself an ideological act as well as a way of exerting power.

FURTHER READING

Burridge, K. (1996) 'Political correctness: Euphemism with attitude', *English Today*, 12(3): 42–3.

Fowler, R. (1991) *Language in the News: Discourse and Ideology in the Press*, London: Routledge.

Lakoff, G. and Johnson, M. (1980) *Metaphors We Live By*, Chicago: University of Chicago Press.

Lucy, J. (1997) 'Linguistic Relativity', *Annual Review of Anthropology*, 26: 291–312.

Lucy, J. (2005) 'Through the window of language: Assessing the influence of language diversity on thought', *Theoria* 54: 299–309.

Majid, A., Bowerman, M., Kita, S., Haun, D. B. M. and Levinson, S. C. (2004) 'Can language restructure cognition? The case for space', *TRENDS in Cognitive Sciences*, 8(3):108–14.

Martin, L. (1986) '"Eskimo words for snow": A case study in the Genesis and Decay of an Anthropological Example', *American Anthropologist*, 88: 418–23.

Orwell, G. (1968 [1946]) 'Politics and the English language', in *Inside the Whale and Other Essays*, Harmondsworth: Penguin: 127–40.

Pullum, G. (1991) 'The Great Eskimo Vocabulary Hoax', in *The Great Eskimo Vocabulary Hoax and Other Irreverent Essays on the Study of Language*, Chicago: University of Chicago Press: 159–74.

Reah, D. (2002) *The Language of Newspapers (Intertext)*, London: Routledge.

Whorf, B. L. (1954) 'The Relation of Habitual Thought and Behaviour to Language', in *Language, Meaning and Maturity: Selections from Etc., a Review of General Semantics*, 1943–1953, S. I. Hayakawa (ed.) New York: Harper: 197–215.

NOTES

1   The Sapir-Whorf hypothesis was not, in the original work, a 'hypothesis' at all. Whorf used the expression 'linguistic relativity principle' (see Lee 1996). We use 'hypothesis' here as this is how the principle is popularly and generally known.

2   The phrase 'prison house' is attributable to the philosopher Friedrich Nietzsche. The philosopher Ludwig Wittgenstein is also associated with the idea. Though he phrases it differently, '*The limits of my language* mean the limits of my world' (proposition 5.6, 1961: p. 115, emphasis in original).

CHAPTER 3

Language and politics

3.1	INTRODUCTION	42
3.2	WHAT IS 'POLITICS'?	43
3.3	POLITICS AND IDEOLOGY	43
3.4	THREE PERSUASIVE STRATEGIES	45
3.5	GRASS ROOTS POLITICS: INTRODUCING MORE LINGUISTIC TOOLS	45
3.6	WORDS AND WEAPONS: THE POLITICS OF WAR	51
3.7	EXTENDING METAPHOR	55
3.8	SILLY CITIZENSHIP	59
3.9	SUMMARY	62

3.1 INTRODUCTION

In this chapter, we consider the importance of language in political contexts. We begin by defining politics, making clear its connection to both ideology and persuasion. We then explore linguistic features that are deployed in order to persuade audiences. These techniques are common across all kinds of persuasive texts, but they are generally easy to find in arguments that are clearly political. The linguistic tools of repetition and parallelism, presupposition and metaphor are introduced by taking examples from the manifesto of a global political movement. These tools will help us see how we are persuaded to accept particular ideologies. To further understand how these tools work, we then consider the language of war using the concepts of euphemism and dysphemism. This allows us to consider the consequences of representational choices. War is clearly political, and may also feel exceptional, rather distant from the everyday for many people. Considering the ideologies communicated by children's toys shows how this division breaks down.

We then move onto the politics of education, specifically, the way the language of commercial transactions is increasingly used in the field of higher education. Because of powerful interests involved in education, it seems very difficult to challenge this ideology. However, we also consider a kind of politics, 'silly citizenship', that is more amenable to individual action.

3.2 WHAT IS 'POLITICS'?

In 2004, the Electoral Commission in the UK created and broadcast an advertising campaign to encourage people to vote and engage in politics. It was an animation, focusing on two male friends. When one friend, Tom, tries to discuss the European Parliament, his friend Mike says, 'I don't do politics'. The animation then follows the friends through a normal city on a normal day. Whenever Mike complains about something, whether it's graffiti or the cost of a drink, Tom waves his finger and remarks 'but you don't do politics'. The advertisement finishes with 'Politics affects almost everything, so if you don't do politics there's not much you do do' (cited in Walker 2004).

When people think about language and politics, it is normal to think about politicians, Parliament and the talk and texts that surround these. We will touch on this kind of material in this chapter, but what we mean by 'politics' is much broader than you might think. Certainly politics includes policy planning and legislation and the discussions of these processes. It also means discussions of social issues by politicians and people who aren't politicians. In this sense, politics is the process by which members of a community discuss and decide about how they are governed. These discussions are clearly connected to power including who is in power, how they are using these powers and whether they should continue to be in power. As the animation points out, we must remember that politics is everywhere.

3.3 POLITICS AND IDEOLOGY

In the previous chapters, we described ideology as a way of thinking and examined how ideology has an effect on both thought and behaviour. When it comes to politics, ideologies are generally connected with beliefs about the proper organisation of society and how to achieve and maintain the goals that this entails. What is striking about this is that these beliefs are found to pattern among people in predictable ways. For example, Jost, Frederico and Napier (2009: 310) explain that political positions we call 'conservative/right wing' and 'liberal/left wing' each have their own demonstrable and predictable belief systems:

> This formulation of the left-right distinction and many others contain two interrelated aspects, namely (a) advocating versus resisting social change (as opposed to tradition), and (b) rejecting versus accepting inequality.
>
> (Jost, Frederico & Napier 2009: 310)

Even a simple description like this, with only two factors, allows people to both explain and justify their political position. A person who thinks society is unequal and that inequality is not desirable, would advocate for social change. If a person believes that inequality is justified or simply the natural order of society they'll be more likely to want to keep things as they are.

Activity 3.1

Regardless of your own opinion, write down the arguments you could use in support of:

a.   retaining the social system you have
b.   changing the social system in a particular way

Note down the feature of society each would involve (this may relate to employment, education, family life, leisure time, the environment and gender roles) as well as arguments for the system generally.
Is this difficult?

When putting together arguments for social change or maintenance of the current system, the points in your argument must be consistent (Activity 3.1). For example, if you want a system that promotes financial equality, this will have consequences for your ideas about wages and employment and gender roles. You probably found it quite hard to come up with arguments for the side you personally don't support. Our beliefs, our sense of what is the 'right' social order has a profound effect on the arguments we find convincing.

Language also has an important role in this kind of discussion. Few people would advocate 'inequality' in simple terms. 'Inequality' has a negative value attached to it; we generally support what is 'equal' rather than 'unequal'. This is considered 'fair'. Notice, however, what happens when we talk about 'fairness' rather than 'equality'. This is an example of a linguistic tool called lexical choice. Equality suggests a straightforward equivalence – that everyone be treated in exactly the same way. 'Fairness', however, allows for other factors to come into the equation. Fairness enables us to consider things such as individual qualities and abilities, whether people have worked hard, whether people 'deserve' something. If you want to argue for maintenance of an apparently unequal system, you're likely to explain this in terms of 'fairness' rather than 'inequality'. Notice that changing one word can change the whole structure of an argument and the points that are needed to defend it (see also Danet 1980).

There are other linguistic tools that can be used to persuade people. In the following, we'll look at some extracts of a manifesto from an emerging political movement in order to show how those tools work. It's important to state at the outset, that the linguistic features we'll see in the manifesto are common across all kinds of persuasive text. They are not of themselves problematic or manipulative; rather, they are typical of persuasive texts, especially in the domain of politics.

3.4 THREE PERSUASIVE STRATEGIES

According to Aristotle (1991), persuasion can take place in at least three ways. He makes a distinction between arguments that rely on **logos**, the words or the argument itself; **pathos**, the emotion conveyed or the emotional connection to an idea or issue and finally, **ethos**, arguments from personality, that is, we trust the argument or ideas because we trust the speaker.

> Identify some texts (they may be written or spoken) that rely on these different kinds of argument. Are there consistent types of arguments that rely on these strategies?

Activity 3.2

Political persuasion, like all forms of persuasion, relies on all three tactics. Employing these tactics is not of themselves deceptive or unusual. Nor are they mutually exclusive. For example, a cosmetics advertisement might use all three. They point out the science behind the efficacy of the cosmetic (logos), employ a celebrity to deliver the message (ethos: a trustworthy speaker) and the advertisement appeals to the desire to look better (pathos).

3.5 GRASS ROOTS POLITICS: INTRODUCING MORE LINGUISTIC TOOLS

The Occupy movement is an international movement, which garnered attention with its actions in the wake of the global financial crisis of the early years of this century. The #occupy movement was inspired by the 'Occupy Wall Street' initiative as well international events such as the Arab Spring (http://www.occupytogether.org/aboutoccupy/#background). It has been taken up around the world and although it is a political movement, it is not a party political movement that is structured in the same way as the political parties we are used to seeing. It is also not clear that it is a singular movement (see *The Occupied Times* 2012). The Occupy movement politics and policies are also very different to those we normally hear and see from governments and mainstream politicians. The movement deals with precisely the same issues that established political parties do, but just as it differs in terms of its structure, it differs in terms of the way problems are identified and in terms of the solutions offered. It is a political movement that has emerged recently, and part of its profile is clearly connected to the increasing use of social media. As such, it seems to represent a shift in politics and the possibility for expressing political views and taking political action.

In order to understand how linguistic choices can have persuasive effects, we look at some of the detail in one of their texts, the 'GlobalMay Manifesto' (Occupy Movement 2012). This manifesto is a statement about the aims and ideals of the movement; though not one that everyone associated with the movement gives their full support to (see *The Occupied Times* 2012). We have discussed the importance of contrasts such as equality and inequality; in this text, we can also identify a number of contrasts. Contrasts set up a clear structure for readers to orient to. Setting up a contrast not only identifies the two things in opposition, it defines them. That is, a contrast doesn't simply describe something that exists already in the world; it also creates the contrast by announcing it.

3.5.1 Contrasts

The manifesto has an introductory section followed by a list of numbered points. Each point has beneath it further bullet points setting out in more detail the consequences of the main point. The first point is shown in Example 3.1.

> **Example 3.1**
> The economy must be put to the service of people's welfare, and to support and serve the environment, not private profit. We want a system where labour is appreciated by its social utility, not its financial or commercial profit.

We find at least two contrasts in Example 3.1. The authors set people's welfare and the environment against private profit. They also contrast social utility with financial and commercial profit. Because social utility, human welfare and the environment all have something in common (a concern with people, where and how they live) these can easily be considered together. Likewise, private, financial and commercial profit all belong together. These two contrasts, then, work to re-enforce each other. Notice that there is another contrast here that depends on the use of 'we'. If 'we want' something it suggests that other people don't. The use of 'we' in this way sets up an us/them distinction. The us/them distinction is perhaps one of the most pervasive in persuasive language (van Dijk 2006).

3.5.2 Three part lists and parallelism

Three part lists (or triple structure) are very common in persuasive texts. They have a pleasing rhythm and as such are easy to remember. They are easy to identify as they have the structure 'a, b and c' (Hutchby & Woffit 2008: 183).

Example 3.2
corporate subsidies and tax cuts should be done away with if said company outsources jobs to decrease salaries, violates the environment or the rights of workers.

Example 3.2 is from the Manifesto and appears beneath Example 3.1. It is an elaboration of the point made there. Notice that the second sentence finishes with a list of three things: outsourcing of jobs, violating the environment, or violating the rights of workers. This is clearly a three part list but this structure could have exploited this feature a bit more fully, through some small changes. For example, 'Corporate subsidies and tax cuts should be removed from companies who outsource jobs, violate the environment or exploit workers' reveals the three part structure more clearly as it repeats the syntactic structure across the three part list by providing a verb and a noun in each part of the list.

Having the same syntactic structure across a number of clauses close to each other is not unique to three part lists. It is also a feature of **parallelism**. Indeed, a three part list is a particular form of parallelism. The parallel syntactic structure encourages a reader to consider the entities in the same place in the same way.

In the final part of the manifesto we find a clear example of parallelism and **repetition**.

Example 3.3
This is a worldwide global spring. We will be there and will fight until we win. We will not stop being people. We are not numbers. We are free women and men.

There is clear parallelism in the second sentence. The parallel syntactic positions are 'be there', 'fight' and 'win'. Notice how this communicates a temporal progression too because of the ordering. When we read a sentence, we understand that the action communicated first happened first and that which is communicated second happened next and so on. Here, the sentence is communicating that we will be 'there' and in this place we will fight and we will stay there until we win; but because of the parallel structure, it can be done in a very succinct way.

There are other examples of parallelism in Example 3.3. Can you identify them? What effect do they have?

Activity 3.3

The most straightforward form of parallelism is repetition. We know from our own use of language that if we want to emphasise something we repeat it. The same holds true in political texts. Repetition across a long text or speech can also help structure it. Just like repetition in a song or poem, it provides a focal point for the reader and allows them to see the structure of the text. Repetition used in this way works as kind of punctuation. The structure that this provides and the way parallelism works can be clearly seen if you list the parallel structures as in Example 3.4.

Example 3.4
We will not stop being people.
We are not numbers.
We are free women and men.

Example 3.4 shows the parallelism clearly and also shows the contrast being made. 'Numbers' are contrasted with 'free women and men' because they occupy the same syntactic position.

Did you notice the unusual noun phrase in the last sentence in Example 3.4? The usual order of 'men and women' has been changed to 'women and men'. As this word order is unusual (marked) it **'foregrounds'** the noun phrase and the position of 'women' in it. Whether it is interpreted as meaning anything depends, first, on whether the reader notices the change and, second, whether the reader attributes any significance to it. While it seems to be standard to place 'men' before 'women' when they are **collocated**, some people understand this as sexist; why, they ask, should 'women' not come first, at least sometimes? This choice can therefore be read as an attempt to point out that 'men' always coming first is problematic and potentially discriminatory. This kind of activism relates to language reform (see Chapter 2 and Chapter 6).

As well as foregrounding, it is also possible to background certain features. Sometimes this is done exactly to draw attention to something rather than to obscure information.

Example 3.5
Maximum income should be limited, and minimum income set to reduce the outrageous social divisions in our societies and its social political and economic effects.

The authors argue that 'maximum income should be limited and a minimum income set'. These points about maximum and minimum income are foregrounded by placing them at the start of the clauses. This is done by using a **passive structure**. As we saw in Chapter 2, the passive tense allows for agent deletion and that is exactly what has been done here. The focus is on the result that the authors want; more equality in terms of income. What they have left in the background, by deleting the agent, is who is required to take up this task. This job would likely fall to the government. As Occupy are calling for a more participatory democracy, one that will 'really represent the variety and diversity of our societies' (Occupy Movement

2012), the agent could also be 'we', as in the government and the people. This is another advantage of the passive voice and the associated agent deletion. It allows writers to express their points without having to specify agents that are difficult to characterise.

3.5.3 Pronouns

Notice that all the sentences in Example 3.4 start with 'we'. Who 'we' are is, therefore, a crucial question. The use of **pronouns**, especially the first ('I', 'we') and second person ('you'), is common in persuasive speeches. In English, 'we' does not specify who 'we' are in that it may include the audience (inclusive we) or exclude the audience (exclusive we). The implicit message in these lines, the argument it implies, is that if you consider yourself a person rather than a number you are also part of 'we'. 'You' is also useful, because in English 'you' does not distinguish between the singular and plural second person.

3.5.4 Presupposition

There is another feature in Example 3.2 here that needs to be discussed. Even if you didn't know about corporate subsidies and tax cuts for corporations, Example 3.2 makes clear that these things exist. Notice that the text doesn't specifically tell the reader that these things exist before discussing them, it simply discusses them. **New information** in a text can be presented as though it is **given information**. Therefore the **semantic presupposition** in the example from the manifesto is that 'Corporate subsidies and tax cuts' for corporations exist. A semantic presupposition is information embedded in the sentence that is taken for granted in the composition and meaning of the text. In order to find presuppositions in a text, there are a number of things you can look for. Possessive pronouns, subordinate clauses, question structures and adjectives (especially comparative adjectives) are good places to focus attention when looking for particular presuppositions. The easiest way to test for semantic presupposition is to negate the sentence.

The sentence that follows (from Example 3.2) is affirmative. Try to negate it. Can you see that the existence of certain entities is not denied when you do this?

corporate subsidies and tax cuts should be done away with if said company outsources jobs to decrease salaries, violates the environment or the rights of workers.

Activity 3.4

In the negated version in Activity 3.4, 'corporate subsidies and tax cuts should *not* be done away with…' the existence of 'corporate subsidies and tax cuts' is retained. This property allows us to distinguish semantic presuppositions from other information that may only be implied. For example, if someone says 'John found a veterinarian for his cat', this presupposes that someone called John exists and that he has a cat. It **implies** that the cat is somehow ill; but there is nothing in the sentence itself that says anything about the cat's health. You might assume that the cat is ill and that this is why the speaker is discussing John's search for a veterinarian, but this relies on your actual experience of the world, what you know about cats and veterinarians. It is background knowledge. It is not a property of the statement itself. This type of knowledge can be referred to as **pragmatic presupposition**. In this book we use the term presupposition for *semantic presupposition* while referring to *pragmatic presupposition* as something implied by the text (see Simon-Vandenbergen *et al.* 2007).

Because of the way semantic presuppositions function, they can be used to efficiently incorporate a 'truth' into a text. This can have powerful persuasive effects. As Simon-Vandenbergen *et al.* (2007) remark, 'The reason why presuppositions are exploitable is that they are harder to challenge' exactly because they are embedded in the text (2007: 49). Semantic and pragmatic presupposition, however, are a natural feature of language and aren't always used to exploit or persuade.

3.5.5 Metaphor and intertextuality

Metaphors create and assert an equivalence between two things. Metaphors state that 'x *is* y'; by contrast, a **simile** simply draws a comparison, saying that x is *like* y. Because they assert and create an equivalence, metaphors don't need a verb; a noun phrase can express the metaphor all by itself. The first sentence in Example 3.3 gives us a good example of metaphor. Here it is again in Example 3.6.

Example 3.6
This is a worldwide global spring.

The **metaphor** in Example 3.6 has become familiar only in recent years. The 'Arab Spring' is a name used to collectively describe popular political movements, often leading to changes in government, that started late 2010. The authors of the Manifesto have borrowed and reframed the metaphor to call for a worldwide shift in political and economic structure – a 'global' spring. This metaphor asserts that the Occupy movement is a global spring, a new start (like spring) for the whole of the world. The authors capitalise on the political meanings that 'spring' already has (i.e. undergoing some kind of positive, new change) and extend this idea of natural renewal to the whole world.

There is one more textual feature to examine in this manifesto. We find an example in the first sentence of Example 3.7.

Example 3.7
Apart from bread, we want roses. Everyone has the right to enjoy culture, participate in a creative and enriching leisure at the service of the progress of humankind.

Clearly the authors do not literally want roses. To understand what the authors mean requires specific background knowledge. We can decipher the meaning by considering the contrast between bread and roses. Bread is food; it is essential. Roses, however, are a luxury, something that people don't need to survive. The contrast between bread and roses is a contrast between surviving and living. This 'bread and roses' contrast, however, has a long history, originating in the campaign of female textile workers in the early twentieth century in Massachusetts (Eisenstein 2013: 32). The authors connect their text to a long line of political struggle for workers. The first sentence here can be discussed in terms of metaphor, but because it has a longer history, it can also be discussed in terms of **intertextuality**. Intertextuality refers to the strategy of drawing on historical, cultural knowledge, as in the example of 'bread and roses'. To fully appreciate the choice made here readers need to know something about this history. Intertextuality also reminds us that texts, and language, have a relation to previous texts and utterances.

> Try to identify other examples of the features described here (parallelism, presupposition, intertextuality, metaphor) in the Manifesto. What other features do you notice? Looking for repetition of particular words, phrases or syntax is a good place to start. What is the text trying to persuade the audience of?
>
> Activity 3.5

3.6 WORDS AND WEAPONS: THE POLITICS OF WAR

War is a domain where we see the political and ideological effects of language. We will explore some examples of how word choices can both reflect ideology and have persuasive effects. We consider the language used to refer to nuclear weapons drawing on our discussion in Chapter 2 about the connections between language and thought. 'Nukespeak', or the language used to talk about nuclear weapons, has long been of interest to linguists (Chilton 1982; Cohn 1987; Woods 2007). One of the reasons for this is that nuclear weapons and the production of nuclear power are fields where **euphemisms** are common. A euphemism is a word used to make something that might otherwise be unpleasant or disagreeable more benign. Euphemisms are also common in the domains of war. 'Collateral damage' for example, is a convenient way of referring to large numbers of civilian deaths, especially during times of war. We tend to use euphemisms in taboo fields, especially in relation biological processes that we'd rather not think about. **Dysphemism**, by contrast, makes something more disagreeable or unpleasant than it might otherwise be. If you call a 'hamburger' a 'cowburger' you might find yourself less hungry than you thought you were.

Carol Cohn (1987) studied the language of nuclear weapons, spending a year with defence professionals in the US in 1984. Seeking to understand how defence policy is formulated, she argues that at least part of it is driven by the way these professionals talk about nuclear weapons. Further, having been exposed to this language for such a long period, she found her own thinking starting to change. Cohn notes that defence policy is a field full of 'abstraction and euphemism, which allows infinite talk about nuclear holocaust without ever forcing the speaker or enabling the listener to touch the reality behind those words' (Cohn 1987: 17). Table 3.1 provides examples of some these abstractions and euphemisms.

Table 3.1 Examples of Nukespeak

Euphemism	Gloss
clean bombs	'weapons which are largely fusion rather than fission and which therefore release a higher quantity of energy not as radiation but as blast' (Cohn 1987: 17)
countervalue attacks	'incinerating cities' (Cohn 1987: 17)
Christmas tree farm	'where missiles are lined up in their silos ready for launching' (Cohn 1987: 20)
footprint	'the pattern in which bombs fall' (Cohn 1987: 20)
cookie cutter	'a particular model of nuclear attack' (Cohn 1987: 20)

Cohn describes her acquisition of this new language related to nuclear weapons and warfare. She felt that knowing how to speak this language gave her a sense of power, in terms of not being so afraid of nuclear war, but also when speaking to those working in the industry. She discovered that if she did not use this new language, the experts would consider her 'ignorant or simpleminded, or both' (1987: 22).

The use of euphemism is not just about making a single object seem more agreeable or about making single actions more acceptable. As with the choice of 'equality' and 'fair', it can structure a whole set of arguments such that some topics can be spoken about in great detail. The choice of a word has consequences.

Woods (2007) explores another way language and nuclear weapons are discussed. He points out the normalisation of the **discourse** of nuclear weapons, but also that there is a competing, strongly anti-nuclear discourse. This alternative discourse emphasises the notion of 'proliferation', the idea that 'the spread of nuclear arms is inevitable, unstoppable and dangerous' (Woods 2007: 94). The word 'proliferation' manages to convey an entire argument and an ongoing process that can't be stopped. Paradoxically, perhaps, Woods suggests that this discourse of 'proliferation' has actually stopped the spread of nuclear weapons because of the form of the word itself.

Discourse in this context means two things. First, discourse refers to texts or language longer than a sentence or utterance. In this sense, nuclear discourse is extended talk or a text about nuclear weapons. Second, discourse describes the ideology underlying and structuring this talk. In the case Woods describes, 'proliferation' and the arguments that this term refers to can be described as a particular discourse about nuclear weapons. That is, the proliferation discourse relies on a set of beliefs and values that are ideological. More broadly, discourse used in relation to ideology is common across a number of fields and topics as we will see in later chapters.

What kind of word is 'proliferation'? Is it a verb, an adjective, an adverb, a noun or something else? Does this have any consequences for how we understand it?

Activity 3.6

The morphology of 'proliferation' tells us that this is a noun. While it is derived from the verb 'proliferate' if we use it in a sentence, it is clearly a noun. The change of non-noun word to a noun is known as **nominalisation**. The reason it is so powerful is related to how we think about nouns. In simple terms, a noun is a naming word; it names a thing. Things have a physical reality, they tend to be stable and to have some kind of concrete existence. This is not to claim that all nouns are concrete; rather, the idea is that when we encounter a noun we tend to orient to the idea that it is a thing. This means that when a verb (or something else) is turned into a noun, we are more likely to think of it as something solid, with a real concrete existence in the world. Once people start talking about 'proliferation' we are in a world of things rather than processes.

Woods argues that we need to understand the discursive formation of 'proliferation' and understand its effects in the contemporary world. He argues that it has serious and far-reaching consequences and is a 'cause of global inequality and double-standards' (2007: 116). It can have these effects because it is such a common sense idea; the belief that 'proliferation' of nuclear weapons is a bad thing is completely normalised in many places around the world. It is part of a dominant ideology in the context of international affairs.

3.6.1 Toys and ideology

The language of warfare and nuclear weapons is linked to the normalisation of particular ideologies. As we saw above, identifying who 'we' refers to is important in understanding persuasive texts. Who 'we' are can also depend very much on who 'they' are. When it comes to war and violence, who is 'us' and who is 'them' is a matter of life and death.

It's worth considering where these ideas come from; how do you find out who 'we' are? As this is a central question for any society, it's hardly surprising that who 'we' are is captured by dominant ideologies. What is a bit surprising is where these ideologies can be found. Linguistic features are not the only evidence of ideology. As we claimed at the start of the chapter, politics is everywhere. A place where you might not expect to find political ideologies is in children's toys. We take this example to show that language is not distinct from other forms of social practice.

David Machin and Theo van Leeuwen observe that toys related to war, such as toy soldiers, guns and other 'play' weapons have 'prepared children for specific kinds of warfare, fought in particular ways fused with specific political ideologies about the meaning of war and society itself' (Machin & van Leeuwen 2009: 52). If we look closely at toys and how they are used, we can find out something about who 'we' are.

Playing with toys may well involve language, but it also requires physical activity. Ideology is not just expressed in language; it is found in every aspect of our lives, including the way children interact with toys. Many plastic toy guns have lights and sounds, including voices shouting at the 'enemy'. The inclusion of 'technology' and the use of sounds makes the toys not only representative of contemporary war but also makes them interactive and so 'allow the child to become physically, actively, involved in the representation' (Machin & van Leeuwen, 2009: 57). Machin and van Leeuwen found that the way children hold guns demonstrates a familiarity with the physical handling of weaponry. Moreover, the children can explain what the guns are for, who the soldiers are and what they do. The children in their study demonstrated fully developed discourses of war, such as knowing that the special forces soldiers are the 'cleverest and best trained' and engage in 'daring missions'. By interacting in this way with these toys, children learn to identify with these soldiers and their weapons, seeing them as representations of their own nation and society. This helps to build a picture for them of the difference between 'us' and 'them'. Who, in particular, 'them', or the 'enemy' represent, in this play is left rather undefined (Machin & van Leeuwen 2009: 58, 59). The children identify an 'enemy' but only refer to the enemy in a generic way, e.g. 'bad people' (2009: 59). For the perpetuation of ideology, this is convenient as it allows for any number of actors, groups or nations to be inserted into this role.

Machin and van Leeuwen argue that particular views of war become part of the children's 'mental furniture' (2009: 59). This has consequences over and above the identification of us and them. For example, the toys emphasise the cultural importance of a particular kind of masculinity, the concept of the daring hero expert soldier and the practice of war as a way of resolving conflict (2009: 59). The values and ideologies that naturalise this way of thinking about the world shouldn't be ignored.

Think of examples of toys made for and marketed to young girls. What do they communicate (see also Boyle 2013)?

Activity 3.7

3.7 EXTENDING METAPHOR

Metaphors are a common part of language. They are 'the omnipresent principle of language' (Richards 1965: 92). We have seen that metaphor creates and states an equivalence; but metaphors are not always obvious. There are many metaphors that are part of everyday language that we might not even notice, such as ARGUMENT IS WAR (Chapter 2 Section 2.4).

As was the case with euphemisms, a metaphor can communicate a lot more than a simple equivalence. Horner remarks: 'Metaphors evoke scenarios; scenarios suggest causal relationships and invite evaluation' (2011: 33). Scenarios, causal relationships, evaluation are all part of persuasive language and of political language. 'Metaphors link ideology with political discourse by providing models for making sense of [the world]' (Horner 2011: 32). We've already seen that linguistic choices people make, the language that is used, can have consequences of how the world is understood. In this section, we consider the consequences of metaphors that are related to money, finance and the market.

It is common to use metaphors when there is a gap in the language. For example, the set of events that constituted the 'Arab spring', described earlier, generated a term to refer to this new phenomenon. The creation of new metaphors is also common when complex political or financial news is being communicated to the public (Horner 2011).

Consider the following terms and decide which action people would be more likely to accept. Why? In answering this question, think about how you might use these words in a sentence.

rescue plan

bailout

intervention

Activity 3.8

While 'intervention' seems reasonably neutral, it still suggests an undesirable situation. We know this because of how the word is used. People talk about 'interventions' in the context of disputes and problems. You don't 'intervene' in a friendly conversation; you 'intervene' in an argument. A 'rescue plan' is clearly a positive thing as it involves saving someone or something from a negative event. Of course, the presence of the negative event makes the term double edged. Finally, what you understand by 'bailout' may well be influenced by the way it was used in the wake of the 2008 financial crisis. In the US, government action, the 'Emergency Stabilization Act', to support the financial markets and banks was referred to using the terms listed. Most widely, it was referred to as a 'bailout'. As Horner notes, this 'evokes images of disaster: sailors bailing water of sinking boats, pilots ejecting from crashing planes' (Horner 2011: 30 following Safire 2008). Far from having some of the positive associations of 'rescue plan', Horner argues that some saw the bailout plan 'as a means of rescuing the guilty from the consequences of their actions' (2011: 31).

Underlying the language used to describe the financial crisis and subsequent intervention, Horner uncovered a series of metaphors that informed thought, language and action. The economy was conceived as a 'system' frequently described with plumbing metaphors. For example, the economic system was 'clogged' and needed to be cleared. The image of clogging was also found in relation to another metaphor: the economy is a human body. 'The circulatory system appeared in several instances of bailout talk to project the danger of a larger system failure should the symptoms remain untreated' (Horner 2011: 35).

Once the economy is portrayed as a human body, a whole range of other metaphors become available. A body has arteries, which if clogged, may lead to a heart attack. If the economy is a body, it also has a heart, which has to be protected (Horner 2011: 35). When people understand that they are part of this body, views of the economy become more personal and more corporeal. No one wants to be sick: literally or metaphorically. Portraying the economy as a body, and by implication a person, is part of a broader set of discourses and representations. Choosing to represent the economy as a body makes discussion of the financial crisis both comprehensible and somewhat personal. As we all have bodies we all understand how they work. As we are all part of the national body we are necessarily part of this economic body too. Constructing the economy as a body also means it may be imagined as a person. The economy, then, can be said to have been **personified**.

Mautner has argues that the market, another name for the economy, has been personified. 'There is ample linguistic evidence that, in general usage, "the market" is reified (i.e., made into a "thing") and at the same time anthropomorphised (i.e., treated as it if it were a human being)' (Mautner 2010:14). The market has a 'will of its own'; it has moods that can be altered by some kind of external action; it can be 'encouraged', 'surprised' and 'misled' (Mautner 2010: 14–15). Once the market is personified, important consequences arise from this. Just as a person in danger should be rescued and a person who is ill should be cured, so too with the market and the economy. Moreover, as Mautner (2010) shows, the market has become the most important person in the world. This is not simply a discourse; it is an idea that has outcomes for real people, for their employment, housing and every aspect of their lives. The construction of the market as a person is a political act.

Even personified, however, 'the market' is rather abstract. Unless a person works directly in financial industries, it might be difficult to see the consequences of this metaphorical personification. Mautner's argument that the market is the most important person, however, can be seen in a domain that may be more familiar: universities.

3.7.1 Student as customer

While in some parts of the world it has long been the norm for university students to pay for their education, this practice has now spread to countries where for many years higher education did not cost a great deal of money. In Australia, for example, Higher Education required no fees between 1974 and 1989 and they were unknown in the UK until 1998. Having to pay fees to the university is only one of the costs associated with higher education and only one of the many things that should be considered when thinking about access to university. Perhaps deciding to levy fees changes the way we think, behave and talk about higher education. Here we explore some features of higher education where fees have been introduced.

For example, students are now increasingly described as 'customers'. Journalist Sean Coughlan writes, 'The market economy in higher education will mean students have to be treated as valued customers. Because, after all, they're paying the bill' (2011). Note the semantic presupposition here, 'the market economy in higher education'. Higher education is now fully integrated into a 'market economy' (see Image 3.1).

When money changes hands, a set of ideas about the relationships between parties comes into focus (see Section 2.4). Consider a normal consumer transaction; buying something like a computer. If you pay a small amount of money for it, does this change your expectations? In the case of something tangible and functional like a computer, expectations and responsibilities are reasonably clear: especially if you pay a lot of money for something, you expect it to work, you expect it to do what the seller told you it would do, you expect that if something goes wrong with the computer that you would be able to get this fixed. This seems reasonable and fair. We buy things all the time and we have a great deal of experience in doing this. While it makes sense to draw on knowledge we already have about consumer transactions, is paying tuition fees for a university education the same as buying a computer? Does the student as customer metaphor fully describe the relationship between universities and students?

© Russell Hugo

Image 3.1 Degree Mart

To answer these questions, we need to carefully examine the propositions that are connected to the 'student as customer' metaphor. This allows us to evaluate these points individually. Only after we have considered all the ideas connected to this metaphor can we assess the ideologies associated with the arguments, and hence, the metaphor itself. Specifically, the student as customer metaphor entails a number of beliefs.

Example 3.8

a.   The relationship between student and university is transactional.
b.   The customer is always 'right'.
c.   The customer should get good value for money (good return on investment).
d.   Services provided should be dictated by market demand.
e.   Only services demanded by customers are valuable.

Consider these entailments. Do you think they apply in a university context? Can you think of other propositions connected to the metaphor?

Activity 3.9

Consider Example 3.8a, the idea that the relationship between the student and university is transactional. A commercial transaction consists of giving money in exchange for goods or services. The student as customer metaphor might suggest that a student simply exchanges money for a degree. In fact, degrees are only granted when the student has successfully completed certain requirements. So, if we were to try to compare the university 'transaction' to a commercial transaction, it is more like buying gym membership than buying a computer. People join gyms to get fit and lose weight. The act of purchasing the gym membership itself does not guarantee any of these outcomes. Joining a gym is purchasing an opportunity to engage in beneficial behaviour, but the customer has to undertake these activities. A university education is similarly interactional. A student must undertake the activities provided by and in fact, required by the university in order to receive the degree as evidence of their activity.

The example of 'student as customer' shows how metaphors can work in extended and powerful ways. While it may seem completely inconsequential to describe university students as university customers, this model is linked to a range of political and administrative decisions as well as to the economic features of the society we live in. The metaphor is connected to propositions that are ideological and difficult to challenge. That is not to say that there aren't other metaphors for the relationship between students and universities.

3.8 SILLY CITIZENSHIP

Discussions of ideology and war, nuclear weapons and the cost of education may suggest that we are politically powerless. The dominance of particular ideologies and the productive power of the language and metaphors connected to them can make us feel powerless. In this final section of the chapter, we consider talk and action that is clearly political but that offers more scope for individual action, for change and for enjoyment. This is an important form of political **agency**.

In Chapter 4 we consider Twitter and YouTube and the way they are changing our consumption of media. Here we will examine how they are also changing the political landscape. Social media and people's access to technology allows them to communicate in new media and new forms. One increasingly popular genre is 'fake news' and 'news satire'. The tradition of critiquing power through humour is not new and can be found in 'Western drama from Aristophanes to Shakespeare. Comedy is the go-to source for civic understanding' (Hartley 2010: 241).

Hartley has coined the phrase 'silly citizenship' to describe certain kinds of 'media citizenship', that is, the playful and humorous ways people produce, consume and engage with the media. Hartley discusses a number of examples such as spoof election ads in Australia and spoofs on political debates in the US (Hartley 2010: 241). 'This kind of silly citizenship has become part of the mediated political landscape, with both professional and amateur creativity expended in the cause of political agency' (Hartley 2010: 241). While this may seem to have little to do with 'real' politics, it is impor- tant to remember that persuasive discourse takes a variety of forms. Hartley describes a YouTube video called the *JK Wedding Entrance Dance* ('Jill and Kevin's big day') in which a bridal party enters the church sanctuary for a wedding dancing to pop singer Chris Brown's song, *forever*. Brown had become infamous for domestic abuse charges regarding his girlfriend. The wedding party 'invited viewers to donate to a charity involved in preventing domestic violence to women and children' and collected US$26,000 (Hartley 2010: 243). As Hartley puts it, 'How civic is that?' (2010: 243). When one considers the amount of attention that these performances can have, and the often viral spread of internet videos and memes, the persua- sive (and therefore political) effects start to look significant. Moreover, what perhaps looks to be 'simply' entertainment may take on a decidedly political edge. Looking more closely at some examples of what might be called 'silly citizenship' demonstrates that while amusing, attention to the language and other choices in these examples exposes contentious ideologies.

3.8.1 'That's just my opinion!'

Our example of silly citizenship comes from a daily television show that is broadcast in the US called The Daily Show with Jon Stewart. The host, Jon Stewart, is well known for his amusing and yet critical assessment of politics and political news coverage. While a transcript of such a performance can never capture all the subtleties of performance, we have provided one in Example 3.9. The segment, appearing early after the new year in 2014, opens with Jon explaining that he won't be starting off the new year by dealing with 'hot button' topics such as religion and politics. He then seems to be at a loss for what to talk about so he makes an apparently casual remark about the record cold weather that the country had been experiencing. The show then plays a series of clips from news reporters commenting on how cold it is. One of the reporters in the clips then says that given all the cold weather it's difficult to see any evidence of global warming.

Example 3.9

[VT of an intro screen from another programme reading 'War on Carbon']

```
1   JS: There you have it (.) War on Christmas is over (.) The war on carbon
2       begins. Global warming just one more liberal conspiracy (.) because
3       even though there is a great deal of scientific data establishing
4       climate trends (.) even though many of the models of global
5       warming predict extremes of weather, not just warming, apparently
6       decades of peer reviewed scientific study can be [higher pitch] like
7       a ficus plant [slower with steadily lower tone] destroyed in one cold
8       weekend.

9   [VT with strap line 'War on Carbon'] Presenter: looks like to me we're
10      looking at global cooling (.) forget this global warming (.) that's just
11      my opinion.

12  JS: Yeah! Your [bleep] opinion! that's your opinion [laughter from
13      audience] it means nothing. [extended laughter from audience] ....
14      it's your opinion! [comic voice] based on its flavor I think lead paint
15      is good to drink that's my opinion! (.) peeing into the fountain the
16      same time as another person is a good way to switch souls with
17      them, my opinion.

18  [VT person being interviewed] if 97 doctors told you that that lump on
19  your lung was something to worry about and **three** scientists [or]
20  doctors told you not to worry about it are you going to listen to the 97
21  or the three

22  [simultaneous talk: inaudible]

23  [presenter in studio] if 97 were **paid** to tell me I had a lump on my lung
24  and it was **bad**.
```

What are the arguments being made here? What linguistic tools is Jon Stewart using to make his argument?

Activity 3.10

One of the reporters in the clip remarks that his disbelief in global warming is 'just his opinion'. Jon Stewart then highlights this point by foregrounding that an opinion is not based on facts. We also find repetition in his formulation of exaggerated and ridiculous 'opinions'. This is then followed by arguments by reporters about expertise and whether the scientific experts on global warming are actually impartial. The argument made by the second journalist (line 23) is that the scientists are not impartial; they are being paid and therefore cannot be trusted (see also Section 4.6).

As the audience laughter (line 13) shows, this is very amusing for at least some people. Nonetheless there are pointed political arguments being made about global warming. This is silly citizenship broadcast across a national television network. As Hartley puts it, 'the stage for citizenship is literally that. It is as much dramatic and performative as it is deliberative' (Hartley 2010: 241).

3.9 SUMMARY

As the Electoral Commission ad we discussed in the introduction points out, politics is everywhere: political movements, higher education, toys, financial systems and humourist talk shows. If we pay attention to language used in these domains, we can uncover the ideologies that underpin the persuasive arguments made. Whether we're looking at repetition and contrasts or presuppositions and metaphor, examining the linguistic choices made gives us a way of understanding the arguments being made and how they are constructed. It then becomes possible to assess these arguments one by one to explore how we can be persuaded by ideologies that aren't consistent with our beliefs.

FURTHER READING

Beard, A. (2000) *The Language of Politics*, London: Routledge.

Boussofara-Omar, N. (2006) 'Learning the "linguistic habitus" of a politician: A presidential authoritative voice in the making', *Journal of Language and Politics*, 5(3): 325–8.

Chilton, P. (1982) 'Nukespeak: Nuclear language, culture and propaganda', in C. Aubrey (ed.) *Nukespeak: The Media and the Bomb*, Comedia Publishing Group, London: 94–112.

Hutchby, I. and Woffit, R. (2008) *Conversation Analysis*, 2nd edn, London: Polity.

Nunberg, Geoffrey (2002) 'Media: Label whores', *The American Prospect*, 13(8) *http://prospect.org/article/media-label-whores* [accessed 11 August 2014].

Simon-Vandenbergen, A.-M., White, P. R. R. and Aijmer, K. (2007) 'Presupposition and "Taking-for-Granted" in Mass Communicated Political Argument: An Illustration from British, Flemish and Swedish Political Colloquy', in A. Fetzer and G. Lauerbach (eds) *Political Discourse in the Media: Cross-Cultural Perspectives, Pragmatics and Beyond New Series*, Amsterdam: John Benjamins: 31–74.

CHAPTER 4

Language and the media

4.1	**INTRODUCTION**	**63**
4.2	**MASS MEDIA**	**64**
4.3	**MANUFACTURE OF CONSENT**	**64**
4.4	**SEMANTIC UNITY**	**69**
4.5	**NEWS VALUES**	**72**
4.6	**EXPERTS AND THE NEWS**	**74**
4.7	**NEWS ONLINE**	**77**
4.8	**NEW WAYS OF 'DOING' NEWS: TWITTER AND THE CITIZEN JOURNALIST**	**82**
4.9	**SUMMARY**	**85**

4.1 INTRODUCTION

In this chapter, we explore the language used in the media. If we consider 'mass media' to be information communicated 'from one sender to a large audience' (Jucker 2003: 132), it is a very broad field. While we will touch on a few aspects of social media, we'll be largely dealing with news media. This might seem to be quite a narrow focus, but consideration of the mass news media allows us to think about how particular ideologies are communicated and maintained, the linguistic choices that help do this, what counts as news, as well as the changes in mass media news reporting. The key theme under-pinning this chapter is one of literacy, that is, the skills audiences need to read and understand the texts they find in the mass media. The changing face of the mass news media means that audiences must continuously learn how to interpret new texts. These skills, these literacy practices, are a form of power. It will become clear that knowing how to read a text is a skill that is a form of symbolic capital.

We examine characteristics of the media that project and perpetuate ideologies before moving on to consider what counts as newsworthy and how news is represented. However, recent changes in technology have altered the way news is produced and consumed. Microblogging sites such as Twitter and the increased consumption of news online are key issues here.

4.2 MASS MEDIA

By definition, the mass media has a large audience. Further, there is often a significant degree of trust in the author of news (see ethos Section 3.4). People would be unlikely to watch, listen to or follow a news site that they didn't think was trustworthy. We expect our news to be true. However, because of this trust and the 'mass' aspect of mass media, these entities can have a significant effect on how a large number of people understand the world. Traditionally, in the time before the World Wide Web and social media, there was 'asymmetry' between producer and consumer. That is, the media outlets were the only producers of news. It was very clear that the mass media could 'largely be described as one-way communication' (Jucker 2003: 132). This asymmetry is our starting point for considering language and the power of the media.

4.3 MANUFACTURE OF CONSENT

As we discussed in Chapter 1, ideologies can be constructed, sustained and re-iterated over a long period of time. News is now broadcast 24 hours a day on a range of different media, including newspapers, radio, television and the World Wide Web. Looking at the language of news can provide important information about how power is created and exercised. While language is not the only consideration when thinking about power, it is extremely important. Fairclough writes:

> It is important to emphasize that I am not suggesting that power is *just* a matter of language. ... Power exists in various modalities, including the concrete and unmistakable modality of physical force ... It is perhaps helpful to make a broad distinction between the exercise of power through *coercion* of various sorts including physical violence, and the exercise of power through the manufacture of *consent* to or at least acquiescence towards it. Power relations depend on both, though in varying proportions. Ideology is the prime means of manufacturing consent.

(2001: 3)

The 'manufacture of consent' that Fairclough refers to is a concept that originates in the work of Noam Chomsky and Edward Herman. In their book

Manufacturing Consent: The Political Economy of the Mass Media, Chomsky and Herman describe how the mass media functions, in both economic and ideological terms (1988). Focusing on the mass media, they point to a number of factors that influence what stories we read and hear and in what form we receive them. They identify five 'filters' that influence the representations finally produced. Because of the way information is altered by these filters, the public's agreement with both the information and the ideologies that structure it is not a 'real' agreement; rather, it is 'manufactured consent'. Chomsky and Herman argue that the news media functions like propaganda, that is, information designed to promote a particular argument or point of view, often one that is beneficial to those in power. The filters are listed below.

a. *Media ownership*
b. *Advertising income*
c. *Where our news stories come from*
d. *How groups and individuals respond to stories, whether they complain, for example, are also filters*
e. *Communism must be avoided at all costs*

The concept of the 'manufacture of consent' is a way of understanding the cumulative effect of these five filters. The filters can be understood as structuring language and content at an ideological level. Though audiences are unaware of these filters when reading or watching the mass media, they are nevertheless important. These filters present events in particular ways. Some events may not be covered at all; others may be given a great deal of importance. The way that stories are told, for example who is to blame or what the key issues are, is also influenced by these filters. Because we are only exposed to the filtered representations, over time audiences find the values of the mass media are normalised; they become part of our collective 'common sense' and, as such, are ideological. Chomsky and Herman argue that such 'common sense' is constructed by the sustained representations of the mass media and that these representations are a product of the five filters they identify. Throughout this chapter, we'll consider examples that demonstrate these filters.

4.3.1 Filtering the facts

We can see how the filters work in the case of Edward Snowden, mentioned in Chapter 1, who revealed classified US information in 2013. The way he was described in the mass media showed a polarised view of the situation. While filters were certainly in operation, the five filters have a different effect depending on the news outlets.

Examine the following news headlines. What positions does the language suggest? What kinds of arguments do you think will be made in the articles that follow? What other linguistic choices will be made in the articles?

a.   NSA whistleblower Edward Snowden says US 'treats dissent as defection' (*Guardian*, McCarthy 2013).
b.   Edward Snowden leaks could help paedophiles escape police, says government (*Telegraph*, Barrett 2013).
c.   Edward Snowden, Russian Agent? (*Huffington Post*, Thomson 2014).
d.   Edward Snowden, the insufferable whistleblower (*Washington Post*, Marcus 2014).

When discussing ideological representations in the mass media, the classic example given is that 'one person's "terrorist" is another person's "freedom fighter"'. The issues raised in relation to Edward Snowden's actions remind us that this example is still relevant (see Section 1.2). Another event of 2013 provided a reminder of this paradigm. When Nelson Mandela, former President of South Africa, died in late 2013, there was an outpouring of grief and admiration for him as he was important in ending apartheid in South Africa. Much of the media overlooked the fact he was labelled in less than heroic terms in the 1980s when the British government named him a terrorist and called for his death (Bevans & Streeter 1996) because of his political work. While we are not making a comparison between Snowden and Mandela in factual terms, it is an important example of how the representations of individuals in the public eye can shift. The fact that these changes are not always remembered or remarked upon is an example of how the mass media exerts its ideological power by framing situations and people in a particular way.

It is worth considering where these ideologies and the particular representations of people come from. It is certainly possible to argue that some choices can be connected to the ownership of the mass media (filter a. in Example 4.1). Whether through explicit direction or something less overt, if the individual who owns a newspaper or media outlet has particular political and social views, it is not impossible that these may influence the content and perspective of the coverage in these outlets. That is, thinking about the significance of advertising revenue to the success of newspapers and television channels, it is tempting to think that this 'manufacturing' is consciously planned by powerful people behind the scenes. This may well happen. However, the choice of the term 'filters' in Chomsky and Herman's model points to the automatic processes that occur without conscious intervention being necessary on the part of the producers. Newspaper editors do not need to be told to print or to withhold particular stories that may make large advertisers unhappy. In terms of running the newspaper, it is common sense to keep advertisers (filter b. in Example 4.1) and owners content. This is how ideology works; the ideology acts like a filter, to remove anything that doesn't fit its values. Nor is this filtering necessarily conscious. To suppose that it is would be to underestimate and misunderstand ideological processes. As we've already noted, when a way of seeing the world is ideological, it appears to be common sense.

In 2010, tuition fees for university students were raised considerably in the UK. In response to this, students and academics protested on the streets of London. Do the newspaper accounts of this event in Examples 4.2 and 4.3 tell the same story? Identify the different lexical choices and describe what they suggest about these events.

Example 4.1
Dozens of computers were destroyed, furniture was broken and fire hoses were turned on when around 200 protesters stormed the Tory HQ after smashing down the large plate glass windows on ground level.

a death was narrowly avoided when one protester dropped a fire extinguisher from the eighth floor …

Police admitted they were unprepared for the scale of the violence …

(Bloxam 2010)

Example 4.2
It was supposed to be a day of peaceful protest, with students exercising their democratic right to demonstrate against soaring university fees.

But anarchists hijacked the event, setting off the most violent scenes of student unrest seen in Britain for decades. Militants from far-Left groups whipped up a mix of middle-class students and younger college and school pupils into a frenzy.

(Gill 2010)

Activity 4.2

It is impossible to know whether Examples 4.1 and 4.2 are an accurate depiction of the events of that day. These extracts suggest that the protest was like a war zone, with uncontrolled violent behaviour; however, this is only one perspective. As it happens, the first author was present at the protest. From her perspective and experience that day, the discussion would look more like Example 4.3.

Example 4.3

A relatively peaceful protest against rising university tuition fees took place in London today. For most of the march nothing particularly remarkable happened. A number of groups were represented, including academics, unions and other members of the public. There was a trivial amount of property damage by a small number of people. According to Lewis *et al.* (2010), near were an estimated 50,000 people on the march.

From Examples 4.1–4.3 you can see that the accounts from eye-witnesses can be very different. Our claim is not that the news is wrong; rather, that it may only be a partial representation of what actually happened. Indeed, the extracts in Activity 4.2 are also only part of the stories by the journalists Bloxam and Gill and, as such, may not represent exactly the narrative they intended.

The next Example (4.4) shows that the manipulation of even one word can change people's understanding of an issue. Lexical choices can bring with them a whole set of propositions, arguments, views and 'facts'. A monthly US magazine, *The Atlantic*, reports that while some Americans support 'The Affordable Care Act' they are opposed to 'Obamacare' in spite of the fact that both terms refer to the exact same legislation about healthcare (Hamblin 2013). They open their story with a short transcript of an interview from an evening television talk show, 'Jimmy Kimmel live', in which members of the public were interviewed about these policies and asked whether they preferred the Affordable Care Act or Obamacare. Example 4.4 is a transcript of one interviewee's answers (in italics) to follow-up questions after he says he prefers the Affordable Care Act.

Example 4.4

'So you disagree with Obamacare?'

'Yes, I do.'

'Do you think insurance companies should be able to exclude people with preexisting conditions?'

'No.'

'Do you agree that young people should be able to stay on their parents' plans until they're 26?'

'They should be able to, yes.'

'Do you agree that companies with 50 or more employees should provide healthcare?'

'I do.'

'And so, by that logic, you would be for the Affordable Care Act?'

'Yes.'

(Hamblin 2013)

How can the person being interviewed in Example 4.4 support the Affordable Care Act but not Obamacare?

This is a very clear example of the confusion that can occur because of different naming choices. The person interviewed had no trouble accepting that the Affordable Care Act and Obamacare were different things (even though they aren't) when they were asked which they preferred. While in one sense this is a leading question, as it **presupposes** a difference between the two things, the people shown in the video were able to offer reasons for preferring one over the other. The way a question is asked can have a significant effect on how people respond (see Loftus 1975).

The naming of this piece of legislation is certainly political. The title 'Obamacare' has been created and maintained by the Republican Party, presumably to discredit and create negativity about the Affordable Care Act precisely because they oppose it. As shown in Example 4.4, the term has served to, at the very least, confuse citizens about the policy. Democrats initially objected to the term 'Obamacare'. Nevertheless Republicans defended it. One Republican politician argued that the term was now part of the language, referring to hits on Google and arguing that it was probably already in the dictionary (Parkinson & Jaffe 2011). This, again, demonstrates the authority dictionaries are thought to have (see Chapter 1). The politician continues: 'It's in the vernacular. In fact', he quipped, 'it's in my spell check.' (Parkinson & Jaffe 2011).

Eventually, President Obama and Democrats accepted the term. Sometimes, a group will begin to use a pejorative term that refers to them in order to take control of it and use it in a positive way. This is called reclaiming (see Section 7.4.1). President Obama acknowledged the Republican strategy of trying to discredit the policy by calling it 'Obamacare'. At a press conference he said 'Once it's working really well, I guarantee you, they will not call it "Obamacare"' (Richinick 2013).

4.4 SEMANTIC UNITY

van Dijk argues that a text is more coherent if it has 'semantic unity' and this 'is obtained by assigning some theme or topic to the discourse or to a fragment of the discourse' (1983: 33). For a text to have semantic unity it has to be consistent in its meaning; it has to tell the same story, rather than having competing views that are not reconciled into a single 'story'. A text with semantic unity communicates a clear message. Such semantic unity may be helped along or act in tandem with larger stories, or themes that frame the more specific details. If a story introduces the topic 'war on terror', this phrase evokes a number of values and implicit **narrative** structures or discourses. For example, we know that 'terror' is by definition bad, therefore a 'war on terror' must be a positive thing. We also understand that wars have a villain and a hero, a good side and a bad (see Chapter 3). This common knowledge or background can be evoked by a word or phrase, and therefore references a discourse or way of understanding any event connected to the 'war on terror'.

4.4.1 Strategic communication

A story from *The Straits Times*, a Singaporean newspaper, provides a nice example of semantic unity. The story is a feature, as well as being part of a series on 'people involved in the war against terror' (Nirmala 2013). The article describes an interview with Kuman Ramakrishna, the Head of the Centre of Excellence for National Security at Nanyang Technological University in Singapore. For readers who already know that this is a series, an overarching theme is already in place. For those reading the feature without this knowledge, the headline will be important. The headline reads, 'Waging propaganda war against terrorists' (Nirmala 2013).

Activity 4.4

A headline often signals an overarching structure for a story. What does the headline 'Waging propaganda war against terrorists' suggest for the content and structure that follow?

As noted, the headline gives the reader a sense of the shape and direction of the story; will it be positive or negative? Who are the main actors? What is this story about? This headline exploits the idea of 'waging war' in two ways. First, it draws on existing discourses of the war on terror, and then represents this as a 'propaganda' war. In such a propaganda war the enemy may be the same, but the weapons will be words and pictures rather than guns and tanks. Setting the story up in this way also sets up a clear contrast between 'us' and 'them'. Once a contrast like this is set up, other contrasting pairs are easier to exploit (see Section 3.5.1). This can be seen in the opening paragraph of the story:

> Emerging from a darkened cinema hall, security expert Kuman Ramakrishna's eyes were gently adjusting to the light outdoors when his mind began decoding an embedded message in a war movie he had just seen, Lions for Lambs.

Because of the headline, the reader can infer that Ramakrishna is one of 'us'. Note, too, the contrast between dark and light. Ramakrishna's eyes adjust to the light at the same time as he starts to see the deeper 'truth' of the war movie he has just seen. Ramakrishna goes on to discuss the meaning of the film with the interviewer. The interviewer refers to the film as 'propaganda' and Ramakrishna reacts.

> With eyebrows furrowed, he [Ramakrishna] advises, 'Don't use the word propaganda as the Nazis gave the term a bad reputation during World War II. Nowadays it's called "strategic communication."'

The rest of the story is a profile of Ramakrishna, describing the research he conducts on social media, social cohesion and the role of society in stopping division and violence. The contrast set up in the headline between 'us' and 'them' is one that continues throughout the story. The sustained use of this and other contrasts creates a clear semantic unity in the story.

He also discusses the important role of entertainment in the propaganda war against the war on terror.

> 'Entertainment is a valuable narcotic for dulling the sensibilities of a propaganda-conscious mind' he preached.

This reminds us that ideologies can be communicated in various media, including films. Ramakrishna is clear that when people are being entertained they are less critical of the messages they receive (see Chapter 3). When we think we're just being told an entertaining story we are less critical of the choices made in how the story is told; we are less likely to look for the filters operating or the ideology that is being communicated.

Notice also that while this is a story in an online newspaper and it clearly contains information and news, there is a focus on the individual being interviewed. This is not unexpected for a profile piece. However, some argue that this shift is more widespread than this. Herbert contends that while in 'traditional print language, the basic unit is the paragraph' (2000: 105), this may well be changing with print journalists writing in a more 'conversational style' (2000: 105). We see this in *The Straits Times* article, with the words of the interviewee being reproduced as direct speech with additional information added to flesh out the feature. We as readers are witnessing a conversation. Herbert sees print journalism as 'becoming simpler, clearer, shorter and more graphic, conversational and informal. All of these qualities it draws from good broadcast writing and language' (2000: 105). It seems to also make these news stories more like entertainment.

The headline in this story sets up the topic and the frame for the story. The ideas of war, language and a clear division between us and them (and good and bad) are set up at the start. These themes and contrasts can be found throughout the article. Of course it is not the case that the headline causes the structure of the feature; rather, the headline points the reader in an interpretative direction.

Having considered the choices made in how events and people are represented in the news, we now examine which events and people are considered newsworthy.

4.5 NEWS VALUES

Allan Bell, a linguist and a journalist, has outlined 'news values' (or 'newsworthiness') of news producers in his book *The Language of News Media* (1991). It is important to note the term 'news values' is used in specific fields to explain what is significant and 'newsworthy' for the people producing the news. It covers actors and events, what is esteemed in the news process and what is relevant for news text. This can be understood as complementing two of Chomsky and Herman's filters: (c.), where our stories come from, and (d.), how we respond to them. While Chomsky and Herman are concerned with the macro level of news production and consumption, from who owns media outlets to audience responses, Bell focuses in more detail on the production of news with regard to what journalists choose to cover. His lists help explain, in a different way from Chomsky and Herman, why some stories are covered and why some aren't.

4.5.1 Actors and events

In terms of actors (subjects of the news) and events, the news values that Bell outlines explain what stories are considered newsworthy and why. Bell, drawing on previous research, identifies the news values below (1991: 156–8).

a.   NEGATIVITY: negative events are more likely to be newsworthy than positive ones
b.   RECENCY: the event should be recent
c.   PROXIMITY: the event should be close by
d.   CONSONANCE: events which can be made to cohere with ideas and understandings that people already have are likely to have high news value
e.   UNAMBIGUITY: the events should be clear; if there is a dispute or a question there should be some resolution
f.   UNEXPECTEDNESS: that which is not routine is more newsworthy than that which is
g.   SUPERLATIVENESS: the worst or best of something is more likely to be covered
h.   RELEVANCE: the audience should be able to see some relevance to their own life in the event
i.   PERSONALISATION: if something can be reported in a personal rather than an abstract way it will be more newsworthy

j. ELITENESS: this relates to the actors in the news; a story about powerful people is more newsworthy than the same kind of story about an 'ordinary' person

k. ATTRIBUTION: whether the facts or the story can be attributed to someone important or trustworthy

l. FACTICITY: figures, dates, locations and statistics are important for hard news.

(Bell 1991: 156–8)

Read today's newspaper online or in paper form. On the first few pages or the home page, try to identify the news values in the headlines and stories.

Activity 4.5

Bell's news values help us understand why we get the news we do, how stories are chosen and which people become the focus of these stories. To really understand which news actors and events will be most important to a story, we also need to know what kind of story it is. There are two distinctions that are often made about news stories. They may be hard or soft news; and they may be fast or slow news.

The first is the distinction between hard and soft news (or stories/ features). Bell explains that the distinction between hard news and soft news is 'basic' for those working in the news (1991: 14). 'Hard news is their staple product: reports of accidents, conflicts, crimes, announcements, discoveries and other events which have occurred or come to light since the previous issue of their paper or programme' (1991: 14). Hard news stories might draw on the news values of RECENCY, NEGATIVITY, PROXIMITY, UNEXPECT-EDNESS, RELEVANCE and FACTICITY. In contrast, soft news might draw on the values of PERSONALISATION, ELITENESS, CONSONANCE, SUPERLATIVENESS and ATTRIBUTION.

We can also distinguish between fast and slow news. Fast news refers to news that needs to be reported quickly but will probably also be out of date just as quickly. A good, though specialised, example of fast news would be the state of the stockmarket or particular stocks. Those who buy and sell shares for a living need sound, up to date information about the prices of shares in order to conduct business. Slow news, on the other hand, is not so time sensitive and refers to events that develop over a longer period of time. The two are not mutually exclusive, however. The voting results in the election of a new head of state will certainly be fast news; audiences will want to know who has been elected as soon as they possibly can. However, the consequences and implications of a change in government or head of state cannot be covered in short sound bites. Careful analysis takes place, opinion leaders are interviewed and consulted, economists and social policy experts are asked for their expert input. While the election result is fast news, the effects of the election will be slower and will last for the full term of office and even beyond.

Activity 4.6

The World Wide Web has changed the way fast news is reported. How do you keep up to date with fast news stories and events?

4.6 EXPERTS AND THE NEWS

When we examine the news media very carefully, in addition how it *represents* events/people, we can also see that the media can play a role in *creating* what is true (FACTICITY). In this section, we examine the representation and construction of expertise in the news mass media. Boyce's (2006) research on the media reporting of the alleged link between the MMR (Measles Mumps and Rubella) vaccination and autism helps us explore the issues and challenges the media encounters when it has to report on a specialised subject. We will see how information that is both RELEVANT and PERSONAL is considered newsworthy in spite of being AMBIGUOUS. The MMR debate also shows us the changing profile of who is considered an expert.

In the UK, as in many other countries children are given a series of vaccinations in the interests of their own health and public health more generally. In 1998, a scientific paper that argued for a link between autism and a 'rare bowel syndrome' was published in a reputable scientific journal, *The Lancet* (Boyce 2006: 892). As Boyce reports, 'The paper in The Lancet did not present evidence linking the MMR vaccine to bowel syndrome and/or autism but at a press conference publicising the research Dr Wakefield [a research scientist] discussed this possible link' (2006: 892). Because of the apparent risk to children this became a big news story. It was NEGATIVE, RECENT and very PERSONAL to anyone with children. In the press conference Professor Wakefield presented the (untested) hypothesis that children should be given the vaccines in three separate doses. However, this suggestion was not supported by the majority of his co-authors nor by any scientific evidence in the published research (or subsequent research, although Wakefield disputes this) (Boyce 2006: 892).

The media, in extensively covering the issue, established an association between MMR and autism. Debate about whether there was or wasn't a causal link ensued as other scientists, in fact, disputed Dr Wakefield's claim, pointing to the journal paper itself that did not explicitly state a link between MMR vaccine and autism. In the media, evidence was portrayed as balanced when in fact there was no empirical support for the link between MMR and autism. The facts were unambiguous (FACTICITY) but this is not how they were represented in the media. But because the story was so emotionally charged, it took on a life of its own.

Nevertheless, because this news story involved children, it had significant effects both in the news media and in the world. First, coverage of MMR in the news increased dramatically (Boyce 2006: 892). More significantly, take up of the vaccine fell. Boyce examined the production, reception and content of stories about MMR in the years following these events. One might think that because this is a story about medicine, illness and vaccines that audiences would be presented with a number of scientific experts. This is not what Boyce found (2006: 896).

The MMR debate is an example of the changing nature of 'expertise' in the media. Particularly in relation to health and medicine, accurate information is crucial. One of the problems in establishing information as factual is, as Boyce argues, 'there has been a real decline in trust of "experts"' (2006: 890). News producers rely on experts to satisfy the news value of ATTRIBUTION and FACTICITY. But in this case, what expertise means is itself contested. If scientists aren't trusted, are parents the experts? What about government bodies? In the absence of (or in spite of) compelling scientific evidence, all these people and institutions can become experts. In terms of news values, which 'experts' are chosen will depend on the facts that news producers want to be foregrounded and conveyed. The individuals they choose to serve as 'experts' will depend on the ideology that the news producer wants to promote and the kind of story they want to construct (see also Example 3.9).

An important issue is not the choice of which experts are spoken to, interviewed or reported, but how the experts are positioned in relation to one another. While it is important to hear the views of parents, their expertise is different from that of a scientist who has conducted direct and relevant research. Boyce (2006) shows that sometimes these very different kinds of 'experts' were treated as comparable contributors to the debate. Example 4.5 is a transcript of a UK ITV evening news story profiling the MMR debate.

Example 4.5

Dr Robert Aston (Wigan and Bolton Health Authority): It makes me deeply sad as a doctor and as a grandfather that a sustained amount of anti-vaccine lobbying, amongst them organisations which claim to be not anti-vaccine, and by sections of the media to keep the controversy going has resulted in the undermining of public confidence in what is probably the safest and most effective of our vaccines. [The MMR vaccine] has done untold good and it prevents diseases, serious diseases and premature death in children.

Stephanie Sherratt (parent): You should be able to have your children vaccinated singly at your own doctors. I object strongly to being told what and when to inject into my children.

Dr Pat Troop (Deputy Chief Medical Officer): We have no concerns about our current vaccine. I think it will send a very strong signal that parents will say, hang on, we think maybe there is a problem around this vaccine why else would you offer us a single vaccine? And confidence would go.

Journalist: Eleven-year-old Nick Williams has autism. His parents believe it dates from the time he had his MMR inoculation at the age of 4.

Parents of Nick Williams: In the November of that year he had his MR booster and by the following Christmas his behaviour was totally different. He was a different child. He wasn't interested in Christmas presents (ITC, 4 February 2002).

(Boyce 2006: 898, 900)

Activity 4.7

How do the speakers position themselves as experts in the transcript in Example 4.5? What arguments do they make?

The speakers in these lines have different kinds of expertise. Notice, however, that they are treated as though they are competing voices, with the same kind of expertise. This is set up by the choice of the first speaker, who refers to himself as both a scientist and a grandfather. Indeed, Boyce's research shows that news consumers were interested in the *personal* views of scientists and other official kinds of experts. In particular, experts were asked whether they would have their children vaccinated rather than being asked about scientific evidence. The importance of the personal value of this story is clear, as Boyce observed that if the experts had no children, their opinion was sometimes represented as less important (Boyce 2006: 898). The story was framed as being about children and parents rather than about science.

The problem was that construction and presentation of the story led people to believe that there was, in fact, a dispute about the facts. Moreover, as Boyce's research shows, people overestimated both the amount of research on both sides and the number of subjects involved (2006). Given the amount and kind of coverage, this is hardly surprising. This story had a serious impact as it resulted in people refusing to have their children vaccinated (Boyce 2006: 892). In terms of media reporting and experts, it also shows that 'expertise' is not something a person simply has, whether by virtue of their experience or their position. Rather, 'expertise' is at least in part constructed by the very process of news production. The mass media can turn a source into an expert, a source who wouldn't otherwise be considered to have expertise on a topic. This may be done in order to present a balanced story. Moreover, this is a process in which such a 'created expert' also has a role. As Thornborrow (2001) shows, 'lay' speakers will provide 'a salient comment on some aspect of their own personal status and identity, before going on to state their opinion, ask their question, or say whatever it is they have to say as a contribution to the talk' (2001: 465). This is not just about identifying themselves, it is about establishing how they are qualified to the comment; that they are somehow an expert on what they are about to say.

The decline of trust in experts that Boyce describes has a number of consequences. It makes it harder for important information to be conveyed as now there seems to be a discourse of distrust, especially around health issues. This means that new stories related to health can be framed as CONSONANT with these discourses of distrust.

4.7 NEWS ONLINE

So far, many of the examples we've been working with come from online versions of newspapers. Most newspapers, and other mass media news outlets, now have webpages; in fact, some news outlets only have an online presence and don't produce a printed version of their 'publication' (e.g. *Huffington Post, Slate*). The changes to news production and consumption that the internet has facilitated have been profound. Jucker identifies six ways in which these changes can be understood in contrast to previous forms of mass media (television, radio and newspapers). First, the internet allows for **hypermedia**, 'the integration of different channels of communication, such as written texts, still pictures, motion pictures and sound' (Jucker 2003: 130). Second, it is also becoming more personal, targeted at particular audiences. This is possible because of the relatively small amount of labour now needed to produce different versions of the same text. Some of this work is done automatically. Third, levels of interaction have been increased dramatically. While it has been possible to write to newspapers or call in to radio stations in the past, the forms of communication between producers and consumers have changed dramatically. This will also have consequences for who counts as an expert. Moreover, even reading material online is a form of interaction, as producers can track exactly what is getting read, what is being shared and so on (Jucker 2003: 139). Fourth, the 'traditional life span of information' is changing (Jucker 2003: 130). People expect up to the minute updates about news and events. Fifth, Jucker argues that mass media communication is now less likely to be asynchronous (there is a time lag between the issue of the message and its receipt); rather, it is **synchronous** (the message is sent and then immediately received). An example of synchronous communication is talking on the phone; **asynchronous communication**, however, would be reading an email that was sent some time ago. Moreover, the forms of synchronous communication have been expanding. Text messaging, online chat and Skype have radically changed the availability of synchronous communication. Sixth,

> the availability of media products is no longer subject to the same physical restrictions as traditional media, and the products, in particular media texts, are losing their fixity because their electronic publication format makes them susceptible to immediate modifications and changes wherever they are received.
>
> (Jucker 2003: 131)

Kautsky and Widholm describe the distinction between printed news and online news. 'Whereas print journalism is mono-linear, from writing, via editing to printing of a final version, news online can be published, edited and re-published again' (2008: 82). Kautsky and Widholm concentrate on what this fast pace of online news production and consumption means for those interested in analysing these texts. We're going to draw on their work not so much to describe how to do the analysis, but to highlight the changing profile of the news in this context. The production of news texts online makes information immediate but also subject to change. The story that was online yesterday may well be gone tomorrow and difficult to recover. Further, sites are updated all the time; the news is now very fast indeed. But how are these choices made? Why is the story that was a headline in the morning harder to find in the afternoon? Table 4.1 concisely outlines the key characteristics in print media and online news (Kautsky & Widholm 2008: 88).

Table 4.1 Media characteristics

	Print media	Online news
Distribution	Periodic	Parallel flow(s)
Presentation form	Yesterday's news	Extended 'now'

Kautsky and Widholm (2008: 88)

As shown in Table 4.1, there are clear distinctions between the kinds of news found in print and online. Printed newspapers are periodic; they come out every day (or sometimes every week, for local papers). The printed page doesn't change. Once the newspaper goes to press, the content and format is fixed. For online news, however, sites are designed so that they can be constantly produced; they are always being updated and changed. The text is not stable.

Over a few days, follow a topic or story on one newspaper website. Does the story remain the same? Are new items added? Are they linked together? Draw a map of the various (versions of) stories and how they link together.

In Activity 4.8, you probably found, like Kautsky and Widholm, that there are differences in how a story is told even over a short period of time. While the same resources may be used (quotes, pictures, sources and facts) they will be presented differently and communicate different messages as the story 'evolves' and as the producers decide to emphasise different aspects of the story. Continuity has to be balanced with novelty. Moreover, different producers will update their sites according to a different timeline. For what was traditionally a daily newspaper, the site may be updated several times a day. For publications that were traditionally published once a month, the updates won't be as frequent or probably as dramatic (until the next month comes).

Many of the techniques used to construct news online are the same ones found in traditional print media. Both print and online news media have content, a structure and a layout. But the move to an online environment provides new constraints and affordances for those producing the news. Bateman, Delin and Henschel identify five areas that we could consider when examining online news (2006: 155).

1. Content structure: what information is included and in what order.
2. Rhetorical structure: what is the relationship between the content elements, what argument does it produce?
3. Layout structure: where are the different parts of the story (the text, the pictures and so on)?
4. Navigation structure: how should the reader move between parts of the story?
5. Linguistic structure: what is the detail of the language used?

These factors will interact. One would expect the headline to be at the top (layout) to be easy to find (navigation) and to entice the reader through its composition (linguistic structure).

4.7.1 Presenting news on the internet

To show the way news stories can be framed online, we consider two articles from *The Times of India* about a publisher, Penguin, withdrawing a book from sale. The book, written by Wendy Doniger, is called *The Hindus: An alternative history*. The stories were both published on the website of the newspaper, on consecutive days, and written by two different journalists (Arora 2014; Singh 2014). We can't reproduce both articles here but Table 4.2 shows a comparison of them. It should be noted that Article 2 is much longer than the Article 1. It was published second so it seems reasonable to conclude that there was more time to gather information, interview people and put together a fuller account of the case.

Table 4.2 Comparison of two news stories

	Article 1: Arora 162 words	Article 2: Singh 677 words
Headline	Penguin to destroy copies of Wendy Doniger's book *The Hindus*	Penguin pulls out of Wendy Doniger's book *The Hindus* from India
1st paragraph	Reports that the book is to be 'withdrawn and pulped' because of a legal dispute	Reports that the book caused a 'stir among various right-wing groups' who claim the book is defamatory. Notes the book will be withdrawn from sale in India
2nd paragraph	Reports that the settlement agreement has been leaked	Reports that there has been a settlement
3rd paragraph	Reports that people started sharing electronic copies of the book online	Outlines the settlement and some background and notes Penguin will withdraw and pulp the book
4th paragraph	Outlines the contents of the settlement; that the book will be withdrawn and pulped	A short extract from the agreement about withdrawing the book
Images and other information	A pdf of the settlement has been included in this page	An image of 'angry tweets' all from people unhappy about the decision to withdraw the book. Article continues with information about the book and more detail about the arguments made in the court case

Table 4.2 shows how the articles report different news while reporting on the same story. Article 1 focuses on the leaking of the agreement by providing a pdf of the agreement between Penguin and the organisation who wanted to suppress the book. Article 2 focuses on the reaction to the leak by presenting a series of 'angry tweets'.

Note, however, that the articles have a lot in common. While the overall rhetorical structure is not the same, the content structure is similar, especially at the beginning. They are using similar information to report the story in different ways. In each article, the headlines are comparable in structure, the crucial first few paragraphs cover much of the same material and the lexis and tone are similar. These first few paragraphs are important because of the way (especially hard) news is structured. Generally, the most important information is reported first. It is only after the 'headline' issues have been covered that more detail about the story is provided. This structure reinforces the main story. There are also more prosaic reasons for the structure. When stories are submitted, they may be shortened from their original length. This story structure is known as the inverted pyramid. Herbert describes it as follows:

> Traditionally the inverted pyramid story begins with all the main facts and relegates the less important details to the apex of the pyramid, and can therefore be cut from the bottom.
>
> (2000: 105)

The pyramid structure is mostly found in print newspapers, which have more limited space than online articles. Although the news story genre was developed and consolidated in the days before online news, it's still important to position the least important information towards the end of the story. This may also be due to reading habits. People tend to read a story from the start but they may not in fact, for many reasons, finish it.

The structure of a story is also related to the layout and the navigation tools available to the news producers. Online newspapers have to deal with very specific layout constraints. Part of this will be determined by the kinds of advertising the publication uses and where this needs to be placed. They will also have to think about their audience and the kinds of devices they may use to read the news. What looks good on a computer screen is very difficult to navigate on a smartphone screen. Thus, it's possible to see changes in the way online newspapers present their information depending on the device that is used to access it. The limits of the screen work in a similar way to layout on the printed page.

Printed newspapers have more tangible layout constraints. The size of the paper they are printed on has consequences for how the news is laid out. With large newspapers that are generally folded, the most important news is usually placed above the fold. This directs readers' attention to the most important story (before they even unfold the paper). 'The newspaper front page is designed around the social constructed concept of news values' (Bateman, Delin & Henschel 2006: 168). While this tells the reader what is important, there is only a little bit of navigation information on this front page, even though these front page stories are rarely complete on the first page (see Jucker 2003: 134–5). They are generally continued elsewhere in the newspaper. The reader will be told which page to turn to for the continuation of the front page story, but other sections of the newspaper will either be separated by the way the paper is folded or indicated on the second page. Of course, printed newspapers have a reasonably stable structure. Regular readers know where the entertainment section or sports pages are to be found.

Online newspapers also have to provide navigation tools. The home page is very important in this respect. It 'is a complex sign, consisting of a range of visual and visual-verbal signs which function as coherent structural elements' (Knox 2007: 23). But because online news isn't printed on paper, producers have to provide more varied tools for navigation around the site (Bateman, Delin & Henschel 2006: 168). This will include headings for different sections, search functions, 'most read' boxes and short snippets of articles that enable readers to click through to the full story. Kautsky and Widholm point out that newspapers online are 'not simply digital versions of newspapers, but a fusion of radio, television and traditional print media' (2008: 84). This means that the organisation and analysis of online news has to take account of the **multimodal** nature of the internet. Further, these changes in technology allow for new modes of communication and new forms of interaction between 'producers' and 'consumers' such that these very categories become blurred. The ability to comment on stories online often leads to conversations between contributors, with very little input from the original writer or producer of the story that led to this comment.

Activity 4.9

Find an online newspaper that allows readers to comment on stories. Look at a range of stories, from national/local news to features. Do they all allow comments? What kinds of things do people write? Are they engaging with the story or with other commenters?

Online newspapers are very different from printed newspapers. It would be reasonable to say that people accessing news online are rarely reading the same publication. This is because of the choices readers have in navigating round the site, following stories back through time and interacting with other readers. Online news changes practices of news production and consumption in significant ways. The previous Activity shows that people can now comment on stories in a new way. Whether this changes what counts as news is not clear, although it shows that the line between producer and consumer is being eroded as well as changing the role of the news consumer. Consumers are now part of the process of news production.

4.8 NEW WAYS OF 'DOING' NEWS: TWITTER AND THE CITIZEN JOURNALIST

Twitter was founded in 2006 and has been taken up by a range of people and institutions for a variety of purposes. Twitter is a micro-blogging application, allowing individuals to author and disseminate messages of 140 characters called 'tweets'. As well as the character limit, tweets have other features. To access Twitter you need a user name and this may allow people to tweet directly to you, by including your twitter handle (which is signified by @). It is also possible to include images and links to webpages in tweets. In addition, hashtags (#) are an important part of Twitter. Hashtags are used to identify the subject or orientation of tweets. For example '#URUvsENG' indicates that tweets with this hashtag are about the Uruguay vs England match in the 2014 World Cup and enables readers to find tweets about that topic. If a hashtag is used enough, its use will be tracked and reported as 'trending'. Events and television programmes also publicise hashtags so that people can follow and contribute to a running commentary about them (e.g. #newsnight). The Twitter interface allows users to see what is trending globally as well as allowing users to follow a subject regardless of who is tweeting. Because Twitter is a platform that relies on **user generated content**, its form and content depends on how people use it (Boyd *et al.* 2010).

Twitter enables more people to engage in **citizen journalism**. Citizen journalism refers to non-professional journalists producing news content. In fact, Twitter has changed what citizen journalism means in that it allows anyone with a smart phone access to the public sphere. While many people publish online, in forums, on websites and so on, because it is possible to monitor Twitter, it can provide an important cue to traditional news bodies about what is happening and what is important. Bruno defines 'the Twitter effect' as that which 'allows you to provide live coverage without any report–ers on the ground, by simply newsgathering user-generated content avail–able online' (2011: 8 cited in Hermida 2012: 663). Hermida points out that this makes verification very important for journalists but also very challeng–ing given the fast pace of contemporary news reporting (2012: 661). 'The process of determining the facts', Hermida writes, 'traditionally took place in newsrooms' (2012: 665). However, 'Arguably, some of the process of journalism is taking place in public on platforms such as Twitter' (2012: 665). The production of news out of user-generated content has changed the construction of news and journalistic practice (Hermida 2012: 666).

There is still, even in the developed world, a 'digital divide'. The 'digital divide' describes the fact that not everyone has access to these technolo–gies. Moreover, knowing what to trust on Twitter is not always straightfor–ward. It requires specific kinds of **literacy** (Murthy 2011). This is clear when we consider the way that news that isn't true may be understood as though it is. For example, in late 2013 and early 2014, a story that the leader of North Korea, Kim Jong-un, had fed his uncle to dogs went viral. It was picked up and reported as fact by a number of newspapers. Keating reported that a blogger, Trevor Powell, traced the story to a satirical posting on 'the Chinese microblogging site Tencent Weibo' (Keating 2014). Keating notes that misidentifying satire as real news is not that uncommon. Even detecting satirical performances face to face is apparently not as straightforward as one would expect.

Because news and information circulates in different ways and can be easily divorced from its point of origin, it's not surprising that sometimes news that isn't true is reported as though it is. What is surprising is that it doesn't happen more often. This may be because, as Starbird and Palen (2010) note, despite the number of people contributing to the mass media stream of information we are still most likely to pay more attention to established or trustworthy news producers.

Activity 4.10

Follow a hashtag for a television programme on Twitter (you'll have to be watching in 'real time' rather than pre-recorded or through an online platform). What kinds of comments are being made?

It's important to note that Twitter is a public space and because we don't know the people tweeting, it can be very difficult to know how to interpret their contributions. While an individual may tweet largely for an audience of family and friends, this does not always stop other people reading the tweet. Some people have got in trouble for their tweets that were misinterpreted (*BBC News* 2012). While friends and family may appreciate an ironic sense of humour and dry wit, they may not be the only audience.

It is worth noting the very positive ways Twitter can be used. Starbird and Palen examine its use in emergency situations. While mainstream media is a significant presence in emergency situations, they also found that the 'most popular retweets among locals [affected by the emergency] were tweets containing much more locally relevant information' (2010: 7). This included information of a timely and local nature, advising people of where help could be secured, what was happening to protect them and so on. They remark, 'Generalizations about the triviality of Twitter communications at the broad level therefore will not necessarily hold for tweets sent, received and retweeted during an emergency event' (2010: 9). Twitter has also been used to track illness and thus plan for demand on local health services. In the UK, the Food Standards Agency (FSA) used information from Twitter to map the spread of the norovirus (a contagious virus causing vomiting). They tracked hashtags such as #winterbug and #barf in order to see whether an increase in use of these correlated with lab reports about levels of norovirus from the same periods and places. Finding that this was the case, they are now able to predict the spread of a virus before lab work confirms it. Twitter enables monitoring of the spread of the virus and managing the resources necessary to cope with outbreaks (Rutter 2013).

4.9 SUMMARY

In this chapter our concern has been with the role that the mass media plays in society and the power it exercises. We have described how the mass media constructs and exercises its power by paying attention to the way information is filtered and represented, how ideology is recoverable through analysis of lexical and syntactic choices, and how news stories are structured in order to present a particular point of view. Concepts such as semantic unity show that individual choices (at the level of lexis and syntax) interact with each other and build to a single interpretation of the facts. What counts as an expert in the mass media was also considered. This demonstrates that experts are constructed by the media, that expertise is not something a person has, but something they are given. This construction of expertise can also be seen when considering Twitter and the citizen journalist. We have also explored the way the traditional media producers choose what to cover. The concept of 'news values' explains why news producers consider some events to be newsworthy while others are not. The move of mass media from print based publications to the World Wide Web has changed some aspects of news production and consumption. However, it is important to remember that even though information is presented through a different technology, the linguistic and ideological choices made are still relevant. Indeed, given the fast pace of news online, the power that such media exert is even stronger.

FURTHER READING

Briant, E., Watson, N. and Philo, G. (2013) 'Reporting disability in the age of austerity: The changing face of media representation of disability and disabled people in the United Kingdom and the creation of new "folk devils"', *Disability & Society*, 28(6): 874–89.
Chouliaraki, L. (2006) 'Towards an analytics of mediation', *Critical Discourse Studies*, 3(2): 153–78.
Irwin, A. (2008) 'Race and Ethnicity in the Media', in N. Blain and D. Hutchison (eds) *The Media in Scotland*, Edinburgh: Edinburgh University Press: 199–212.
Miller, L. (2004) 'Those naughty teenage girls: Japanese Kogals, slang, and media assessments', *Journal of Linguistic Anthropology*, 14(2): 225–47.
Philo, G., Briant, E. and Donald, P. (2013) *Bad News for Refugees*, London: Pluto
Thornborrow, J. (2001) 'Authenticating talk: Building public identities in audience participation broadcasting', *Discourse Studies*, 3(4): 459–79.

CHAPTER 5

Linguistic landscapes

5.1	INTRODUCTION	86
5.2	DEFINING THE LINGUISTIC LANDSCAPE	86
5.3	SIGNS AND MULTILINGUALISM AND POWER	96
5.4	SIGNS AND IDEOLOGY	99
5.5	TRANSGRESSIVE SIGNS: GRAFFITI	101
5.6	ONLINE LANDSCAPES	102
5.7	SUMMARY	107

5.1 INTRODUCTION

In Chapter 1 we considered the question 'what is language?' In this chapter, we are concerned with the question 'where is language?' Language is all around us. When we speak we use language, when we write and read we're also using language. Recently, linguists have become particularly interested in the use of language in the everyday semiotic landscape, in what might normally be considered banal or mundane contexts. We begin by explaining what the linguistic landscape is, and in contrast to the abstract signs we investigated in Chapter 3, explore types of concrete signs and their authors. We consider multilingual linguistic landscapes, the ideologies that signs communicate and the different meanings of graffiti. The importance of the virtual landscape is then examined to show how signs communicate in this context as well as how the division between online and offline linguistic landscapes is collapsing.

5.2 DEFINING THE LINGUISTIC LANDSCAPE

In cities and towns around the world, there is an abundance of linguistic and other **semiotic** material. Alongside official signage indicating street names, traffic regulations and building numbers, there is an abundance of material that people may or may not pay attention to. Advertising billboards, posters and hand written notices are placed all around us; they are all part of the linguistic landscape.

Scholars working in the field of Linguistic Landscapes (LL) and Semiotic Landscapes (SL) have directed their attention to the use of language and other meaningful objects in the construction of space. It's worth taking a moment to think about what 'construction of space' means.

Imagine you're blindfolded and taken to a public space somewhere. When the blindfold is removed, how would you know where you are?

Activity 5.1

In this scenario, you would probably quite quickly figure out what kind of place you were in. You might look for street signs, the names of roads and directions to other places. From this, you may be able to orient yourself. If you happened to be placed in another country, you would be able to deduce this simply from the way the signs were composed, from their typeface, colour and size. You might look for shop signs, to try and find something familiar. The surroundings may be easy to understand. You would be able to tell if you were in a government office, for example, or a bus station. Language and other semiotic features help us understand what kind of space we're in.

Research in LL studies the way 'linguistic objects ... mark the public space' (Ben-Rafael *et al.* 2006: 7) and the '*symbolic construction of the public space*' (Ben-Rafael *et al.* 2006: 10, emphasis in original). Researchers consider signage, the languages in which they are written, who produced them and to whom they are directed. It is useful to draw a distinction between official and non-official signs. For example, official signs are usually produced by the government, local councils or the owner of a building or site. The messages that they convey can be described as 'top down' discourses (Ben-Rafael *et al.* 2006: 10). On the other hand, signs produced by individuals or small groups can usually be identified on the basis of the message and the form of the sign. These can be described as 'bottom up' discourses. Image 5.1 is an example of a top down message because it is posted by the government. In Wales, all official signage is bilingual so the text is in English and Welsh. Note that the use of 'bottom up' and 'top down' does not relate to the placement of English and Welsh on the sign itself.

Image 5.1 Bilingual Welsh sign

The difference between 'top down' and 'bottom up' discourses can be seen in Image 5.2 and Image 5.3.

Image 5.2 Official no smoking sign

Image 5.3 Hand-drawn no smoking sign

Immediately one can see that Image 5.2 is an official sign. The standard typeface, the normal no smoking icon and the reference to 'this station and its platforms' immediately communicates that it is official and a top down discourse. It has been professionally produced and the use of the **passive voice** 'have been designated' points to the authority authoring the sign. In addition to asking people not to smoke, it demonstrates its authority to make such a request.

In contrast, the picture in Image 5.3 is a hand-drawn sign on a single piece of A4 paper. It is immediately identifiable as a bottom up discourse. This sign was posted outside a university building, next to an official no smoking sign. It would be reasonable to hypothesise that this sign has been created by an individual wanting to add their voice to the official signage on the same wall. It is then possible to interpret it as a personal plea not to smoke in this space.

Kress and van Leeuwen argue that we can apply the following reading strategies to further interpret visual material. We can treat it in a similar way to reading written texts. In writing, we expect a writer to start with what is already known or 'given' before moving to new information. Thus, the left hand side of an image or a page can be understood as 'given' and that on the right as 'new' (1996). Kress and van Leeuwen argue that we can understand content at the top as 'ideal' and content at the bottom as 'real'. This works particularly well for large billboards or full page advertisements in magazines. The claims for the product will often be at the top while information about how to contact the vendor will be at the bottom.

These strategies vary across cultures, however, because of different reading practices; not all languages are written left to right. As Scollon and Scollon argue, 'there is always a danger of overgeneralizing from closely situated semiotics to [160] broader social, cultural, or universal categories' (2003: 159–60).

5.2.1 Space and meaning

The signs in Image 5.2 and 5.3 tell us something about the space in which they are located and about the signmaker. Paying attention to the features of these signs is to attend to the 'symbolic functions of language [which] help to shape geographical spaces into social spaces' (Leeman & Modan 2009: 336). The very presence of the signs alters the space where they are found. The meaning the sign conveys also depends on where it is placed. This is why Scollon and Scollon emphasise the 'material placement' of signs as a key concern when analysing them. They call this mode of analysis geosemiotics.

> **Geosemiotics**: the study of the social meaning of the material placement of signs in the world. By 'signs' we mean to include any semiotic system including language and discourse.
>
> (Scollon & Scollon 2003: 110)

Note that language is just one of many semiotic systems. Other things, like placement of a sign, the typeface used, the colour, images and so on, also create and communicate meaning. Because signs are so varied across the linguistic landscape, we need to pay attention to all these semiotic choices.

Where a sign is placed tells us something about its meaning and the intentions of the sign maker. It is also worth noting the importance of where signs are placed in two other respects. First, signs need to be well-placed in relation to the information they convey. We have all had the experience of looking at a sign with an arrow and not being sure where it is pointing. The **deictic** nature of these signs means they need to be carefully placed in order to fulfil their informative function (see Denis & Pontille 2010); '*the sign only has meaning because of where it is placed in the world*' (Scollon & Scollon 2003: 29 emphasis in original). A stop sign in the middle of a field, even though it has all the features of an official traffic sign, has a very different meaning to one at a street corner. In fact, an official sign out of place may well be considered transgressive. This depends on the relationship between the sign and where it is placed.

> All of the signs and symbols take a major part of their meaning from how and where they are placed – at that street corner, at that time in the history of the world. Each of them indexes a larger discourse whether of public transport regulation or underground drug trafficking.
>
> (Scollon & Scollon 2003: 2)

This is particularly clear in terms of regulatory and top down signs. Official signs index, or point to, the authority able to create and place these signs. Moreover, the placing of signs can define a boundary.

Mautner argues that physical signs can function as 'boundary markers … playing an important part in carving up space into public and private areas, and into zones where it is permissible to enact some social roles (e.g., cyclist or angler), but not others (e.g., busker or dog-walker)' (2012: 190). The drawing of these boundaries depends on the deictic function of signs as is the case in Image 5.4.

Image 5.4 No parking sign

As well as creating boundaries and defining space, signs index other meanings, discourses and messages. As we noted previously, Scollon and Scollon suggest that signs index a 'larger discourse' (Scollon & Scollon 2003: 2). For example, the no-smoking signs (Image 5.2 and 5.3) point to at least two other discourses. The first is the rather widespread ban on smoking in public spaces. In many countries it is now illegal to smoke in workplaces, public buildings and even on public streets. The presence of a conventional, official no smoking sign indexes the laws that brought these bans into effect. The second discourse is the stigmatisation of smoking. Since widespread smoking bans have taken effect, smoking is now a more stigmatised practice than it was. This may explain the hand-drawn image in Image 5.3. In any case, the illegality of smoking in many places has perhaps made it more acceptable to ban it in other spaces.

In public spaces, people are often urged to behave in a particular way. Whether this relates to putting rubbish in bins, covering your mouth when coughing or safely crossing the road, many of these interventions are useful in spaces with multiple users. Traffic signs, to take the most obvious example, allow road users to co-exist in a reasonably safe manner. While traffic signs have an important regulatory function, they also provide motorists and pedestrians with a clear understanding of what is appropriate and what is not. The line between law and good behaviour in this domain is not always clear. A pedestrian can cross a road without a designated crossing in many countries without breaking the law. She may nevertheless be breaking the rules of what counts as good behaviour from a pedestrian. In other transport domains, particularly public transport, signs may urge passengers to behave in appropriate ways. In order to have maximum effect, these signs may be organised into a wider campaign (see Section 5.4).

All signs, but particularly top down official signs, structure space through boundary marking and by indexing other discourses. As Mautner argues, signs carve space into 'zones where it is permissible to enact some social rules … but not others' (Mautner 2012: 190). Such structuring of space is an exercise of power and is ultimately ideological. This does not mean, however, that it might not have positive intentions or effects.

5.2.2 Different kinds of signs

When attempting to understand the range of signs we encounter in the linguistic landscape, considering the distinction between top down and bottom up, even with attention to materiality, is not enough. Scollon and Scollon (2003: 217) provide four categories of sign:

1. Regulatory discourses – traffic signs or other signs indicating official/ legal prohibitions
2. Infrastructural discourses – directed to those who maintain the infra-structure (water, power etc.) or to label things for the public (e.g. street names)
3. Commercial discourses – advertising and related signage
4. Transgressive discourses – 'a sign which violates (intentionally or accidentally) the conventional semiotics at that place such as a discarded snack food wrapper or graffiti; any sign in the "wrong space"' (Scollon & Scollon 2003: 217).

Note that these categories may overlap. The hand-drawn no smoking sign in Image 5.3 seems to be regulatory, but as it's not top down, it can also be considered transgressive.

If we consider these categories together with the other characteristics of signs we considered above, it is possible to be quite specific about the kinds of signs we find.

When you travel to the university, try and document the signs you encounter on the way. This can be done on even a very short journey – and this is preferable as some spaces have a great proliferation of signs. Note the signs you see and mark on a map where you found them. How many are official top down signs? How many are bottom up and of what kind? It may help to use Scollon and Scollon's four categories: What does this tell you about the space you're in? What kind of people are in the space? What kinds of activities take place there?

Activity 5.2

5.2.3 Top down and bottom up as a continuum

It is not always easy to know where to draw the line between top down and bottom up. Ben-Rafael *et al.* (2006) suggest the signs on individual shops are 'bottom up' as these allow for personal choice in their composition and display (2006). However, within the context of the shop itself they could be regarded as top down. Leeman and Modan (2009) argue that the

> distinction between top-down and bottom-up signage practices is untenable in an era in which public-private partnerships are the main vehicle of urban revitalization initiatives in urban centres in many parts of the world, and when government policies constrain private sector signage practices.
>
> (2009: 334)

Nevertheless, if the distinction is thought of as a continuum whose orientation points may shift in different contexts, it is still helpful in understanding how signs are constructed and consumed.

The distinction between top down and bottom up can also be supplemented by other factors in order to figure out how to read the sign. For example, the materiality of a sign may give some clues to its status and legitimacy. This is the case with the sign in Image 5.3 (the hand-drawn no smoking sign). However, sometimes official signs, authored by the government or a local government body, depart from the austere choices we may associate with top down discourses, as in Image 5.5. This sign, found at a pond in a nature reserve, appears to be addressed to dogs. Another sign directly above it (not included here), gently urges pet owners to stop their dogs from playing in the pond.

Image 5.5 Woof Woof, Staffordshire Wildlife Trust

It is also likely that we attend to signs with specific features more than we might otherwise. The sign in Image 5.6 was found in a women's bathroom in a theatre in Vancouver, British Columbia. The fact that it is metal and screwed to the wall tells the audience it is permanent and therefore, perhaps, important. The use of a standard serif typeface and the use of the symbol conventionally used to prohibit something (a red circle with a line through it) all suggest that authority stands behind what is ultimately a request to consider the experience of others.

Image 5.6 Ladies' bathroom sign

Image 5.6, the sign in the women's bathroom urges women to be considerate of other patrons. This kind of signage doesn't specifically prohibit something; rather, it asks the audience to behave in a particular way. Public transport spaces also contain many such signs. See if you can find examples on buses, trains or trams or in transport hubs (bus and train stations, bus stops and so on).

Sometimes, the top down and bottom up are found on the same sign. This is clear when an official sign (top down) is altered in some way by the public (bottom up). These alterations may pass judgement on the authors of the sign and their actions or on a social issue of wider significance (see Image 5.7).

Image 5.7 Stop sign

Additions to signs such as the one in Image 5.7 bear some resemblance to graffiti. Whether or not you think such alteration is acceptable depends very much on your attitude to the original sign and to the intervention of individuals in public sign space. We consider this later in this chapter.

Image 5.8 High fives, Ryan Laughlin

Image 5.7 and 5.8 exploit the conventions of top down signs to creatively intervene in the everyday space of signs. What is particularly striking about examples like this is that the audience may not immediately notice that there has been an intervention. Because traffic signs are part of our everyday semiotic landscape, we expect to see signs telling us to stop or give way or indicating the speed limit. Therefore we don't read them in detail because we don't need to. The artists' interventions capitalise on the conventional nature of traffic signs in order disrupt the everyday LL. This may well be entertaining, invite passers-by to look at their environment in a new way and may also critique the top down control of the built environment.

5.3 SIGNS AND MULTILINGUALISM AND POWER

Scholars studying LL are often concerned with questions of multilingualism and uncovering the everyday communicative strategies of the people who actually use a particular space. It is important to consider a whole range of signs and semiotics in relation to each other, across a landscape. This is particularly valuable when considering power. Considering multilingualism in LL can also tell us about the languages used by inhabitants of those spaces and whether this 'matches' up with the 'official language'. While multilingualism is a rich field of research in LL we can explore it only briefly here.

In Image 5.1, we saw a sign from a nation that is officially bilingual. The inclusion of both Welsh and English on this official, top down sign shows that there are now two official languages in Wales (May 2011). Official recognition of a language is an important marker of power and acknowledgement by those in authority. In places where the official language is contested, which languages are included on this kind of top down signage is a subject of intense debate (Heller 2006). Official language policies do not represent all aspects of the linguistic landscape (Ben-Rafael *et al.* 2006). Regardless of what those in power claim about the linguistic profile of their community, the linguistic landscape is a testament to the languages actually being used in a place. That is, it is not the case that the only languages used in a community are the 'official' languages. Close examination of the linguistic landscape can reveal languages that would otherwise be invisible.

5.3.1 Invisible language

Some research on linguistic landscapes focuses on the range of different languages with specific attention to their presence and the ways they are used. This can provide insight into linguistic diversity not captured by official top down discourses or even by official audits (e.g. a census). Blommaert describes the linguistic landscape of his local community in a part of Antwerp, Belgium. This area, Berchem, is 'predominantly Turkish and Belgian … both groups being the most visible (and audible) ones there' (2013: 46). While he notes that there has been some Chinese migration to the area, 'it is not Chinatown' (2013: 46). When conducting his ethnography, however, he documents a handwritten sign in Chinese script found in the window of an empty shop. It advertises a flat to rent. Because it is written in Chinese, it is clearly addressed to a Chinese audience. But careful examination shows that its meaning is not straightforward.

The Chinese sign is written 'in a mixture of traditional Mandarin script (used in, e.g. Taiwan, Hong Kong and most of the traditional Chinese diaspora), and simplified script (used in the People's Republic)' (Blommaert 2013: 45). Blommaert points out that this may suggest that the author is not fully competent in either form or is trying to cater to a likely audience. Because this sign is placed on the inside of a window, it communicates more than simply a flat for rent. It adds to the semiotic landscape and claims ownership of the space in which it is placed (even if only a very small space) (Blommaert 2013: 46), suggesting an emergent, or otherwise invisible, Chinese network.

Multilingualism in a community may have several sources. We show how it might happen by considering the language and sign choices in Image 5.9.

Image 5.9 Mondo macho

Image 5.9 was taken in Arles, France. From the sign directing people to hotels we can already deduce something about this place. The names of the hotels are in French; we know we are in a French speaking area (though this need not be France). That there are directions to six hotels suggests that this is a tourist area. The design of these signs suggests they are not made by each individual hotel; they are not just advertising signs, or commercial signs in Scollon and Scollon's terms. They are more like official street signs, directing people to the relevant local tourist infrastructure – hotels. They have an 'informing' function (Blommaert 2013: 54).

The shop front in the background, however, is a form of advertising, with a 'recruitment' function (Blommaert 2013: 54). This shop sign, like many others, announces '(a) the kind of transactions performed in that place, (b) the kinds of audiences targeted for such transactions' (Blommaert 2013: 54). For many people it may not be difficult to understand that this is a clothes shop for men because of its name: Mondo Macho. When one considers that Arles is situated on the French Mediterranean coast, together with the hotel signs that tell us that Arles is a tourist destination, it seems reasonable to think that this store may want to cater to this holiday market.

Activity 5.4

Have a closer look at the signs for hotels and the shop front in Image 5.9. Did you notice the other texts? How would you classify them?

There is also some regulatory text on a barrier behind the hotel sign. Whether this is barrier out of place (waiting to be moved to and thus regulate another space) or it belongs there is not clear from the photo. Finally, there is more text on the shop window. Unlike the signs painted on the glass, one is written 'femme' (woman) directly on the glass by hand and the other has been written on a piece of paper and then fixed to the inside of the window. This sign is in French, 'Boutique a vendre', communicating that the shop is for sale. As this is written in French, it seems to be addressed to the local, rather than tourist, population.

5.4 SIGNS AND IDEOLOGY

So far we have considered single instances of signs; but signs can also be part of a broader communicative strategy. If this strategy is directed towards a particular goal, it might be called a 'campaign'. For a set of signs to constitute a campaign they should be somehow recognisably related (in terms of design, colour and language) and serve the same general aims. A good example of this is a campaign from Singapore. Michelle Lazar has analysed the National Courtesy Campaign that was launched by then Prime Minister Lee Kan Yew 'with the goal of changing the boorish habits of Singaporeans and recreating a society of people who would be more courteous and gracious towards others, especially strangers' (Lazar 2003: 201). This was a campaign that covered not only public transport, but public behaviour more generally. The campaign urges people to be 'courteous' to their fellow people.

Lazar notes that Singapore has launched other similar prescriptive campaigns advising citizens about bad behaviours such as littering, spitting and drug abuse and 'persuasive' campaigns about language use and family planning (2003: 203). The National Courtesy Campaign (hereafter CC) was extensive in terms of both duration and the issues it covered. It started in 1979 and lasted for over 20 years. 'The idea was to gradually transform all sectors of Singaporean society to become "naturally" courteous' (Lazar 2003: 202). The use of 'naturally' reveals the ideological force of the campaign. The campaign sought not simply to control behaviour in particular situations, but to change people's 'nature'. While Lazar focuses on the road and public transport part of the campaign, it also encouraged schoolchildren, retailers, employers, employees and Singaporeans studying abroad to be courteous.

The campaign is at least partly constituted by its signs. For a campaign to work, its signs need to be arranged in specific ways. For public transport and road users, for example, it is important that the audience is able to see the signs while they are using transport or driving on the roads. Indeed, the signs were placed on and around buses, taxis and trains as well as on cars and roadways. CC messages were also printed on tickets for public transport. The signs and their messages became routine and ubiquitous (Lazar 2003: 208).

While the campaign is clearly a top down discourse, since it comes from the government, it makes use of a discourse of 'community', which, as Lazar notes, has become a 'new *means* of governance' (204). That is, responsibility for particular aspects of social and political life is handed to the community, making success or failure its responsibility. Crucial in such a technique is the creation of a community, whether at the national, regional, local or some other level. The CC sought to create this community by using informal language and images. Lazar calls this 'informalised authority' to make clear that while it seems to be inclusive and to minimise social distance it nevertheless comes from a place of authority (2003: 205).

Two figures were used to create this informal tone and to build the courteous community. The first is a yellow smiling face called 'Smiley'. The second figure was a humanised lion called 'Singa' (Lazar 2003: 209). Singa is a cartoon lion whose name means 'lion' in Malay (Lazar 2003: 209). The name of Singapore itself is from the Malay 'Singapura', lion city, thus Singa serves as a symbol of the country (Lazar 2003: 210). Singa is both courteous and friendly, and yet is a figure of national authority in the most informal of guises; a cartoon lion (Lazar 2003: 201). Lazar notes that smiley faces, in different colours, were placed in a range of places, often completely covering a bus or train carriage and thus 'enveloping [the vehicle] symbolically with courtesy' (2003: 209). They were also placed at strategic points so that travellers saw them when boarding a bus or train. The intention was that 'commuters [would be] prodded into a friendly state of mind when boarding the bus and coming into close contact with fellow travellers' (2003: 209).

In addition to Smiley and Singa, instructions were also given to transport and road users. These included:

> Be polite. Signal early.
>> Think of other road users.
>> Let passengers alight first
> Please let passengers alight first
>> Please mind the platform gap
>> Please do not alight when doors are closing
>
>> (Lazar 2003: 212, 214)

While these might seem to be **face threatening**, in that they tell people what to do, these clear instructions are important in establishing conventions of courtesy and constructing a community (Lazar 2003: 212). Other messages are more general:

> Courtesy paves the way, makes your day.
>> Courtesy. The key to a pleasant journey

While on the face of it, all these messages do is urge people to be courteous; their very presence changes the linguistic and social landscape. The attempt to create and address a community through the use of informality and persistence change the way people orient to the spaces they are in and people around them. If someone chooses not to be courteous in this linguistic and social landscape that choice is more meaningful and more inconsiderate than if the campaign had not existed. The campaign doesn't just seek to change behaviour, it seeks to change people's ideas about what counts as appropriate behaviour. Far from simply being about 'good manners', campaigns like this are a form of control; 'individuals are not overtly constrained, but also are not entirely free' (Lazar 2003: 219).

The courtesy campaign in Singapore was wide ranging and long lasting. As we have seen, it sought to change public behaviour and conceptions about what counts as good behaviour in public. Changing ways of thinking about good behaviour is an important ideological shift. For it to work, the campaign really does have to be taken up by the community it addresses. There is tangible evidence that the campaign has had a lasting effect. Specifically, in Singapore, there is a permanent exhibition called the 'Kindness gallery' to document and archive campaign materials and explain what the movement is (http://kindness.sg/get-involved/the-kindness-gallery/).

5.5 TRANSGRESSIVE SIGNS: GRAFFITI

We defined a transgressive sign 'as a sign which violates (intentionally or accidentally) the conventional semiotics at that place such as a discarded snack food wrapper or graffiti; any sign in the "wrong space"' (Scollon & Scollon 2003: 217). Here we focus on one kind of transgressive sign, graffiti, in order to demonstrate some of the different meanings it can have. We're especially interested in transgressive signs because they provide marginalised people a voice in public space. Transgressive signs thus provide a measure of agency for people without conventionally recognised power.

Carrington (2009) notes that graffiti is 'an unsanctioned urban text' one that 'sits in direct competition with the sanctioned texts displayed in the production of commercial advertising, shop front signs, street signs and noticeboards' (2009: 410). The fact that graffiti is present at all may suggest that the space is contested in some way (see Image 5.7); and while Carrington describes graffiti as 'vernacular', we can also understand it in relation to the bottom up scheme described above. As these signs are not top down, they allow the viewer to see the contributions of other people to the built environment. Graffiti points to the existence of people engaged with their environment in an active way.

A sign may contain both 'commercial graffiti' and 'non-commercial graffiti' (Lee 2000 cited in Carrington 2009: 411–12). The former is 'about authority and control of public spaces and buildings in a consumer culture and can be found on most city surfaces' while 'non-commercial graffiti' is 'an alternative system of public communication' (Lee cited in Carrington 2009: 411–12). Both mark out space and ownership of space. Both comment either on that space or the world more generally. But while we generally know how to read commercial graffiti, and generally agree on how it should be understood, not everyone reads non-commercial graffiti in the same way. One of the key differences between them is that commercial graffiti is paid for; the textual space is purchased in some way and is therefore considered to be legitimate.

Carrington argues that the 'imperative for these ways of writing on the city revolves around voice, identity and space' (2009: 417). Graffiti seeks to claim back space that has been colonised by commercial signage, and for ordinary people to mark and comment on the spaces they inhabit.

> It is loud: it screams from the walls 'I am here and I want you to know.' It screams 'I don't respect your boundaries – textual or spatial.' It is hyper-visible – large, messy, prominent, spatially transgressive, dismissive of private ownership and corporate power – and therefore directly reminds us of the inter-medial nature of text. Our eyes *see* its visual qualities as well as convert it to meaning chunks.
>
> (Carrington 2009: 418)

Graffiti is a way for disempowered people to make a visible mark, to disrupt the landscape that is increasingly occupied by the increasingly powerful. Carrington argues that it creates a **narrative** and is a form of 'participatory culture'. The people who live in the space provide evidence of their experiences, views and actions. In this sense, it is a form of citizenship, not unlike the silly citizenship described in Chapter 3. It allows for the visibility of a hidden community and permits this community to see itself in its environment.

5.6 ONLINE LANDSCAPES

The World Wide Web, social media and computer mediated communication all involve language in a virtual landscape. These virtual spaces are also linguistic landscapes. Seeing these things as landscapes, rather than just language, allows us to pay full attention to the semiotic choices made as well as the new spaces created in these environments. This LL has changed rapidly over the last few years. The kinds of interaction available due to improvements in and access to technology has transformed the way people communicate. YouTube is one of these innovations. Because it is an online format that allows anyone with a computer to interact with society, it is a varied and accessible landscape.

5.6.1 YouTube

It's difficult to generalise about how people actually use YouTube. The site itself, however, at least tells us what is possible. The search function indicates that people can look for something specific (either a person or a topic). The ability to share links indicates that people can tell their friends about what they are looking at, or direct them to suitable content. The listing of similar content beside and after individual clips suggests that some viewers may browse through a range of linked and interrelated material. The existence of 'channels' and the ability to 'follow' a film maker or **vlogger** indicate that some viewers might be loyal to particular YouTube spaces and people.

If you've spent any time on sites like this, you'll know that there is a wide range of material. From professionally produced material and animations to outtakes from personal or real time event recordings, there is no such thing as a YouTube 'style'. When it comes to material produced specifically for YouTube, generalisations may be made, although even here, commonalities among vlogs will depend on genre and type.

Go to YouTube and find several videos representing each of the following genres:

- ◼ tutorials (e.g. how to knit, fix a leaking pipe)
- ◼ animations
- ◼ ·music.

Are there common features within each genre of video? Are there common features shared by all three of the genres?

Activity 5.5

While there is certainly some similarity between YouTube and television, it has also been described as being a form of 'post-television' (Lister et al. cited in Tolson 2010: 278). Using Nick Couldry's research on traditional media, Tolson (2010) sets out the differences between television and YouTube. First, while television tends to be 'centred', with content being filmed or broadcast from a studio, YouTube is 'decentred'. Those producing and broadcasting content only need to have access to recording equipment and a computer that is linked to the World Wide Web. Second, connected to the centrality of this production, television tends to have a 'hierarchy of discourse', with some channels and programmes being more prestigious than others. This may depend on the 'institutional voice' of the channel or programme or the kind of people producing the content. YouTube, however, is not hierarchical. While content is searchable and ordered so that viewers can find material, none of it is presented by the platform as more prestigious than anything else. In addition to this, rather than having an 'institutional voice', the voices on YouTube are 'individual voices', with ordinary people becoming the 'celebrities and experts'. Third, what a viewer can watch is dictated by the television programme schedule; that is, without having recorded content in some way, it's not possible to watch the 6pm news at

9am. YouTube provides very little direction about what to watch when. Just as producers can choose what to broadcast, viewers can choose what to watch and when to watch it (Tolson 2010: 285).

YouTube allows anyone with a visual recording device to have a public profile. While some users' purpose is just fun, others try to capitalise on the large YouTube audience for more practical purposes. YouTube allows for a different kind of citizenship and contribution to social justice via campaigns such as Thinkbeforeyouspeak.com, an online campaign to discourage the use of words that insult homosexuals and other marginalised groups. On the other hand, YouTube is also used for commercial purposes by large corporations for advertising and marketing campaigns.

5.6.2 Twitter

Having discussed Twitter in Chapter 4 we can think about how our access to technology has changed our linguistic landscape. Because of smart phones, the online linguistic landscape is part of the everyday. The distinction between being offline and online is breaking down. Because of the easy access to the internet via smart phones users can be online all of the time. The virtual landscape, therefore, is ubiquitous. What this virtual landscape looks like depends on the technology but also on the choices the user makes. An individual's experience of Twitter, for example, will depend on who they are following, which hashtags they are interested in, and so on. Moreover, the way people use Twitter can vary widely. It may be used for keeping up with developments in your work and career, making sure your train is running on time, following your favourite singer or interacting with friends. Twitter, and other online platforms, provides opportunities (though always with some limitations) and resources for making choices in how we create a personalised linguistic and semiotic landscape. Gillen and Merchant refer to these choices in terms of constructing a 'point of view' (2013: 51). Further, because of the **user generated content** on Twitter, users are changing the very landscape they inhabit. While this may be most visible in citizen journalism (Chapter 4), it is also true more generally, even given the small amount of space allowed for each Tweet (140 characters).

It's important to remember that while many people have access to the technology that provides access to this new linguistic landscape, this is not universal. There is still a significant digital divide even in the West with people excluded from the online world because of the money or physical attributes necessary to access it (Murthy 2011: 785).

The division between 'online' and 'offline' is becoming harder to chart. This will continue to change and evolve. While this has consequences for how we perceive our personal space, it will probably also mean changes for the linguistic landscape. Already advertising appears on screens, with some spaces being sensitive to movement around them and activating when human presence is detected. The constant access to Twitter, news feeds, updates on screens in public spaces can all be described under the term 'ambient journalism' (Hermida 2012). This can be compared to 24-hour news channels in some respects, but the recent changes in access to technology represent a radical shift in what 'ambient' means. In dealing with and thinking about the linguistic landscape, then, we are no longer just thinking about signs, posters, billboards and notices.

5.6.3 Memes

One of the things that the World Wide Web makes possible is the quick circulation of 'memes'.

> Memes are contagious patterns of 'cultural information' that get passed from mind to mind and directly generate and shape the mindsets and significant forms of behavior and actions of a social group. Memes include such things as popular tunes, catchphrases, clothing fashions, architectural styles, ways of doing things, icons, jingles and the like.
> (Knobel & Lankshear 2007: 199)

In the online context, '"meme" is a popular term for describing the rapid uptake and spread of a particular idea presented as a written text, image, language "move," or some other unit of cultural "stuff"' (Knobel & Lankshear 2007: 202). Memes are a striking example of extensive, bottom up activity that changes the linguistic landscape.

Memes are a new kind of text production and consumption: they point to a new kind of **'literacy'** (Knobel & Lankshear 2007: 203). What these skills are can be examined by looking at the 'doge' meme. This meme consists of a picture of a shiba inu dog accompanied by a series of words and short phrases. The words are in Comic Sans font and in bright, fluorescent colours. Anyone producing a doge meme would follow these formatting conventions. The construction of the phrases in the meme follows the pattern intensifier +adjective/noun. Intensifiers are usually words like 'so', 'very', 'much' and 'many'. This pattern is found in various examples of the meme and for those who are literate in the conventions of this meme; the phrases are immediately recognisable as doge phrases (McCulloch 2014).

What makes doge phrases distinctive is that they don't obey the normal conventions of combination (McCulloch 2014). Intensifiers normally used with nouns are used with adjectives and vice versa; thus we find 'much happy' and 'very word'. While the doge meme is clearly an internet phenomenon, it has not stayed within these virtual walls. Image 5.10 is a photo taken in a university library.

Image 5.10 Doge graffiti

Image 5.10 includes a doge phrase, 'much surprise' and a picture of a dog. Written beside it, 'You thought Doge would not appear?' makes clear the move from appearing in virtual space to a table in a library. While we certainly don't want to condone drawing on library furniture, this transgressive use of language suggests that the conventions of doge are not only well established but also well-travelled.

Knobel and Lankshear argue that 'replicability' is important to consider for online memes (2007: 208). This means they should be easy to copy. They should also have the feature of 'fecundity', which refers to the 'rate at which an idea or pattern is copied and spread' (2007: 202). Research on successful memes, that is, those that are picked up and reported on by mainstream media, suggests that memes should be humorous (though they may contain an element of satire or social commentary), richly **intertextual** (referring to other texts, cultural products or practices) and contain some kind of 'anomalous juxtaposition', that is, the placement of two mismatching or incongruous elements together (Knobel & Lankshear 2007).

There are exceptions to this. Knobel and Lankshear report on The Dog Poop Girl meme. This meme is a good example of people exercising their agency online in order to express disapproval and seek justice. It began when a woman in South Korea travelled on a train with her dog. 'The dog had fouled the train carriage and its owner refused to clean up the mess, even after being asked a number of times to do so' (Knobel & Lankshear 2007: 216). Another passenger photographed the woman and her dog. This image became a meme, as it was extensively circulated and commented on in order to both find and shame the dog owner.

What is striking about memes is the linguistic and semiotic creativity involved in their creation and consumption. Their success, indeed their existence as memes, depends on a number of people consuming, circulating and building on the meme. They are indicative of a kind of semiotic democracy because the conventions they rely on are generated from the bottom up and shared by a large number of people. Memes rely on a particular kind of literacy, a fluency in the codes and rules that inform the meme. Due to the online nature of these memes, they also require some facility with software, the manipulation of text, image and sound. Consuming the memes helps to learn these rules and thus replicate and reproduce the meme by following the rules established by a collective.

5.7 SUMMARY

Understanding the linguistic landscape is important for understanding the spaces in which we live. While many of the signs we encounter on a typical day seem normal and inconsequential, they nevertheless construct the space in which we live, communicate messages and convey ideological information. While some signs are clearly the preserve of the powerful, there are spaces in the linguistic landscape where other voices can be seen. These spaces may be understood as contested, but they show that space and place are more varied than we normally think. Examining signs, both in the 'real world' linguistic landscape and the virtual landscapes of the World Wide Web, shows us how people make meaning and understand the contributions of others. The increasing access to technology has made individual agency more visible; but we find these voices only if we know how to look. The tools described in previous chapters, together with those introduced here, allow us to examine the world we live in new ways.

FURTHER READING

Gawne, L. and Vaughan, J. (2011) 'I Can Haz Language Play: The Construction of Language and Identity in LOLspeak', in M. Ponsonnet, L. Dao and M. Bowler (eds) *Proceedings of the 42nd Australian Linguistic Society Conference* 97–122; ANU Research Repository – http://hdl.handle.net/1885/9398
Jaworski, A. (2011) 'Linguistic landscapes on postcards: Tourist mediation and the sociolinguistics communities of contact', *Sociolinguistics Studies*, 4(3): 569–94.
McElhinny, B. (2006) 'Written in sand: Language and landscape in an environmental dispute in Southern Ontario', *Critical Discourse Studies*, 3(2): 123–52.

CHAPTER 6

Language and gender

6.1	**INTRODUCTION**	**108**
6.2	**WHAT IS GENDER?**	**108**
6.3	**INEQUALITY AT THE LEXICAL LEVEL**	**110**
6.4	**DIFFERENCES IN LANGUAGE USE: DOING BEING A WOMAN OR A MAN**	**116**
6.5	**GOSSIP**	**118**
6.6	**GENDER AND POWER**	**123**
6.7	**GENDERED TALK: PERFORMING IDENTITY**	**126**
6.8	**SUMMARY**	**130**

6.1 INTRODUCTION

In this chapter, we examine language and gender. We begin by considering the meaning of 'gender' by contrasting it with 'sex'. We then turn to issues of inequality of the sexes in language. We explore the use of the generic 'he' and other **lexical items** that represent women less favourably than men as an example of inequality. We then look at different kinds of talk in addition to the form of communication known as gossip, in order to evaluate whether and how men and women use language differently. To examine the language of more deeply entrenched ideologies associated with gender, we then consider whether women talk more than men. Finally, we investigate how gender identity is performed through language and the connection between gender and sexuality.

6.2 WHAT IS GENDER?

There is a strong relationship between language and gender. In order to explore these relationships there are a few key things to remember as you read on. Firstly, we must establish what we mean by 'sex' and 'gender'. 'Sex' is the biological state of male or female. Many linguists have used the term in this way in their research. In the first wave of linguistic studies of variation, academics were usually interested in broad patterns, across a large population. In this context, it makes sense to divide people according to their sex. However, later models used to explain the linguistic differences found between individuals culminated in recognition that sex is not always the best category of analysis. So, while sex is biological, gender is socially constructed. Women and men can demonstrate their identities in various ways too; that is, it is not the case that all men (or all women) share the same fundamental qualities simply because they are of the same biological sex. Instead of assuming biological categories, referring to *socially constructed gender* allows us to make different distinctions, and to talk about people as being masculine or feminine.

Analysing behaviour as connected to socially constructed gender rather than sex is crucial in understanding the different ways people perform their identity as well as how they are judged. Sex is not the same as gender. Sex, as a biological category, has little influence on gender: it isn't the case that all women and all men behave exactly like the other members of their biological sex group. Gender, then, is not something a person has, it is something they accomplish through their behaviour, clothing, habits and speech. Scholars often characterise this as 'performing' gender. Talking about gender allows an understanding of people's behaviours in nuanced and detailed ways; and while it is true that a wide range of genders and gender performances are available, this does not mean they are all understood as equal. The current inequality of sexes (discussed as follows) is evident in the performance and interpretation of gender identity. We will see that there are certain expectations of people according to biological sex. Very often, however, in reality people don't always conform to those expectations. The gender norms in a society generate conventions that people are judged against. It is of course possible not to conform to these gender expectations, but there are often consequences for the individuals who do this.

We will see through our exploration of gender and language that inequality is an important factor underlying the linguistic patterns we find. Although most countries have legally recognised the equality of men and women, there are still pervasive examples of everyday **sexism** and they can be easily found in language. For example, in 2013, while on official business in Malaysia, London Mayor Boris Johnson remarked that women only go to university to find husbands (Topping 2013). Another British politician remarked on the differences between men and women, claiming that women are better at finding 'mustard in the pantry' while men are better at parking cars. He described feminism as 'a passing fashion created by "shrill, bored, middle class women of a certain physical genre"' (politics.co.uk).

Find out how many of your political leaders are men and how many are women. What does this mean for the leadership of your city/province/country? Are all citizens equally represented?

It is very important to understand that despite the advances in equality of sexes, complete equality has not yet been achieved.

Activity 6.1

6.3 INEQUALITY AT THE LEXICAL LEVEL

6.3.1 Marked terms

Activity 6.2

Consider the meaning of the following pairs of words:

bachelor / spinster
master / madam
waiter / waitress
host / hostess

What does each pair of words refer to? Does each of them refer to exactly the same thing?

There are a few differences between the terms referring to men and the 'equivalent' terms for women. If we consider the difference between 'bachelor' and 'spinster', while both mean 'unmarried adult' these terms represent different types of unmarried adults. If we consider how these terms are used, it becomes apparent that bachelor is positive while spinster is negative. For example, common **collocations** for bachelor are 'eligible bachelor' or 'bachelor pad'. These collocations reflect a positive view of single life for men; their lifestyle is desirable and they too are desirable. 'Spinster' on the other hand, is more likely to be collocated with 'lonely' or 'old' and suggests an image of an older, unattractive woman. The two different terms for unmarried adult suggest more generally that being unmarried is a positive characteristic for a man but negative for a woman. The difference between 'bachelor' and 'spinster' and terms similar to these can be discussed in terms of lexical **asymmetry** because terms that are meant to be referring to equivalent positions for women and men are not actually used in the same way. These patterns of asymmetry generally go in one direction; the negative judgements are related to the female role (Schulz 1975) but not the male one.

The same negativity that attaches to 'spinster' is found in connection with **marked terms** referring to women. A term is marked when it has a relationship with a seemingly 'neutral' and generic counterpart. For example 'actor' referred to as an 'unmarked' term because it refers to a male and actors in general. 'Actress', however, refers only to a female 'actor'. By having a different form to indicate only a female 'actor', it is 'marked'. In the context of gender, we find that terms referring to men are generally unmarked and considered neutral while those referring to women are marked for sex. Similar examples are prince/princess, waiter/waitress, host/hostess and so on.

This marking would not be problematic if it were not for the asymmetry. Female occupation terms often have negative connotations. This can be seen in the 'master / mistress' pair. While 'master' is a position of authority, 'mistress' has undertones of loose sexuality.

Asymmetry is found in other domains too. Consider some of the titles available to men and women in Example 6.1.

Example 6.1

Female	Male
Miss	Mr
Mrs	
Ms	

One might think that in the modern world, with high levels of divorce and the recognition of alternative life styles with respect to relationships, the use of titles would be less important. But many organisations still require you to indicate your title on a subscription form, order form, over the phone and so on. While women's titles indicate their marital status, the most common title available to men is 'Mr', which provides no information about his relationship status at all. Occasionally 'Master' will be available for males, although this tends to be restricted to young boys. The difference between Miss and Mrs is straightforward; Miss means an unmarried woman and Mrs signals that the woman is married to a man. The meaning of 'Ms', interestingly, is rather more contested. It was initially proposed as a replacement for both 'Miss' and 'Mrs' so that women, like men, would only have one title that didn't refer to marital status. As often happens with words, Ms has taken on a range of other meanings according to the way it is used and how people understand it. It is often thought to indicate that a woman is divorced, a feminist, a lesbian or unmarried (Schwarz 2003; see also Lawton, Blakemore and Vartanian 2003). The result is that whatever choice of title a woman makes, information about her will be revealed. If she chooses 'Miss' it will be assumed that she is unmarried. The fact that men don't have to make this choice shows again the importance society places on marriage for women (as shown in the discussion of bachelor and spinster). If a woman chooses 'Ms', she may have very little control what people think this means, exactly because of the range of meanings that Schwarz has identified. Again, this is not a choice men are subject to. There is asymmetry in having to make a choice as well as what these choices may communicate.

6.3.2 'Generic' he

In relation to some terms, especially occupation terms (e.g. host/hostess, manager/manageress), it is often argued that the male term is not really sexed, but rather is generic and refers to both sexes. This, however, raises the question of why female marked terms are required at all. Some of the problems with supposed generic terms become clear when considering pronouns.

a. Every student should bring his books to class.
b. Every student should bring their books to class.
c. Everyone should cast his vote on polling day.
d. Everyone should cast their vote on polling day.

Do the sentences in Activity 6.3 include women?

Prescriptivists might argue that a and c above are the only acceptable forms. The suggestion that one could use 'their', as in b and d in these contexts is met with the objection that such use would result in disagreement in terms of number (i.e. 'every' and 'everyone' suggest the singular form). This is despite the fact that singular 'they' and 'their' has a long history of use in this way. Prescriptivists have argued that number agreement is more important than representing both sexes (Bodine 1975). However, Baranowski investigated the use of generic pronouns in the British and American press and found that '*he* is no longer the preferred singular epicene pronoun in English' (2002: 395) and 'they' is the most common and encouraged by guides on writing styles (e.g. The National Council of Teachers of English (NCTE) (2002), Linguistic Society of America (1996)).

It is important to note that numerous attempts have been made to encourage the use of existing generic pronouns (e.g. they) or to invent new pronouns (e.g. ze) (see Baron 1981) that are not marked for sex. New pronouns have not been particularly successful. While new words are taken up in language very easily, closed linguistic groups, such as pronouns and other grammatical particles, are much more resistant to change (see Section 2.6).

6.3.3 Sexism in word order

The recent acceptability of 'they' as generic does not mean that sexism in language has been eradicated. Even the order of words can demonstrate gender inequality. Heidi Motschenbacher (2013) examined the patterns of ordering when both a male and a female are mentioned in a noun phrase. While one often hears 'ladies and gentlemen' when an audience or other large gathering is addressed, this ordering is unusual. It is far more common for the male noun to be placed first; as in 'man and wife' (see Table 6.1).

Table 6.1 Gendered order preference in personal binomials
(adapted from Motschenbacher 2013: 223)

	Order f-m	Order m-f
General nouns		
woman/man	285	2,375
girl/boy	125	425
female/male	7	233
Address terms		
lady/gentleman	161	5
madam/sir	0	10
Mrs/Mr	0	546
Nobility titles		
queen/king	1	126
princess/prince	0	154
duchess/duke	0	65
lady/lord	1	49
countess/earl	0	15
Heterosexual roles		
wife/husband	66	551
widow/widower	16	1
bride/(bride) groom	115	3
Kinship terms		
mother/father	278	170
mum (or mum)/dad	349	7
mummy/daddy	35	7
aunt/uncle	55	44
niece/nephew	14	22
sister/brother	31	505
daughter/son	41	288
Occupations/functions		
actress/actor	0	42
hostess/host	0	19
policewoman/-man	0	108
other woman/man compounds	0	136
Pronouns		
she/he	60	554
her/him	17	411
herself/himself	3	81
her/himself vs him/herself	7	41
hers/his	8	14

Activity 6.4

Table 6.1 describes the results of Motschenbacher's (2013) research. What does her research show about which sex most commonly occurs first in personal binomials? What does this order suggest about our cultural norms for women and men?

In the majority of cases of personal binomials, Motschenbacher (2013) found that the male form comes before the female. The instances where this does not occur are domains that are considered feminine; specifically, parenting and children. This tells us that there are some fields that 'belong' to women.

Marked terms (Section 6.3.1) also demonstrate cultural conventions of this kind. The collocation 'lady doctor' or 'female doctor' is reasonably common as is 'male nurse'. These terms suggest that the 'default' sex for a doctor is male and the 'default' sex for a nurse is female.

The ordering of **binomials** is so deeply ingrained that women included in a binomial may not be given priority even in a text where women are the focus. For example, in the Convention on the Elimination of All Forms of Discrimination against Women (CEDAW, UN 1979), the noun phrase 'men and women' occurs 28 times while 'women and men' occurs only once. It may be that these orderings are simply conventional such as 'fish and chips' or 'salt and pepper'. Nevertheless, Motschenbacher demonstrates the ordering of other noun phrases where power is clearly at issue. The data from her research in Table 6.2 suggests that the more powerful subject will come first.

Table 6.2 Order of personal cojuncts in relation to power (adapted from Motschenbacher 2013: 216)

Cojuncts	More power/less power e.g. 'master and servant'	less power–more power e.g, 'servant and master'
Master/servant	22	2
Employer/employee	59	19
Mother/child	156	17
Father/child	22	0
Parent/child	306	81
Teacher/pupil	146	73
Doctor/nurse	146	23

Motschenbacher's research suggests that the ordering of such words is linked to power. The conventional ordering, with men first and women second, may be an indication of women's less powerful position in the social hierarchy. There is a range of linguistic evidence that supports this idea. We now consider the way words associated with women often become less positive over time.

6.3.4 Semantic derogation

Further examples of sexism, and especially gender inequality, can be seen in cases of semantic derogation. **Semantic derogation** refers to the process by which a word comes to have negative meanings over time. Some of the terms we've already examined have been subject to this. Around the year 1362, 'Spinster' (Section 6.3.1) referred to a person who spun yarn (OED). While this term could be used about men, it most often used to refer to women, probably because this work was typically done by women.

'Slut' too has been subject to derogation. In 1402 it meant 'A woman of dirty, slovenly, or untidy habits or appearance; a foul slattern' (OED). Only later did it become linked to loose sexual morality. Although this word has always been used to judge women in relation to an expected standard, whether this is related to keeping house, maintaining appearances or being chaste, 'slut' is currently in the process of being **reclaimed** (see Section 2.6). Women have begun to use the word to refer to themselves to resist the sexist usage of the term (Attwood 2007). It is also noteworthy that there is no term that refers to males in exactly the same way. While a 'stud' is a sexually promiscuous male, this is not negatively evaluated in the way 'slut' is.

Further examples of semantic derogation relating to women can be found in the domain of animals. Shulz (1975) shows that animal terms acquire negative connotations (e.g. pig, dog, cow) once associated with women.

Derogation and sexism toward women through language is not always obvious. Hines' (1999) research on associations of women with food shows how difficult it can be to notice and appreciate the ways women are objectified in language. Hines documents the 'WOMAN AS DESSERT' metaphor, drawing attention to the way women are conceptualised as something sweet to be eaten and shared. She provides a list of desserts that are also used to refer to women below.

- cheesecake
- cherry pie
- poundcake
- cookie
- crumpet
- cupcake

(Hines 1999: 152)

There are many semantic fields in which this kind of derogation occurs. As Schulz remarks:

> Again and again in the history of the language, one finds that a perfectly innocent term designating a girl or woman may begin with totally neutral or even positive connotations, but that gradually it acquires negative implications … after a period of time becoming abusive and ending as a sexual slur.
>
> (Schulz 1975: 65)

This is true not only in English, but in other languages too (Fontecha & Catalán 2003). Although gender inequalities have been addressed in significant ways since Shulz's research in 1975, the different treatment of men and women at the lexical level continues today (Hastie & Cosh 2013; Mills 2008; Parks & Roberton 2004).

6.4 DIFFERENCES IN LANGUAGE USE: DOING BEING A WOMAN OR A MAN

In 1975, Robin Lakoff published *Language and Woman's Place*. While this book has been criticised for its introspective nature (e.g. Dubois & Crouch 1975), the questions it raised and the features of 'women's language' that Lakoff identified led to a great deal of research on women's language. Lakoff argues that women's language is characterised by a number of features including the avoidance of swear words, the use of hedges or fillers ('you know', 'sort of'), the use of tag questions, empty adjectives, intensifiers, specific colour terms, more standard syntax, rising intonation on declaratives and high levels of politeness (Lakoff 1975). Subsequent research on what women actually do linguistically doesn't always match up with Lakoff's claims. However, nearly 40 years later, if we understand Lakoff's features as typifying a kind of 'ideal' woman against which real women are measured the list continues to work well. In this way, Lakoff's features provide us with an account of what people *expect* from women in their language use. An important feature of the concept 'women's language' is not that there actually is a way that men and women use language differently but that society expects them to do so without questioning this expectation. The belief that women speak one way and men another is strongly entrenched.

Lakoff's list of women's features has had other benefits. It provided linguists with a clear research agenda. Academics proceeded to gather data from women to find out whether they really did use more tag questions, colour terms and so on. Here we consider the research on one feature: tag questions. Tag questions are an ideal feature to examine because they are associated with uncertainty, lack of power and women (Lakoff 1975). They also demonstrate that assumptions about the function of linguistic features can be wrong. Research on tag questions allows us to see the key issues in language and gender; first, that we have ideologies about how men and women use language and, second, the complexity of linguistic features requires careful examination before we come to any conclusions about how people use language.

6.4.1 Tag questions

A tag question turns a declarative sentence into a question by 'tagging' or adding something onto the end.

> **Example 6.2**
> a.   She's a good looking girl, *isn't she* ?
> b.   That's not right, *is it* ?

In Example 6.2, 'isn't she?' and 'is it?' are the tag questions. Some tag questions express uncertainty about the declarative that it follows, as in b (an **epistemic** function). 'That's not right, is it' might be used by someone who really isn't sure whether it's right or not. But there are other functions tags can have. Consider example b. Imagine a teacher saying this to a school student. Is the teacher expressing uncertainty? In such a scenario, the teacher would be inviting the child to reconsider their position and to respond in some way.

Lakoff identified tag questions as part of 'women's language' (1975). Women's use of tag questions was interpreted as expressing uncertainty and a lack of confidence. Linguists started researching tag questions in order to establish whether women use them more than men. In the process of doing this work, however, they also discovered that tag questions have more than one function. As the examples in 6.2 show, tag questions don't just indicate uncertainty. Tag questions can have a **modal** or **affective** meaning. Modal in this context refers to the amount of certainty the speaker is expressing while affective tags signal the speaker's attitude to the addressee or even the topic being discussed. People use tag questions to express uncertainty, but they also use them to invite another person to speak, or to signal that what is being discussed or said is sensitive.

Research shows that while women use more tag questions, they are more likely to be affective tags that facilitate conversation (Holmes 1984). In Holmes' research more than half of women's tag questions were of this type. In contrast, the majority of tag questions used by men were modal; that is, they expressed uncertainty. In fact, tag questions can have even more functions if considered in conversational context. Consider Example 6.2a. given previously. Depending on the context, this might be a way of inviting a shared appreciation of an attractive woman or a way of expressing displeasure at the wandering eye of a boyfriend. The analysis of tag questions shows that while a linguistic form may have a conventional function; it may have other functions too. Therefore we must be very careful about making claims about what use of a tag question means (Holmes 1986, 1987).

A troubling aspect of tag question hypothesis is that, for some observers, the claim that 'women use more tag questions because both are associated with uncertainty' seemed to be self-evident. All cultures have ideas about how different groups of people should use language. People take as given the difference between men and women; one of the consequences of this is that we have no trouble accepting the idea that women and men use language differently. What we see in the detail of these assumptions is that women are thought to use less powerful language as a reflection of their lower position in the social hierarchy. Even though it is not true that women use 'less powerful' language (Conley, O'Barr & Lind 1978), the ideology remains. Taken together with the lexical asymmetries and **semantic derogation** described earlier, these linguistic features are a reflection of the lower rank women hold in the social hierarchy. The same ideologies about the difference between men and women's speech in addition to the negative value attached to women's speech can also be seen in the case of gossip.

6.5 GOSSIP

Gossip usually refers to talk about other people. It is often considered to be meaningless unreliable information and sometimes even malicious. In popular discourse, gossip is particularly associated with talk that women engage in with other women.

Deborah Jones defines gossip as 'a way of talking between women in their roles as women, intimate in style, personal and domestic in topic and setting' (1980: 194). According to Jones, 'gossip' is something that women do with close friends, often in their homes or other private settings. While Coates argues that Jones' claim that gossip revolves around women's roles as wives, girlfriends and mothers is too strong (2011: 201), this kind of talk allows women to explore and negotiate what it means to be a woman in a variety of contexts. Coates found a wide range of topics covered in the women's talk she collected. She observes 'it seems to be typical of all-women groups that they discuss people and feelings, while men are more likely to discuss things' (2011: 201). This characterisation of gossip seems rather different to the popular conceptions of gossip. Far from being scathing and malicious, women's talk among themselves deals with their relationships with other people and their feelings and opinions about events in the world. Linguists have taken up gossip as a legitimate object of study and found that first, gossip is a very complex form of communication and second, both men and women equally engage in this form of communication.

Several key linguistic discourse strategies typical of talk involving groups of women can be seen in Example 6.4.

Example 6.3

1. C: I didn't go over for my father/ I asked my mother
   B: it's so odd that you should

---

2. C: if she wanted me / I mean . I – I immediately said

---

3. C: 'Do you want me to come over!/ - and she said

---

4. C: 'Well no I can't really see the point / he's dead

---

5. C: isn't he?' / <LAUGHS> . and .   [and she
   A: mhm/
   B: well that's right/ [that's

---

6. C: said no / I mean   {{xxx}}   [no point in
   B: what John was saying/ that they
   E: [you've got

---

7. C: coming/   so
   A: [yeah
   E: terribly forward-looking parents you   [see/ it

---

8. E: depends on the attitude of- . mean is- is his

---

9. C: [I don't
   B: %I don't know%
   E: father still alive?   [Because

---

10. C: think – I don't think they had a funeral either/
    E: that would have a very big bearing on it/

---

11. D: if they were religious I mean/ yes/ [it would all
    E: [yeah

---

12. C: yeah I don't thnk they had a funeral/
    D: depend/   [if there were life
    E: yeah/ . I mean [if there was – if there

---

13. C: they had a memorial service/
    D: after death/   [then they'd KNOW
    E: was-   [if they- if-

---

14. D: that you hadn't come/
    E: that's right/

(Coates 2011: 205)

Normally in a conversation, we expect that only one speaker will talk at a time (Sacks, Schegloff and Jefferson 1974). This is not what we see in Example 6.3. First, more than one person is speaking at once without any members of the conversation expressing an objection to that. This is called a **shared floor** (rather than a one-at-a-time floor) (see Talbot 2011 [1992]). Second, the use of **minimal responses** (stave 5, 7 and 11) signals that participants are paying attention to the speaker. This is also known as

back-channelling. They do this by providing small utterances, such as 'mhm', 'yeah', without disrupting or interrupting the current speaker. Third, speakers use expressions such as 'I mean' (stave 2 and 6) that can be understood as signalling that the speaker knows this is a sensitive topic and is trying to express respect for other speakers' points of view. This strategy is called **hedging**. These strategies are typical of women's conversations with each other (Coates 1996). Women tend to be co-operative in this context; they construct a shared floor, provide support for the speaker, and carefully manage any points of conflict or disagreement (Coates 1996).

This conversational structure facilitates a particular type of discussion. In the case of Example 6.3, Coates points out that 'At one level, individual speakers are dealing with their own feelings about the topic under discussion' (Coates 2011: 205) but they do this in order to explore more general ideas: who is a funeral for, do other people's expectations matter, is distance a good reason not to attend a funeral? The discussion of these more general ideas can be seen as part of the process through which the women discover and articulate their own values.

This engagement with personal attitudes and their relation to broader social norms and conventions is often part of conversations that are considered 'gossip' in the popular sense. For example, discussing a friend's decision to leave her husband or someone's dating habits might seem like pointless speculating. Further, such talk can seem intrusive because it may require a great deal of very personal contextual information (did the husband do something, and so on). But among friends, such talk can also be a way of reflecting on social norms and conventions and one's own attitude towards them. These conversations are very often part of sustaining relationships (establishing if there is agreement on these matters) and figuring out one's own position on social rules. Coates argues that the function of gossip is 'the maintenance of good social relationships' (2011: 202). Talk is an important way of building and sustaining relationships between people; the relational function of phatic talk is clear in the case of gossip.

6.5.1 Gossip and men

Earlier in this chapter, we considered women's talk, or 'gossip'. This is not usually a form of communication associated with men, but that doesn't mean they don't engage in it. Cameron (2011 [1997]) examined the speech of an all-male group of college students. While their talk can be discussed in terms of the 'typical' features of male talk, we can also examine it in terms of functions of 'gossip' that we discussed previously. Example 6.5, from Cameron's research, is a transcript of the talk of five young white middle class men while watching sports. 'Sports talk' is considered to be a masculine activity, but as a number of scholars have noted, it bears many similarities to women's talk (Johnson & Finlay 1997; Kuiper 1991). Moreover, Cameron's data shows a male discussion that contains more than simply 'sports talk'. The men discuss their day, decide who will go grocery shopping; they discuss wine and exchange stories about women. They also engage in

> discussion of several persons not present but known to the participants, with a strong focus on critically examining these individuals' appearance, dress, social behaviour and sexual mores. Like the conversationalists themselves, the individuals under discussion are all men.
>
> (Cameron 2011: 181–2)

Example 6.4

BRYAN: uh you know that really gay guy in our Age of Revolution class who sits in front of us? he wore shorts again, by the way, it's like 42 degrees out he wore shorts again [laughter] [Ed: That guy] it's like a speedo, he wears a speedo to class (.) he's got incredibly skinny legs [Ed: it's worse] you know=

ED: =you know like those shorts women volleyball players wear? it's like those (.) it's l[ike

---

BRYAN: [you know what's even more ridicu[lous? when
ED: [French cut spandex]

BRYAN: you wear those shorts and like a parka on ... (5 lines omitted)

BRYAN: he's either got some condition that he's got to like have his legs exposed at all times or else he's got really good legs=
ED: =he's probably he'[s like
CARL: [he really likes

BRYAN: =he
ED: =he's like at home combing his leg hairs=
CARL: his legs=

BRYAN: he doesn't have any leg hair though=   [yes and oh
ED: =he real[ly likes

ED: his legs=
AL: =very long very white and very skinny

BRYAN: those ridiculous Reeboks that are always (indeciph) and goofy white socks always striped=   [tube socks
ED: =that's [right

ED: he's the antithesis of man

(Cameron 2011: 183–4)

Activity 6.5

What social norms do you think this discussion represents for the participants?

The young men's discussion presents two key characteristics of gossip; discussion of non-present people in some detail and discussion of a topic of importance to the speakers.

The men are discussing a classmate who they are apparently not friends with. At one level, they are discussing this person's clothing and his personal appearance in a detailed and negative way, but at another level, the men are dealing with their own ideas and feelings about social norms: in this case, social norms of what it means to be a man. For the men participating in the discussion, the man they criticise is not performing his masculinity appropriately; he is 'the antithesis of man'. In this talk we can see the participants identifying characteristics of the social norms young heterosexual men are expected to follow.

6.5.2 Features of men's talk

We saw in Example 6.3 that the women had a shared floor, used hedging strategies and provided support to speakers with minimal responses. Research shows that men's talk tends to have different features (Coates 2002). Cameron describes male talk as

> competitive, hierarchically organized, centres on 'impersonal' topics and the exchange of information, and foregrounds speech genres such as joking, trading insults and sports statistics.
>
> (Cameron 2011: 179)

Saying that men are competitive is linked to the observation that men seem to prefer a one-at-a-time floor. Holding the floor is esteemed; this is why there might be competition for it. Men are also said to signal that they are listening by remaining silent. For women silence may signal a breakdown of communication, for men it appears to be acceptable (Pilkington 1998). While competition and silence can be found in men's talk, there are two things we need to bear in mind. First, as the conversation in Example 6.4 shows, these features are not always present. Second, the way some of these features are characterised may not reflect how conversational participants understand them. For example, it has been shown that men seem to prefer topics such as cars, technology and sport (Coates 2002). These topics are described as 'impersonal' topics, but it may be that these topics are intensely personal for the men who talk about them. Certainly they are not 'personal' in the way that emotions are (a topic found in women's talk and not so often found in men's talk), but characterising them as 'impersonal' may misrepresent what they mean to the participants and to the conversation in which they occur. Moreover, other research finds that the distinction between how men and women use language is not clear, and that both sexes employ both co-operative and competitive features depending on the context (Mullany 2007; Schleef 2008; Woods 1989).

See if you can find, in Example 6.4, examples of the conversation features just described. Do people talk at the same time (shared floor) or not? Are there silences? Does this look like competitive talk?

Activity 6.6

It is possible to find evidence of competition in the talk in Example 6.4. The young men all contribute observations about their fellow-student in a critical or humorous way. There is some **simultaneous talk**, which might be seen as interruptive, but there is no evidence that the speakers object to this. These can be referred to as **overlaps** rather than interruptions. There are no silences or breaks in the conversation. They also support each other in their conversational contributions. For example Bryan suggests that the student may have really good legs. Ed furthers this by commenting that he must spend time combing his leg hairs. This topic is then taken up by Bryan.

6.6 GENDER AND POWER

From the discussion of gossip we see that while the structure of this type of talk may be different among gendered groups, it serves the same purpose for each. Gossip is way of exploring, negotiating and contesting social norms for many speakers. We have to wonder, then, why is gossip only associated with women although everyone engages in it? Additionally, why is gossip negatively evaluated? The answers can be found in the androcentric rule (Coates 2004: 10). This rule states that anything women do linguistically will be negatively judged and everything men do with language will be seen as normal. In essence, the androcentric rules means that men's language is unmarked and women's language is marked.

The androcentric rule is a gender specific statement of the more general process of **linguistic subordination** (Lippi-Green 1997). Wolfram and Schilling-Estes (1998: 6) describe this as a principle whereby the speech of socially subordinate groups will be interpreted as linguistically inadequate by comparison with that of socially dominant groups.

This 'principle' operates widely and will inform our understanding of language, society and power in several other chapters of this book. Next we explore another feature of so-called women's language. We'll see, again, how inequality is present in understanding linguistic behaviour.

6.6.1 Do women talk more than men?

Many cultures claim that women talk a great deal:

- Women's tongues are like lambs tails — they are never still. (English)
- The North Sea will sooner be found wanting water than a woman at a loss for words. (Jutlandic)
- Where there are woman and geese there's noise. (Japanese)
- Nothing is so unnatural as a talkative man and a quiet woman. (Scottish)

(Holmes 1998: 41)

Activity 6.7

Consider the proverbs above. What do they say about women and their linguistic behaviour? What do they imply about men and their linguistic behaviour?

You might have heard that women use 20,000 words a day while men only use 7,000. This claim has been circulating in the media for some time. Like the 'Eskimo words for snow' myth (see Chapter 2 and Pullum 1991) it is reported frequently in the media and is generally accepted as true. Linguist Mark Liberman (2006) attempted to find the source of these figures for word use by men and women. His exhaustive research found no study to support these figures. In fact, he found that these numbers are often used without reference to any source or supporting evidence at all (see also Cameron 2007).

Activity 6.8

In Chapter 4 we discussed media and expertise. What parallels do you see between the claim that women use 20,000 words a day and the issues we discussed in Section 4.6?

The belief that women talk more than men is a pervasive one. As the proverbs listed above suggest, many cultures pass judgment on how much women talk. As with tag questions, above, exploring actual linguistic behaviour and the possible reasons for that behaviour will help us understand some of the issues behind language society and power.

A very important point when considering the issue of 'who talks more' is knowing there are different types of talk (Coates 2004). Giving a full account of different types of talk isn't possible here so we'll simply say that *where* the talk takes place is a key feature of this issue. We must consider whether the talk takes place in the public or private domain because these domains have different qualities. Public talk has the purpose of informing or persuading and is often associated with higher status/power (e.g. one generally has to be 'invited' to participate in public talk in some way). Private talk serves interpersonal functions such as making social connections, developing relationships, and so on.

Which type of talk (public or private) do you think is more valued by society?

Activity 6.9

Not all kinds of talk are the same. Some talk is highly valued. Examples of highly valued talk include talking in public, at a formal meeting, giving a presentation or in the mass media. In these public contexts, research suggests that men talk more than women (Holmes 1995; Woods 1989). Talk in the public sphere is undertaken by powerful people; it is one of the ways they express, claim and perform their power. This kind of language tends to involve expressing facts or information, persuading an audience or making some kind of change in the wider world. In the private domain, however, women talk more than men (DeFrancisco 1991; Fishman 1980).

Private talk such as to family members, consoling children or talking with friends involves looking after people, building relationships. Talk in the private sphere, in domestic or other private settings, is not as highly valued as public talk. For example, consoling a child is not as esteemed as giving a speech.

If research has established it isn't the case that women talk more than men (in the public sphere at least), then why is the belief that they do talk more so pervasive?

6.6.2 Silence is golden

Spender (1980) suggests that the belief that women talk too much is explained by the fact that any talk from a woman is considered 'too much'. That is to say, women do not need to speak very much in order to be perceived as speaking too much. This belief is demonstrated by Herring, Johnson and DiBendetto's study (1998) of an online discussion list. They examined the participation rates of men and women on the discussion list. This list was a professional discussion list for academics teaching and working in the field of composition and rhetoric. Herring *et al.* hypothesised that the mode of communication (computer mediated communication) and the type of list would allow for equal participation of men and women. They tracked participation on the list, in terms of contributions made, and found that normally, women provided 30 percent of the material (1998: 198).

Herring *et al.* found an even more striking pattern when they examined a specific discussion. This discussion began with a request from a male user for suggestions for readings for a class on 'men's literature'. The discussion lasted several days. On two of the six days of this discussion (in which all contributions increased), women's contributions exceeded those of men (1998: 200). But over the course of this particular discussion, men provided more contributions overall. Some of the men on the list reacted vociferously to the increase of women's contribution by expressing their intention to leave the list, claiming they felt 'silenced' (1998: 198). They claimed that the discussion had 'degenerated into insults, vituperation and vilification' (1998: 202). Herring *et al.* looked closely at the discussion and found little evidence of such contributions from women (1998: 202). Herring *et al.* suggest that this increase in contributions by women 'was ultimately responsible for male perceptions of having been "silenced" and of women having dominated the discussion' (1998: 201).

Herring *et al.*'s study shows that women do not need to truly dominate a conversation in order to be perceived as doing so. As Spender has argued, 'The talkativeness of women has been gauged not in comparison with men but with silence. Women have not been judged on the grounds of whether they talk more than men, but of whether they talk more than *silent* women' (Spender 1980: 41; italics in original). That is, it is not the case that women talk more than men but are *perceived as doing so*. Part of this has to do with different purposes and types of talk. It is also related to the cultural norm that public talk belongs to men; women do not have equal rights to the floor in the public domain (Coates 1996).

6.7 GENDERED TALK: PERFORMING IDENTITY

6.7.1 'Dude'

In this section, we focus on the way individuals perform their gender identity. This may be done in a range of ways, through choices about clothes, hairstyles, how one walks and sits, or any number of physical activities. Language is also an important way people perform their gender, and while the gender a person performs can be understood as the sum total of all these choices, here we focus on what the use of one word tells us about how to do being a (heterosexual) man.

Kiesling (2005) describes how young men in a fraternity use the word 'dude'. 'Dude' is a very useful form of address. It can be used at the start or end of an utterance (Example 6.5a and b) and has a range of meanings depending on the intonation the speaker uses (Kiesling 2005: 291).

Example 6.5
a.   dude it was like boys in the hood man ai:n't no: lie: (Kiesling 2005: 294)
b.   Everybody plays that damn game, dude. (Kiesling 2005: 295)

Do the men (or women) you know use the term 'dude' to address their male (or female) friends? Do they use a different term? List the different ways the term can be used and how it is said. What do these different uses do?

Activity 6.10

While 'dude' may serve many purposes such as help speakers follow the structure of conversation, express positive or negative evaluation or even signal agreement, it is the relationship between speakers that 'dude' invokes that it is of interest here.

When talking or using language, we express feelings about our relationship with that person by the language we use. Terms of address are an important way of doing this. For example, we express respect by using 'Sir' or 'Madam' or express affection by using 'honey' or 'darling'. Kiesling argues that 'dude' projects a stance of solidarity and camaraderie 'but crucially in a nonchalant, not too enthusiastic manner' (2005: 282). That is, 'dude' can be used to express friendship without being too affectionate by projecting a 'stance of cool solidarity' (2005: 282). Societal expectations for heterosexual men are such that they shouldn't express too much closeness in their friendships, especially with men. According to societal expectations, if a man were to express his positive regard for a male friend, he risks being perceived as homosexual. Expressing solidarity among friends therefore is potentially in conflict with those societal expectations. Kiesling suggests that 'Dude allows men to create a stance within this narrow range, one of closeness with other men (satisfying masculine solidarity) that also maintains a casual stance that keeps some distance (thus satisfying heterosexism)' (2005: 283).

The example of 'dude' shows us two important things. First, it demonstrates that even a single lexical choice can have a range of functions, including the performance of gender. Second, it shows that gender performances depend on social expectations (ideologies) about what appropriate performances of being a man or a woman look like. Further, these ideologies rely on the position that heterosexuality is unmarked (see Example 6.4) and that homosexuality is marked.

6.7.2 Local ideologies: gender and sexuality

Jones (2011) explores the talk of women who make reference to what it means to be a 'proper' lesbian. She examines the conversation of a hiking group in the north of England of gay women who call themselves the Sapphic Stompers. Her focus is a particular group of women, on a particular day in a particular context (a **community of practice**, see Chapter 9). Jones explains that it is not the case that all lesbian women speak in the same way or 'perform' being a woman in the same way; that is to say, we perform our identities and these identities are not stable but shift according to context. One of the ways we perform our identity is through language. Previously, we made a distinction between sex and gender and explained that gender is socially constructed. We have also seen, in the example of 'dude' (Section 6.7.1), that gender performance is informed by ideologies about what constitutes a 'normal' sexuality.

Example 6.6 is a transcript of the women discussing two television shows (Jones 2011: 728). One of the shows is called *Cagney and Lacey* and was broadcast in the 1980s. It portrayed two female police officers in their professional and personal lives. While both Cagney and Lacey were heterosexual, their toughness and strength gained them much admiration from women looking for different ways of being women at that time. The second programme is *The L Word*, a drama series, focusing on the lives of lesbian women.

Example 6.6
Claire (C), Marianne (M), Sam (S) Author (L)

1	M: I wasn't impressed with it
	C: /It's not exactly- Cagney and
	L: What the L Word?/

| 2 | S: [I still haven't got] I still haven't got past the pilot I've got the |
| | C: Lacey [wasn't exactly the L Word] |

| 3 | S: first series but I just (.)   They just so do not look like lesbians/ |
| | M: (XX)   /I |

4	M:
	C: But the **L Word** is **genius** as **well**
	L: That's that is the problem (.)

5	M:	[They all- they all
	C:	[They're **a::ll** unrea[listic (.) Cagney and
	L:	ridiculously like (.) feminine [and

6	M:	they're all talking how] I've never heard any lesbian talk [about
	C:	**La::cey** were unrealistic.] They said [that

7	M:	other women]
	C:	there would] never be two **female** police officers who were partners that (.)

8	L:	there is **one** who (.) looks like she **is** (.) and **she's** the one that everyone

9	M:	[That is] bisexual? No? Oh
	L:	[fancies] No she's the one that everyone fancies though

10	S:	[Which one is she?]
	C:	She's [not **rea::lly**] androgynous::s
	L:	because she's like androgynous looking

11	S:	Oh that
	C:	/**Sha::ne**
	L:	She's er/ she's also the one that sleeps around a lot

12	S:	one [Shane.] Shane
	C:	Yeah the one who
	L:	[Yeah] (.) ri**dicul**ously thin though. Shane yeah

13	S:	[Well yeah she's the only one who looks] vaguely like a dyke
	C:	really **is** [bisexual is]

14	S:	actually
	M:	True.
	C:	[I thought Guinevere-]
	L:	But you see and everyone **fancies** [her which suggests-] (.) that

15	S:	[that she's the only dykey one {laughter}]
	C:	Guinevere Turner's [in it as well and she's a lesbian]
	L:	Which one's Guinevere?

The women in Sapphic Stompers don't often explicitly discuss their sexuality or their politics. However, Jones asserts that members of the group are both feminist and lesbian. The conversation in Example 6.6 shows the women negotiating what it means to be a 'proper' lesbian. They discuss the characters in the television shows and discuss how each of them seem or do not seem 'lesbian' in terms of the actors' physical and linguistic performance. In stave 5, the discourse suggests that to be too feminine may not be conducive to being a 'real' lesbian. The Stompers seem to be conscious of the discourses and representations of lesbians in society generally. Jones argues that in their talk, some of the Stompers appear to make a distinction between 'women' as 'heterosexual women' and 'lesbians' (stave 6–7). The position seems to be that being a 'lesbian' is not the same as being a 'woman' as in this conversation, the identity 'woman' is associated with heterosexual norms. Just like the male students' gossip (Example 6.4), expectations of how to attract the attention of a 'proper' member of the opposite sex include having specific physical characteristics. When the Stompers claim that a character in *The L Word* is too feminine (stave 5), they are resisting dominant, heterosexual definitions of beauty and negotiating what it means to be a lesbian. They do not appear to be endorsing these dominant definitions and discourses of homosexuality, nevertheless those discourses have to be invoked in order to be resisted.

It's important to remember that Jones is not claiming that there is actually a way to be a 'proper' lesbian; nor is she arguing that the Sapphic Stompers insist on particular performances of lesbianism. The Sapphic Stompers' discussion is considered not only in relation to the specific context (on a hike with a group of fellow lesbian hikers), but also in relation to the topic under discussion (what a lesbian looks like). For example, any one of Sapphic Stompers might discuss looking like a lesbian in a different way if they were at an after-work party. Jones' interest is in how identity is performed and constructed in particular contexts.

As we described in the introduction, gender or sexual identity is not an inherent characteristic. The women in Example 6.6 perform their identity, as lesbian women, by taking particular positions on topics, making particular value statements and expressing particular views. They can claim and perform their sexual identity by 'doing things' with language.

6.8 SUMMARY

In this chapter, we have considered a range of issues in the field of language and gender. This has shown that inequality between women and men is still an important concern in contemporary society and that women continue to have less status than men. This status difference is reflected in other examples we have considered, including beliefs about quantity of talk and who has rights to the floor in different contexts. While claims are made about the differences between the way men and women use language, men and women also do very similar things with it, as the example of gossip shows. Moreover, differences in language use are best explained by the way people are expected to perform their gender, rather than because of any innate difference between men and women. The performance of identity, including gender identity, is complex and important. We continue to examine this performance in the following chapters.

FURTHER READING

Cameron, D. and Kulick, D. (2003) *Language and Sexuality*, Cambridge: Cambridge University Press.
Coates, J. (2013) *Women, Men and Everyday Talk*, Basingstoke: Palgrave.

Frable, D. (1989) 'Sex typing and gender ideology: Two facets of the individual's gender psychology that go together', *Journal of Personality and Social Psychology*, 56(1): 95–108.

Khosroshahi, F. (1989) 'Penguins don't care, but women do: A social identity analysis of a Whorfian problem', *Language and Society*, 18(4): 505–25.

Pauwels, A. (2001) 'Non-sexist language reform and generic pronouns in Australian English', *English Worldwide*, 22(1): 105–19.

Pauwels, A. (2003) 'Linguistic Sexism and Feminist Linguistic Activism', in J. Holmes and M. Meyerhoff (eds) *The Handbook of Language and Gender*, Oxford: Blackwell: 550–70.

Talbot, M. (1992) '"I wish you'd stop interrupting me!" Interruptions and asymmetries in speaker-rights in "equal encounters"', *Journal of Pragmatics*, 18: 451–66.

CHAPTER 7

Language and ethnicity

7. 1	**INTRODUCTION**	**132**
7.2	**WHAT DO WE MEAN BY 'ETHNICITY'?**	**133**
7.3	**ETHNICITY, THE NATION STATE AND MULTILINGUALISM**	**134**
7.4	**RACISM AND REPRESENTATIONS OF ETHNICITY**	**135**
7.5	**ETHNOLECT**	**137**
7.6	**ETHNICITY AND IDENTITY**	**141**
7.7	**DISCOURSES OF AUTHENTICITY**	**146**
7.8	**CONSEQUENCES FOR ETHNOLECTS**	**149**
7.9	**CROSSING**	**153**
7.10	**SUMMARY**	**155**

7.1 INTRODUCTION

Holmes notes that people may 'signal their ethnicity by the language they choose to use' (2008: 183). In this chapter, we examine the various ways ethnicity may be expressed and communicated through language. We'll consider how the position of ethnic groups in the social hierarchy is reflected by language use. As with other variables such as class and age, a person's ethnicity has at times been treated as a simple part of their essential nature; stable, determined and unchanging. It is true that some research shows a correlation between particular **linguistic variables** and ethnicity. However, we will see that it's not always quite so straightforward. How individuals articulate their ethnicity and how it is understood may vary because of the communicative context they're in and the people they're interacting with. Ethnicity may also interact with other aspects of identity such as age, sex and so on.

7.2 WHAT DO WE MEAN BY 'ETHNICITY'?

It's useful to have a sense of what the term 'ethnicity' includes. Allan Bell notes that ethnicity 'is one of the most slippery social dimensions' (2014: 173). He continues:

> [Ethnicity] has to do with a group sharing sociocultural characteristics – a sense of place, ancestry, a common history, religion, cultural practices, ways of communicating, and often a language. When socio-linguists question their informants about ethnicity, they are nowadays most likely to ask what ethnic group a person identifies with, indicating the socially constructed [174] nature of ethnicity.
>
> (2014: 173–4)

How do you define your ethnicity? How do you distinguish between your ethnicity and that of other people? Compare the features that define your ethnicity to the ones Bell mentions.

Activity 7.1

If you are part of the ethnic majority, you probably don't even consider that you have an ethnicity. But as with accents, we all have an ethnicity. Again, if you are part of the ethnic majority, the only time you think about ethnicity might be when filling in forms that specifically ask you for your background. The categories that are chosen and the way they are labelled can reveal a great deal about the make-up of a particular nation and the characteristics it sees as relevant. They can present a challenge though as they often treat 'race' as synonymous with ethnicity. While 'race' is connected to biology and physical characteristics, ethnicity is far more appropriate in understanding how people align with sociocultural groups, how they construct their identity and how they use language to do this.

Ethnicity is not a straightforward concept. Just as women don't all speak in the same way simply because they are women, people who by some defini-tion belong to the same ethnicity don't necessarily speak in the same way.

It is important to highlight the distinction between race and ethnicity. The relationship between these two categories is analogous to that between sex and gender. Ethnicity, like gender, is socially and culturally constructed. In addition, as Harris and Rampton (2003) have argued, the roots of linguis-tic difference related to social categories are very similar regardless of the social category. For example, linguistic subordination (see Chapter 6) is a factor in some way in most social categories.

Earlier in this chapter, we used the phrase 'the ethnic majority'. While this will vary from place to place, the ethnic majority is generally **unmarked**, that is, it is perceived as the norm. Indeed, the majority doesn't need to be a numerical majority, it just needs to be the unmarked ethnicity. What the unmarked ethnicity is depends on a variety of political, social and historical factors. Whether an ethnicity is labelled as such also depends on the conception of the 'nation', the idea that people have about who they are and their cultural backgrounds. 'Ethnic' tends to be reserved for groups that are at some level thought of as marked or 'other'. What happens as a result is that the terms 'ethnic' and 'ethnicity' typically only refer to minority groups. In short, groups we describe in terms of 'ethnicity' are very often 'the other'; invoking an oppositional relationship of a 'them' to an 'us'.

7.3 ETHNICITY, THE NATION STATE AND MULTILINGUALISM

One of the most important 'boundaries' in the modern world is that of the nation state. We don't deal with multilingualism and language policy here in detail, however, the relationship between nation, language and ethnicity is an important one. While the three are often thought to exist in a stable relationship, such situations are far more complex.

There is a persistent idea that nations should be ethnically and linguistically homogenous (Irvine & Gal 2000), but this is very rarely the case. Nevertheless, we can see this ideology at work in calls for migrants to learn the majority language, for the designation of an official language and in demands for cultural assimilation of minorities more generally. In the UK, the idea that immigrants should learn English as soon as possible is seen as 'common sense'. One politician remarked, 'A community of broken English is no community at all' (Pickles 2013). In this particular case, funding was proposed to help people learn English. The idea that learning English is 'common sense' signals that this is part of the dominant ideology. The underlying argument is that a community should be linguistically homogenous; that it can't be a community otherwise.

Although some people think that nation states *should* be this way, it is not usually the case. Thus, when people propose language legislation or complain about 'deterioration' of or need for an official language, this may be a covert way of expressing negative views of 'the other'.

As Canagarajah observes, 'In social practice … language has always been a hybrid and fluid repertoire of semiotic resources that people can employ strategically for their diverse interests, needs, and objectives' (2012: 252). This view sees language as a resource for meaning and identity-making and prompts us to examine the full range of what people can do and what they actually do to perform these identities and create meaning in specific contexts. 'We can agree that ethnic identities are socially and linguistically constructed, and yet affirm the importance of these identities' (Canagarajah 2012: 255). Language policies that effectively demand the eradication of a person's first language prevent people from freely expressing their identity.

Find out what the language requirements are for immigration and/or citizenship in your country. Is competence in a particular language required? Which language(s)? How is this assessed? What does this signal about the identity of the nation?

7.4 RACISM AND REPRESENTATIONS OF ETHNICITY

In this section, we consider how different ethnicities are represented. Because minority ethnicities are not generally afforded positions of power in the social hierarchy, it is not surprising that representations of these groups are not positive. Racism consists of 'the everyday, mundane, negative opinion, attitudes and ideologies and the seemingly subtle acts and conditions of discrimination' (van Dijk 1993: 5). When a group is singled out, it draws boundaries and allocates people to membership in categories they might not themselves have chosen.

Teun van Dijk has worked extensively on racist discourse and defines it as follows: 'Racist discourse is a form of discriminatory social practice that manifests itself in text, talk and communication' (2004: 351). Framing this discourse as a 'social practice' reminds us that speaking and writing are actions, and that in using racist discourses we are *doing* something. van Dijk argues that there are two forms of racist discourse: '(1) racist discourse *directed at* ethnically different Others; (2) racist discourse *about* ethnically different Others' (2004: 351). One of the most obvious ways that racist discourse manifests is in pejorative words about the other.

van Dijk (2004: 352–3) identifies three further ways that people construct racist discourse about the 'other':

a. *difference* –the 'other' is not like 'us'
b. *deviance* –the 'other' behaves in a way that 'we' feel is amoral
c. *threat* the 'other' is dangerous.

Example 7.1 from the British press about immigration demonstrates racist discourse (from van Dijk 1999: 103).

Example 7.1
Our traditions of fairness and tolerance are being exploited by every terrorist, crook, screwball and scrounger who wants a free ride at our expense . . . Then there are the criminals who sneak in as political refugees or as family members visiting a distant relative.

(*Daily Mail*, 28 November 1985)

At first glance, Example 7.1 looks like an argument about immigration and illegality; however, we can see van Dijk's three strategies of racist discourse at work here. *Difference* can be seen with the identification of 'our traditions', creating a contrast with 'them'. *Deviance* is found in the mention of 'terrorist', 'crooks' and so on. Further, the particular kinds of deviance identified suggest these figures are a *threat* to 'us' and 'our traditions'. Note that ethnicity is not explicitly mentioned.

The backgrounding of anything explicitly racist is another common tactic in discourse that it is in fact racist. van Dijk (1993) observes that people go to great lengths to deny that they are racist by presenting themselves positively. A common way of doing this is through an explicit denial: 'I'm not a racist, but … ' followed by a statement about an ethnic group in negative terms (Bonilla-Silva & Forman 2000).

The belief that immigrants are criminals, terrorists or looking for something for nothing seems to always be present in public minds, applied to any group that happens to be moving to a country. Example 7.1 was printed in 1985. Example 7.2 is the first line of a 2013 story about Romanians arriving in the UK following the removal of immigration restrictions.

Example 7.2
The first coachload of Romanian migrants left for the UK yesterday — with some boasting of plans to beg and steal from 'generous' Brits.

(Flynn 2013)

Activity 7.3

Look closely at Example 7.2 and explore the way this extract speaks about the 'Other'. See if you can identify examples in each of van Dijk's three topic categories. What do you think the rest of the story reported?

7.4.1 Reclaiming terms

Whether or not discourse can be racist depends on context, including who is speaking. For example, a term may be racist when a person from the out-group uses it, but a positive identity marker when used by the group itself. In other words, terms that were originally used to demean a group can be reclaimed for use by the in-group as a positive marker of identity. Although reclamation of negative terms may be relatively unconscious action by a group, it can be considered a form of agency (see Section 6.3). One example of this is the word 'nigger', an extremely derogatory word used to refer to African Americans in the US. The term is so inflammatory that US speakers typically use the euphemism 'the N-word' in public discourse about the term (Rahman 2012). When used by African Americans to each other, the term 'nigger' can mean a variety of things, however, that are not always pejorative (Croom 2014; Kennedy 1999). Thus, this marginalised group takes charge of the use and meaning of a word that had been used by out-group members to demean them. This process allows a marginalised group to reject the majority group's portrayal of them.

A similar case of reclamation exists in Australia where 'wog' is a term used to refer to migrants (and their children) from Italy, Greece and the Mediterranean generally, including Lebanon and the Middle East. While it was once a derogatory term, it has since been reclaimed and 'used to claim a common migration experience and background' (Kiesling 2005: 4). As a marker of identity, 'wog' began to be used to positively (by in-group members) affiliate with a particular ethnic identity. This was so much the case, that the group even parodied their own language, their ethnolect, and other cultural behaviours, in productions for television and theatre, such as *Wogs out of Work*.[1]

Can you think of other previously pejorative terms that have been reclaimed? You might know some that aren't connected to ethnic identities, but to some other aspect of identity. Do your colleagues agree that they have been reclaimed? Can everyone use these terms or are they restricted for the use of certain people?

Activity 7.4

7.5 ETHNOLECT

7.5.1 'Wogspeak'

Like age, class and gender, it is possible to find some correlations between ethnicity and specific **linguistic variables**. While we need to be careful about how we define ethnicity and how we interpret these correlations, Scott Kiesling's (2005) research on 'wogspeak' demonstrates the importance of considering the interaction of a number of features that occur when language is used to indicate identity.

Migration to Australia has occurred in various waves from various places since colonisation by the British in the 18th century. In the mid-20th century, significant numbers of Italian and Greek workers arrived in Australia with further waves of migration since. The children and grandchildren of migrants from the Mediterranean may now call themselves 'wogs'. Kiesling (2005) studied the ethnolect of this group, which he calls New Australian English (NAusE). Kiesling's data comes from interviews with four ethnic groups conducted by a Greek Australian student in Sydney. Kiesling examined a number of linguistic variables, notably vowels in High Rising Terminal phrases (HRT). HRT is used to describe the way a speaker's intonation will go up (rise) at the end of word or utterance. It is similar to the intonation pattern for questions, but used in a declarative statement. Specifically, he examined the vowel sound in Australian English ('ah'), like at the end of 'better', to ascertain whether it was pronounced differently by Anglo and ethnic groups. Kiesling's data did, in fact, show a difference in the pronunciation of 'ah' in HRT (Figure 7.1). The data showed a difference in two aspects of voice quality ('openness' and 'length'). However, there is also variation in use in individuals (Figure 7.2).

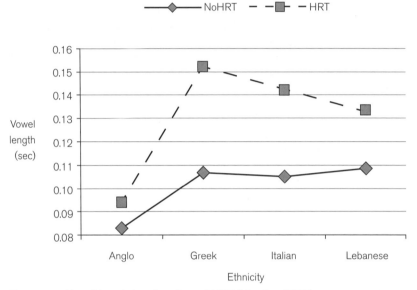

Figure 7.1 Vowel length by ethnicity and HRT (Kiesling 2005)

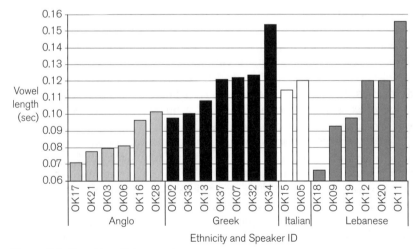

Figure 7.2 Vowel length by speaker

In spite of the variation among individuals, we can make some generalisations if we cluster the individual results into groups. Kiesling summarises as follows:

1. Greek-Australian speakers, when using HRT on (er) ['ah'], exhibit a dramatically longer average length [of the vowel] than all other groups.
2. Lebanese-Australian speakers are also significantly different from Anglos but exhibit much more variability than Greek-Australians.

(Kiesling 2005: 20)

The first conclusion means that when high rising terminals occur with the sound ('ah'), the length of this sound is longest for Greek Australian speakers. Kiesling emphasises that the features shouldn't be examined in isolation. Rather, together, vowel length *and* openness with regard to HRT create the **style** identified by speakers in Australia as 'wogspeak' (Kiesling 2005: 20).

Kiesling also points out that the ethnicity of the interviewer who gathered this data has to be taken into account when analysing the data. Interviewees might take various stances towards the interviewer based on whether their experiences as migrants are similar to hers or not. Taking into account the context of communication (e.g. the identity of the speaker and addressee) is vital in understanding the varieties speakers use (see Section 9.4.2). Identity is not fixed; rather, it is emergent and negotiated in the context of specific encounters.

7.5.2 African American English

One of the most well-documented ethnolects is African American English (**AAE**) (e.g. Bailey, Baugh, Mufwene & Rickford 2013; Labov 1972c; Wolfram 1969). As the name suggests, AAE is associated with an African American ethnicity; however, not all Americans of African descent are speakers of AAE.

AAE shares many features with other varieties of US English such as pronunciation and morphology. In fact, there are few features that are unique to AAE; the distinguishing features of AAE rely on particular combinations of features such as the co-occurrence of copula deletion and habitual be. Some of the more salient features to out-group members tend to be structural. Table 7.1 provides some examples of features of AAE (Wolfram 2009: 330).

AAE is not homogenous across geographic regions; thus, AAE varies depending on where speakers acquire it, just like other varieties of US English (Wolfram 2009).

Table 7.1 Features of AAE (adapted from Wolfram 2009: 330)

Linguistic feature	AAE	European American English
Copula deletion: deleting the verb 'to be'	He late	He is late
	They running	They are running
Habitual 'be': to indicate habitual or intermittent activity. Usually in the 'be' +-ing form	Sarah don't usually be there	Sarah isn't usually there
	John be late	John is always late
Absence of 'possessive s'	John hat	John's hat
	Jack car	Jack's car

Labov and many other scholars have described the perception in society that AAE is somehow linguistically deficient; that it is a 'faulty' version of standard English (Labov 1972b). Although linguists have shown that AAE is a logically structured language just like any other language, it is strongly disfavoured. This negative attitude toward AAE is an example of the strong roots of language ideologies and linguistic subordination. In Chapter 2 we explored the structure and power of language ideologies. With regard to AAE, perceptions show that people think it is not a language, but simply a degenerated form of English (e.g. Lippi-Green 1997, Smitherman 1977, Wolfram 1998).

> All linguists agree that nonstandard dialects are highly structured systems. They do not see these dialects as accumulations of errors caused by the failure of their speakers to master standard English. When linguists hear black children saying 'He crazy' or 'Her my friend' they do not hear a primitive language.
>
> (Labov 1972c: 237)

The belief that AAE speakers are unintelligent or cognitively lacking in some way is a common misconception about speakers of non-standard varieties. Clearly, this misconception can have serious consequences in terms of education, access to employment and how one is generally perceived. Research tells us that even a few features of AAE are enough to trigger an identification of a speaker as being of African American ethnicity (Purnell, Idsardi & Baugh 1999). This suggests that in these speech communities, AAE is a salient variety.

At the same time, like many marginalised varieties, AAE also carries a great many positive connotations within its community of speakers. This puts speakers in a difficult position. Rahman (2008) studied the views that middle class African Americans have of AAE and how they use it. She sets out the central concern:

> The dilemma for many African Americans is that language that serves as a symbol of ethnic identity may also serve as the focus for discrimination in mainstream society and language that can be useful for socio-economic advancement may lead to suspicion in the African American community.
>
> (2008: 142)

She refers to this dilemma as a 'linguistic push-pull' (Rahman 2008: 142), a problem that many speakers of marginalised sociolects face. As we will discuss, sociolects can be very important for speakers in performing their identity.

7.6 ETHNICITY AND IDENTITY

A person might claim membership in an ethnic group based on where their parents were born, for example, but whether this will be accepted or acknowledged by other members of this group may depend on what kind of evidence of membership is provided. Identities based on ethnicity sometimes have to be ratified by other members of the group. Some of this evidence might be constituted by linguistic variables: a certain proficiency in a language may be enough to have an ethnic identity accepted; however, there might be other identity markers that need to be addressed in other ways, or even shown with different signs, by wearing certain clothes, having bodily markings and so on.

Crucially, groups don't always assign value to the same things, thus ideological differences may result in the positive evaluation of a language variety in one community, but not in another. Labov's concept of 'covert prestige' makes this more clear (1972a). The notion of **'covert prestige'** acknowledges that some speech communities, usually ones that don't have a great deal of power in relation to other dominant groups, value different kinds of speaking, often involving non-standard varieties (such as AAE). For those communities these non-standard varieties are 'covertly' prestigious, or valued within the community but not outside it. **'Overt prestige'** is awarded to varieties that are valued according to **hegemonic** norms. Thus, speaking the standard variety of a language confers prestige in wider society but may not within particular communities. These features relate directly to the 'linguistic push-pull' that Rahman (2008) refers to (see Section 7.5.2).

7.6.1 Lumbee English

Schilling-Estes describes the performance of ethnicity in Robeson County in North Carolina in the US. Robeson County is located in the American South 'where a bi-racial classification system has long been firmly entrenched' (2004: 166). The two groups in this system are Black and White. But in North Carolina, as in many other parts of the world, there are indigenous people too. In Robeson County, the Lumbee Indians have always been a significant part of the population and have 'struggled to assert themselves as a separate people who are neither White nor Black' (2004: 166). The Lumbee have also faced difficulties because of ideas about what it means to be an 'authentic' Indian tribe. The Lumbee have been variously described over the years in terms of ethnicity. Prior to 1885 'they were referred to simply as "mixed", "free persons of color", or, occasionally, "free White"' (Schilling-Estes 2004: 167). The Lumbee, themselves, have resisted this biracial classification. For them, being identified as Black was to be subject to all manner of discrimination and identifying as White would be to erase their indigenous ethnic identity (Shilling-Estes 2004: 167). Describing ethnicity sometimes involves disassociating from the groups and values one doesn't want to be identified with. This complex positioning of groups is well demonstrated in Schilling-Estes' research. She analyses conversations between two young men, one African American, Alex, and the other Lumbee, Lou. While both ethnolects share common features, there are differences in both the level and range of use. For example, both AAE and Lumbee English make use of uninflected 'habitual be', as in 'He be talking all the time' (Schilling-Estes 2004: 168). In Lumbee English, however, unlike AAE, 'be' can be inflected: 'He bes talking'; and 'in certain non-habitual contexts', for example: 'I might be lost some inches' (Schilling-Estes 2004: 169).

The conversation ranged over a number of different topics. The two men knew each other from university and so at times would be talking about people they both knew or past events they both participated in, but they also discussed politics, race relations and the American civil war. Another one of the linguistic features Schilling-Estes examined was **rhoticity** after vowels.

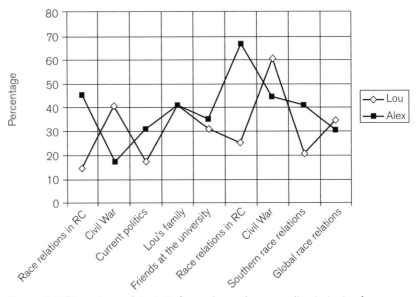

Figure 7.3 Percentage of rhoticity for each speaker according to topic of discussion (Schilling-Estes 2004: 173)

Both AAE and some varieties of Southern English are non-rhotic in some contexts. The Lumbee, however, show a slightly lower percentage of non-rhoticity when compared with both Whites and African Americans (Schilling-Estes 2004: 171). Figure 7.3 shows the percentage of non-rhoticity in the speech of Lou and Alex according to topic of conversation.

Figure 7.3 charts the usage of percentage of non-rhoticity for each speaker when discussing different topics. What do you notice about the patterns of usage? Consider the upper and lower values of each speaker. When are the two levels of use closest? What explanation might there be for this?

Activity 7.5

As Schilling-Estes notes, Alex generally uses a higher percentage of non-rhoticity than Lou. But for this variable (Schilling-Estes also looked at others), Alex and Lou are closest in their level of usage when discussing family and friends. If language is connected to ethnicity, how are we to make sense of this? It's not the case that Alex and Lou's ethnicity changes over the course of the interview. Schilling-Estes writes,

> One explanation for the linguistic distance in the sections on race relations is that considerations of ethnic group membership may be more salient when the two are talking directly about the subject than when talking about family and friends, at which point considerations of personal friendship are uppermost.
>
> (2004: 177)

The change in language in Alex and Lou's conversation may indicate both distance from and closeness to the other person.

7.6.2 Gang identity

Mendoza-Denton's (1996) research on Latina gangs in Northern California describes the use of language and other practices to construct an identity that is linked to a particular type of ethnicity and femininity. Mendoza-Denton undertook an **ethnographic** study of Latina gangs in California, spending a lot of time with and around the gangs in order to understand the way they construct their identities. There were two gangs in her field-site. The first group, Sureñas/os (Southerners) are generally recent migrants from Mexico. In contrast, the Norteñas/os (Northerners) tend to be American born. These groups orient to the world in different ways: 'they are in deep conflict over the politics of identity in their community, and this conflict is reflected in their language attitudes, discourse patterns, and eventual success (or lack thereof) in the American educational system' (1996: 52). Sureñas tend to orient to Mexico and Mexican culture, while Norteñas value the cultural products and practices associated with the US. The importance of these identities is seen very clearly in the social practices that the Sureñas and Norteñas use to display these identities. Here we consider a range of semiotic resources including language these women use to perform a specific local identity.

Mendoza-Denton describes one of the gang member's use of a linguistic feature called 'creaky voice' 'in narratives for the construction of a hardcore persona' (2011: 266). Creaky voice describes a type of vibration (a type of phonation) of the vocal chords (vocal folds) while talking. Creaky voice is also known as 'vocal fry'. In other English-speaking communities it has been associated with a variety of social characteristics (Mendoza-Denton 2011: 265). Mendoza-Denton's research documents the speech of one young Norteña, 'Babygirl'. Babygirl uses creaky voice to perform a tough, female persona, but not all the time, as the following shows (creaky voice indicated in bold).

Example 7.3

Transcript: Babygirl at home (0:56) (Mendoza-Denton 2011: 267).

```
1    All my homeboys respect me a lot//
     they **never** / you know //
     they always look up to me / and they're always **like**/ you know //
     tell me what's up / you know //
5    and they always protect me / you know //
     it seems like //
     I'm like the only female there //
     but they always seem to protect me //
     you know //
10   from other guys //
     you know //
     from other **dudes** //
     so it's like they're //
     it's like / we're like a whole big fa**mily** //
15   you know //
     we could uhm //
     we could talk about uhm . . . //
     we could talk about uhm . . . //
     it's like a– we're–
20   we could talk about **like**//
     we could talk about **like**//
     what happened / at home / you know //
     how do you **feel about things** at home you know //
     and we could talk **about** //
25   anything
```

Mendoza-Denton argues that creaky voice is found at points where emotion is being managed. 'In this young woman's narrative, creaky voice participates in a local economy of affect centred around being silent, being hard of heart (hardcore), and being toughened through experience' (2011: 269). Mendoza-Denton describes how creaky voice signals toughness among Norteñas when used in conjunction with other semiotic resources such as makeup (Mendoza-Denton 1996). Norteñas and Sureñas both use makeup and clothing to signal group membership (see Table 7.2). Norteñas, for example, use both solid and liquid liner to create a strong, hard and long line, sometimes almost to the temples. It is understood as an expression and marker of power and toughness. The same is true of other practices as Babygirl suggests in the transcript in Example 7.4.

Example 7.4
We never wear earrings
just in case we get in a flight
It's not our style to wear earrings ? me entiendes? (you know?)
Don't even smile
That's the weak spot
Don't ever smile

(Mendoza-Denton 1996: 56)

Table 7.2 Semiotic resources for indicating group membership in Norteñas and Sureñas (adapted from Mendoza-Denton 1996: 53)

	Norteñas	*Sureñas*
Colour	Red burgundy	Blue navy
Hairdo	Feathered hair	Vertical ponytail
Eyeliner	Solid first, then liquid	Solid only
Lipstick	Deep red/burgundy	Brown

Mendoza-Denton argues that 'creaky voice assists these gang girls in the construction of a hardcore persona in the context of a locally-defined economy of affect' (2011: 266). The performance of the hardcore identity exploits existing language resources in order to construct an identity that is locally relevant and appropriate to Babygirl's audience. This kind of creativity is not unusual among adolescents. As we will see in Chapter 8, this period of life is one of experimentation with social roles, ideas and personal presentation; thus, it is hardly surprising that language can be one of the resources that is creatively exploited for this purpose.

7.7 DISCOURSES OF AUTHENTICITY

7.7.1 Mexican ethnicity

In this section, we focus on research by Petra Scott Shenk that examines how individuals claim a Mexican ethnicity through their discourse. Shenk takes up a theme that is current in contemporary sociolinguistic research; that is, what is authenticity? She notes that authenticity, in this case in respect of ethnicity claims, is not predetermined. Rather, individuals appeal to ideological constructs of that ethnicity in order to formulate defensible claims to authenticity. Shenk argues that 'positioning oneself as authentic often depends on positioning the other as inauthentic' (2007: 198). She also notes that power is crucial here, even if it is a local power structure, as 'the authentically positioned participant has the authority to delegitimize the authenticity of the other participant' (2007: 198).

Shenk's research examined Spanish-English code switching among a small group of bilingual Californian university students. We use the term **code-switching** to refer to the use of two or more linguistic codes within a conversation or even within the same utterance. Shenk writes, 'In these data, Spanish linguistic proficiency, place of birth, and purity of bloodline are evoked as ideological tests for authenticity' (2007: 199). Not all of the informants were born in Mexico, and they don't all have Mexican-born parents. Finally, none of them are fluent in Spanish. Shenk argues that all of these individuals are 'on the margin of the group' (2007: 199) that could claim Mexican ethnicity according to the three tests just mentioned. That they all know this means that claims to authentic ethnicity are important but also problematic. This kind of non-central membership is far from unusual. What it means, though, is that rather than ethnicity being a binary category (where you either belong or you don't; you're part of 'us' or 'them'), we find 'internal hierarchies of ideology and power that cannot be completely separated from the ideologies of the external dominant culture' (2007: 200). Thus, potential members of this group are positioned both by authentic/core members of the ethnic group as well as by values of the exterior majority.

The relationship of these in-group tests for membership to out-group norms is clearly demonstrated in the case of purity of bloodline. Even though Colonial American institutions valued 'European blood' over anything else, mixed European and indigenous bloodlines meant impurity and a lower place on the hierarchy of power. Indeed, Spanish was seen as 'white' and Mexican as 'mixed'. While the informants here have a concept of 'pure' Mexican bloodlines (as opposed to the colonial view of their ethnicity as mixed and impure) there has nevertheless been an incorporation of the broader ideological position in relation to blood and its purity. We can see appeals to purity and birthplace in the following exchange (Shenk 2007: 206–7) shown in Example 7.5 (Lalo is a man and Bela a woman).

Example 7.5

11	Bela: Este,	*Okay,*
12	Bela: mira mira,	*look look,*
⌈13	Bela: [no empieces] {smiling voice}	*don't you start {smiling voice}*
⌊14	Lalo: [hhh, {laughter}]	[hhh, laughter]
15	Bela: T´u ni siquiera eres original	*You're not original either.*
16	Lalo: M´as original quet u {smiling voice}	*More original than you {smiling}*
17	Lalo: (.) Both of my	Both of my
⌈18	Lalo: [parents are-]	[parents are-]
⌊19	Bela: [Mas origi]nal?	*[More origi]nal?*
20	Lalo: (.) are Aztec BLOOD	(.) are Aztec BLOOD
⌈21	Bela: Ay cal[mate] {smiling} [Tu]?	*Oh calm down. {smiling}.You?*
⌊22	Lalo: [hhh {laughter}] [{laughter}]	
23	Lalo: {laughter}hhh.	
⌈24	Bela: donde nacis [te] [En don-]	*where were you born. Wher-*
⌊25	Lalo: [Soy] [PURO]	*I'm PURE*
26	Lalo: Yo soy PURO.	*I am PURE*
⌈27	Bela: Cual [PURO:] {smiling voice}	*What (are you talking about) PURE.*
⌊28	Lalo: [Soy nacido]-	*I was born-*
29	Lalo: Soy nacido aqu´i pero,	*I was born here but,*
30	Lalo: soy PURO	*I'm pure.*
⌈31	Bela: Ay [sí mira mira] {mocking}.	*Oh yeah look look. {mocking}*
⌊32	Lalo: [Please man]	Please man
33	Bela: Donde nacieron tus papas	*Where were your folks born.*
34	Lalo: Z:acatecas Jalisco,	Z:acatecas Jalisco
35	Lalo: that's like the HEART.	that's like the HEART
⌈36	Bela: [Zaca]tecas Jali:sco .hhh {laughter}{mocking}	
⌊37	Lalo: [Ye]-	
38	Lalo: Yeah,	
39	my mom's from Zacatecas,	
40	my dad's from--	
41	(-) from Los Altos {smiling voice}	
42	(.)That's the HEART fool.	
43	That's where the REAL Mexicans come from.	
44	Bela: Ay mira y tu? {smiling voice}	*Oh look and you?*
⌈45	Bela: (.)De donde [saliste] {smiling voice}	*Where are you from.*
⌊46	Lalo: [Psh that's-]	*Psh that's*
47	Lalo: % that's my land fool %	
48	(-) I came from my mother's WOMB.	
49	Bela: [laughter]	

Adapted from Shenk (2007: 206–7)

We can see that both acknowledge that they're not 'original' and so the dispute begins to establish who is 'more original' (line 16 ff). Lalo links this to his 'Aztec blood' as 'the Aztecs, as precolonial and hence pure-blooded Mexicans, ideologically represent the archetype of Mexicanness for many Mexican American people' (Shenk 2007: 208). It is somewhat strange that when Lalo provides evidence for his 'more original' position, he switches to English. It may be that he considers his lineage such strong evidence for his ethnicity that any performance in Spanish becomes redundant. Indeed, Shenk points out that the Spanish he uses here is not idiomatic. Thus, his switch to English may be to background his problematic position in relation to the requirement for Spanish fluency. Nevertheless, competence in a language is common as a discourse to claim ethnicity as well as a resource to display it.

7.7.2 African American ethnicity

Cutler (1999) studied a white middle class teenager, Mike, who at times in his life adopted features of AAE in order to project a particular kind of identity. Cutler suggests that Mike uses AAE features to take advantage of the prestige associated with African American youth culture (Cutler 1999: 429). Mike seems to be demonstrating an alignment with hip-hop. It should be said, that hip-hop is certainly not synonymous with African American culture. Rather, hip-hop itself might be said to draw on the cultural value of features of AAE and its association with a cool toughness, especially for young men. As well as adopting phonetic features of AAE, Mike also uses some of the **lexical items** associated with this language.

> **Example 7.6**
> a.   Mike (age 16; 1996): You ever hear of Frank Frazetta? Dis is some **phat** shit, yo. **Yo,** when the dude dies, dis book will probably worth like a thousand dollars. **Yo,** tell **that shit** is not **phat**! (Cutler 1999: 422)
> b.   Mike (age 16; 1996): Dis is gonna sound **mad** weird, yo. Don't worry, don't worry. I'll put **THE SHIT** OFF! Don't touch it. **Chill,** DON'T TOUCH IT! DON'T TOUCH IT! I got this over here! (Cutler 1999: 423)

For Mike, the use of linguistic features was coupled with other behaviours. He joined a gang, tagged his name in graffiti and generally tried to behave in ways inconsistent with normative expectations of what a middle class white boy might do. While at one point in his life he seemed to be trying to perform an African American identity, over time this changed. While he retained some AAE linguistic features, 'this was no longer an attempt to construct a black identity' (Cutler 1999: 435). This makes sense when remembering that hip-hop draws on the linguistic features of AAE without requiring that these index some kind of 'objective' ethnicity, or indeed be related to ethnicity at all. Thus Mike is able to draw on various semiotic resources associated with African American identity as he develops his own identity.

7.7.3 Welsh turfing

Language proficiency can be a clear and expedient indicator of belonging and of having verifiable and demonstrable roots; at the same time, it takes considerable effort to acquire such competence for L2 speakers. Yet linguistic competence isn't the only way of claiming an ethnicity. There are other forms of cultural capital that can be developed and exploited. For example, a study of Americans who claimed a Welsh identity found 'the higher informants' competence in Welsh, the more intense affiliations to Wales they reported' (Coupland, Bishop, Evans & Garrett 2006: 363).

Wray *et al.* (2003) argue that it is possible to 'turf' an identity, that is, create connections even though there is no historical personal link to the ethnic community.

> Turfing entails the deliberate attempt to revitalise a historically 'rooted' community by encouraging outsiders to adopt aspects of its cultural identity. We use the metaphor of turfing because the outward manifestations of the culture are not, as with the original rooted community, an expression of a pre-existing identity. Rather, they are put into place before the affective identity arises, in the hope that 'roots will grow down', anchoring the new community members permanently into the adopted identity.
>
> (2003: 49)

The research subjects, American college students participating in a Welsh choir, are thus able to 'turf' an identity, in part by enacting salient practices: singing; specifically, singing in Welsh at their college in the US, and also during trips to Wales. We can also understand how people seek to trace their family history, especially those from former colonies, as a way of establishing a claim to an ethnic identity. It should be noted that the creation and maintenance of such identities is labour intensive. Individuals generally perceive some kind of cultural capital resulting from this labour.

7.8 CONSEQUENCES FOR ETHNOLECTS

There are a variety of negative consequences for speakers of ethnolects. These consequences could be as innocuous as minor misunderstandings or as serious as educational discrimination and incarceration. We describe examples of miscommunication to demonstrate the varying effects of cross-dialect interaction.

7.8.1 Caribbean English

The potential for misunderstanding always exists in cross-dialectal interactions. Nero (2006) describes the differences between Caribbean English (CE) and Standard American English (SAE) with a particular interest in educational contexts. As he points out, documenting and exploring these differences has consequences not only for particular interactions and settings, but also for what we mean by 'language' and 'ethnicity' (2006: 501). Caribbean English can be discussed in terms of Global Englishes (see Chapter 10). We don't address those issues here. An important detail, however, is that CE speakers are found throughout the world and come from different parts of the Caribbean, including Jamaica and Guyana (2006: 503). As with many Creoles and non-standard Englishes, there is more than one kind of CE. It is possible to distinguish between the basilect, 'an English based Creole', a mesolect, 'between English and Creole' and an acrolect 'regionally accented varieties of the standard language' (2006: 502). Nero includes other distinctions that can be made in the particular case of CE, but this three way distinction serves us well here.

As it is closest to standard English, the acrolect may present fewer opportunities for misunderstanding. But this puts speakers in a difficult position as 'the basilect and especially the mesolect are often used to assert "true" Caribbean identity in informal and private domains' (2006: 503). However, the basilect is also stigmatized, as it is associated with lack of education and a low socio-economic position (2006: 503).

Nero argues that one of the most common ways in which miscommunication occurs between CE speakers and SAE speakers is confusion about **lexical items.** Some words have the same form across languages, but their meanings are very different (see Table 7.3).

Table 7.3 Lexical items in CAE and SE (adapted from Nero 2006: 506, Table 1)

Word	Meaning in CE	Meaning in SAE
Hand	Part of the body from the shoulder to the fingers	Part of the body from the wrist to the fingers
Foot	Part of the body from the thighs to the toes	Part of the body from the ankles to the toes
Tea	Any hot beverage	Specific beverage made from tea leaves

Misunderstanding is also attributed to accent, although this can usually be resolved by listening carefully or through context (Nero 2006: 506–7). In an educational setting, where a great deal may depend on pronouncing words 'correctly', however, this can have negative consequences in terms of perceptions of ability and learning trajectories.

The lexical differences will have effects for writing and the importance of writing in educational (and other contexts) is well known. While this may not lead to severe misunderstanding, it may lead to misunderstanding intended politeness or simply be attributed to faulty use of the language. In an educational context, Nero argues that teachers responsible for the education of CE speakers should be trained in the specific features of CE, have a full understanding of Caribbean culture and be familiar with communicative norms. In terms of the latter, for example, Nero points out that 'direct eye contact with the teacher or an adult is considered rude in Caribbean schools' (2006: 508). Not knowing this may lead a teacher to attribute an attitude to a student that they don't actually mean to convey. One might summarise the many useful recommendations that Nero provides as 'don't assume'. He suggests that teachers should probe student's intended meaning, provide opportunities for the use of different varieties of English and be open to the different conventions of languages both when selecting teaching materials and activities and interacting with students (see also Labov 1982). Language itself can then become a topic for discussion and learning rather than being an obstacle to understanding. This is a constructive strategy in any educational context, especially given that most varieties of English are not in fact 'standard' (see Chapter 10).

7.8.2 Australian Aboriginal English

Eades (2003) studied the way indigenous Australians are treated in the legal system. She found that the conventions of Aboriginal English (AE) put indigenous people at a serious disadvantage in a legal system that relies on and enforces Anglo conventions of communication. Eades points out some of the causes of misunderstanding are discourse strategies such as silence, gratuitous concurrence, question formation and interruption. For example, silence is 'important and positively valued' (2003: 202) by speakers of AE. It signals the importance of the topic under discussion and as such can be understood as a sign of respect and attention. The rules of the courtroom, however, construe silence from a witness or suspect as evidence of deception or lack of co-operation.

Gratuitous concurrence describes how speakers of AE may answer 'yes' to **closed questions**, 'regardless of either their understanding of the question or their belief about the truth or falsity of the proposition being questioned' (Eades 2003: 203). In any communication context, this convention may lead to miscommunication with non-AE speakers. In a legal context, this can be very damaging and lead to serious injustice. There are other aspects of questioning conventions that differ for speakers of AE. Eades notes that it is not unusual for a declarative with rising intonation to be understood as a question that invites more than simply a 'yes/no' response. It is treated as 'an invitation to explain' (2000: 172). But because speaking rights in the courtroom are restricted, any extended speech may also be construed negatively in the legal context. Because of the differing discourse strategies of AE and Anglo speakers, AE speakers are often interrupted and silenced in the court. Eades finds that such interruptions are often made by the judge. Example 7.7 is a transcript of an interaction between an AE witness and an Anglo judge. The judge's interruptions are linked to the witness trying to provide a detailed response to what is, for non-AE speakers, a closed question.

Example 7.7
31. J: Have you spoken to them since?
32. W: Oh [(xxxxx)
33. J: [Since this event?=
34. W: =at court I did yeah– last=
35. J: =Have you indicated to them what you're telling me that you feel it was unwarranted and that you're sorry for it?
36. W: Yeah– yeah it's=
37. J: =You've said that to them?
38. W: Yeah– yeah.
39. J: You tell me that truly?
40. W: Yeah (1.2) I said it when I got charged that that was– you know– my stupidness

(adapted from Eades 2000: 174)

The question asked in line 31 could be answered with a simple 'yes', and given that the judge keeps asking the question, it is clear that this is what he wants. When the witness tries to provide more than this, the judge interrupts. Had the witness been allowed to speak at line 32, the judge may not have needed to ask so many questions. These misunderstandings occur because of different communicative conventions in what look like the same language. When obviously different languages are involved in the same communicative context, it is at least easier to anticipate misunderstandings.

Activity 7.6

Can you think of other contexts where cross-dialect miscommunication may occur? What are the consequences of this?

Misunderstandings occur all the time, even between speakers of the same variety. Sometimes this can be resolved with **metalinguistic** talk. In the case where varieties have significant differences, however, difficulties may be harder to resolve. As Eades' work shows, the common conventions of communication that would inform such metalinguistic talk may not be present. A misunderstanding when making a purchase in a store is benign;

however, a misunderstanding when being arrested is dangerous. As we have already noted (Chapter 1), discrimination linked to cross-dialect communication has been found in the areas of education, housing, employment and the general accumulation of social capital.

7.9 CROSSING

Code-switching (see 7.7.1) demonstrates membership of a particular language community on the part of the speaker. There are a variety of reasons why a speaker may switch linguistic codes, whether consciously or unconsciously. It may be related to the topic or it may occur if another person joins the conversation who can only speak a particular code or variety. A switch may, therefore, also indicate solidarity and inclusion or, conversely, distance and exclusion (see Milroy & Gordon 2003: 209).

Crossing, 'language crossing' or 'code crossing', on the other hand, describes the practice of using language that is associated with, or belongs to, ethnic groups that the speaker doesn't belong to. As we have seen in Section 7.6, competence in a language, or the 'right' to use it to claim membership of a group, may have to be ratified. The sociolinguist Ben Rampton demonstrates how crossing involves 'borrowing' a variety and perhaps trespassing on language territory that one can't authentically claim. Rampton's preliminary definition is that crossing 'refers to the use of language which isn't generally thought to "belong" to the speaker' (1997: 2). Rampton thus differentiates crossing from code-switching by stating that crossing involves a 'disjunction between speaker and code that cannot be readily accommodated as a normal part of ordinary social reality' (Rampton 1995: 278). That is, according to the normal 'rules' of communication, the speaker should not be able to use the code. Therefore, the speaker can only use this code when the ordinary norms of 'social reality' and communication do not apply. As Rampton puts it, 'crossing either occasioned, or was occasioned by, moments and activities in which the constraints of ordinary social order were relaxed and normal social relations couldn't be taken for granted' (1997: 2).

Rampton's research study involved two years of **ethnographic** fieldwork with teenagers in a South Midlands town in England. He recorded conversations, interviewed participants and also asked them to comment on the data he'd recorded. He analysed instances of crossing into Panjabi, conversations involving stylised Asian English and those where Creole features were evident. He found that there were three different contexts where crossing occurred:

1. when the teenagers interacted with adults
2. when they were with their peers
3. events such as listening to bhangra[2] music, which was very influential among the young people in the neighbourhood (1997: 3)

Rampton concluded that crossing performed a variety of functions for the speakers. For example, it indicated resistance to adult norms, challenge of expectations about ethnicity, and indication of identities not related to ethnicity. Significantly, crossing appears to be connected to 'liminality' and the 'liminoid' (Rampton 1997: 7). **Liminal** spaces exist in between recognised, ratified spaces. Liminal spaces are often defined by what they are not. For example the language of the participants in Rampton's study took place in the school playground. The playground is potentially a liminal space because while it is on school grounds it is not subject to the normal school rules of the classroom. Because it takes place in liminal spaces, 'crossing never actually claimed that the speaker was "really" black or Asian' in the way that code-switching does, and it also suggests that in 'normal' spaces, 'the boundaries round ethnicity were relatively fixed' (1997: 7).

While researchers first looked at teenagers, Rampton's research suggests that the mixing of different styles isn't just a feature of adolescent speech. Even though there may be a perceived connection between such stylisation and a particular period of life, other data suggests that older speakers also employ different styles (see Rampton 2011b).

Shankar (2008) also found crossing among students in her study at a California high school. Example 7.8 is a transcript of three South Asian (Indian subcontinent) American students interacting at lunch time.

Example 7.8

Setting: 'a lunchtime conversation [where] Kuldeep (M) uses Spanish in an exchange with Uday (M) and Simran (F)' who use Punjabi (Shankar 2008: 274). Bolded words are South Asian Accented English, italicised words are Punjabi, underlined words are Spanish.

1. Uday: *Saleya eh* **garbage** *can vai*? [Is this a garbage can, stupid?]
2. Kuldeep: No habla Inglés [I (sic) don't speak English].
3. [*loud round of laughter*]
4. Kuldeep: **Don't know what you say . . .**
5. Simran: Throw that fuckin' shit out!
6. Kuldeep: *Oh balle! Hon boleya!* [Oh wow! At least you're talking to me now!].

In line 2 Kuldeep reacts to being scolded by Uday (line 1) (for not throwing his rubbish in a bin) by saying in Spanish that he does not speak English. Everyone laughs at Kuldeep's Spanish response in part because they often use Spanish when joking with each other, and also because Uday's reprimand was in Punjabi and therefore did not rely on knowing English. Kuldeep then responds that he doesn't understand Uday, using South Asian American Accented English. Simran reiterates the reprimand in English and Kuldeep responds sarcastically in Punjabi. This use of Spanish in line 2 represents crossing; these students learn Spanish at school but do not use it in everyday life. Shankar explains:

By occasionally speaking in Spanish in a school environment where they are routinely mistaken for Latinos, [these] boys use Spanish as a way to mock faculty who cannot easily differentiate between them and Latinos. Ridiculing this misrecognition is a continual source of humor for [these] teens.

(Shankar 2008: 274)

In Example 7.8 we see a range of varieties used in a single interaction to do different kinds of things. The use of Punjabi can be understood as signalling their shared ethnicity, while the use of Spanish in this humorous way signals their shared understanding of what Spanish means in this context. As Shankar explains, it also indirectly comments on the way they are misidentified in the school context. The use of Spanish helps them manage their status as 'other' at the school. What looks like a simple conversation has a number of layers and meanings.

7.10 SUMMARY

Language can be used to demonstrate or claim an ethnicity. However, because the link between language and ethnicity is not straightforward, any claims to an ethnicity may be challenged. Such a challenge may be directly posed by an 'authentic' member of the group. The claim may also not be acknowledged because of lack of understanding of the linguistic features and semiotic resources used to signal ethnicity. Further, what looks like a claim to ethnicity may in fact be something else, as we saw in the case of crossing. How claims are made, how ethnicity is performed, depends on the local context, including the interactional situation, and the features available for exploitation. Moreover, it is important to consider the range of features a speaker relies on, as it may be the use of a specific combination of features that makes the claim to ethnicity and identity. Being able to use a linguistic variety brings with it cultural capital. In the case of ethnolects, this might be minimal because of linguistic subordination. In addition, linguistic subordination also means that ethnolects are disparaged, misunderstood and result in speakers being vulnerable to a variety of risks that can be more or less serious.

FURTHER READING

Cheshire, J., Kerswill, P., Fox, S. and Torgensen, E. (2011) 'Contact, the feature pool and the speech community: The emergence of Multicultural London English', *Journal of Sociolinguistics*, 15(2): 151–96.

Eades, D. (1996) 'Legal recognition in cultural differences in communication: The case of Robyn Kina', *Language & Communication*, 16(3): 215–27.

Gumperz, J. J. (2003) 'Cross Cultural Communication', in R. Harris and B. Rampton (eds) *The Language, Ethnicity and Race Reader*, London: Routledge: 267–75.

Labov, W. (1972c) 'Academic ignorance and Black intelligence', *The Atlantic*, 72 (June): 59–67.

Shenk, P. S. (2007) '"I'm Mexican, remember?" Constructing ethnic identities via authentication discourse', *Journal of Sociolinguistics*, 11(2): 194–220.

van Dijk, T. (2004) 'Racist Discourse', in E. Cashmere (ed.) *Routledge Encyclopaedia of Race and Ethnic Studies*, London: Routledge: 351–5.

Warren, J. (1999) 'Wogspeak: Transformations of Australian English', *Journal of Australian Studies*, 23(62): 85–94.

NOTES

1 This was a popular stage show that toured in Australia in the 1990s.
2 A kind of Panjabi music.

CHAPTER 8

Language and age

8.1	INTRODUCTION	157
8.2	WHAT DO WE MEAN BY AGE?	158
8.3	EARLY LIFE STAGE	159
8.4	ADOLESCENT LIFE STAGE	160
8.5	MIDDLE LIFE STAGE	166
8.6	LATER LIFE STAGE	167
8.7	THE CREEP OF AGEISM	175
8.8	SUMMARY	176

8.1 INTRODUCTION

In this chapter we explore the way age plays a role in the **stratification** of society. We are particularly interested in how that stratification is represented in the *use* of language and how language is used *about* and *in communication with* different age groups. One way that different usage of language according to age group can be seen is in patterns of language change. Another pattern of language variation can be found in age groupings across the lifespan. These kinds of variation are reflective of an age group's place in the social hierarchy. In addition to examining how different age groups use language, it's also important to consider how language is used to communicate to people of different ages. For example, the terms used to refer to people of different ages tell us something about how we perceive age in our society. As we saw in Chapter 6 and 7, the way a person is described reveals a great deal about their position in the social hierarchy and thus how much power they have.

8.2 WHAT DO WE MEAN BY AGE?

When we talk about age and language, it's important to remember that although chronological age is relevant to some degree, what is even more important is the **life stage** that a person has reached. Eckert (1997: 151) explains: 'age and ageing are experienced both individually and as part of a cohort of people who share a life stage, and/or an experience of history.' The life stage perspective considers the various culturally constructed age group-ings a person passes through in their life, called 'life stages', such as childhood, adolescence, adulthood. Life stages do not make specific reference to chron-ological age since not all people experience these stages at exactly the same age. In addition, the life stage perspective allows us to consider the culturally constructed expectations about each life stage that may be unique to particu-lar social groups. The transition from adolescence to adulthood can be marked at a variety of chronological ages depending on the social group. For example, this may be marked by entering the workforce or by finishing formal education. For some people that may happen at age 18 when they finish secondary education while for others it may begin at age 23 when they get a university degree. In addition, the way people divide up age groups and the objective chronological age attached to these groups depends on the age group making the divisions. Younger people, for example, are more likely to set the threshold for 'elderly' lower than older people (Giles & Reid 2005: 398). This is a reflec-tion of the social construction of age. As we stated earlier, our chronological age may not be the same as our 'subjective' or 'contextual' age. In sociolinguis-tics the life stage perspective has been an approach taken by scholars such as Penny Eckert (1988) and Gillian Sankoff (2005) whose research demon-strated that considering life stages can sometimes provide a better explana-tion of speakers' language behaviour than chronological age.

Activity 8.1

Look at the table below and discuss with your colleagues where you would place the chronological age of these groups. What does society expect of these groups of people in terms of behaviour, language and habits?

Lifespan period	Chronological age	Cultural expectations
Childhood		
Adolescents		
Adult		
Older adult		

Now think about people you know who fit into these age groups; do they match the cultural expectations you noted down? Does this change how you might categorise these individuals?

8.3 EARLY LIFE STAGE

The early life stage refers to the stage where a large amount of parental intervention is necessary for existence. This usually includes babies and young children. Children are not yet fully capable members of society, which contributes to a special status in Western society. One of the expectations of this life stage is that because of their vulnerability they need to be protected from certain kinds of ideas and representations (Sealey 2000).

8.3.1 Language used to talk to children

It's not difficult to see that the way people speak to children differs from the way they speak to older people. In many languages, talking differently to children is routine. We call the language that adults use only with children **'child directed language'** (CDL). Example 8.1 is a transcript of a mother talking to her baby.

Example 8.1

Mother	Ann (3 months)
	(smile)
Oh what a nice little smile!	
Yes, isn't that nice?	
There	
There's a nice little smile	(burps)
What a nice wind as well	
Yes that's better isn't it?	
Yes	
Yes	(vocalises)
Yes	
That's a nice noise	

(Snow 1977:12 in Ochs & Schieffelin 1994: 475)

Peccei (1999: 56) describes some of the features of CDL, a few of which are evident in Example 8.1. She suggests CDL often includes the use of the child's name, directing attention to current tasks or the immediate environment and the use of full nouns rather than pronouns. Other features of CDL suggest that adults consider speaking to children as educational; they are teaching them to use the language.

The language used to speak to and about children is closely linked to the ideas that we have about children and their linguistic and social development. Sealey (2000) examined the portrayal of children in the public sphere such as in newspapers, radio and advertising. She suggests that children are frequently characterised as 'targets of harm', 'beneficiaries of care' and dichotomously as both 'angel and demon' (2000: 69). This is not universal, however, and Sealey reminds us that these characterisations are limited to the location and time in which they were observed. For example, Ochs and Schieffelin (1994) note that while the Kaluli of Papua New Guinea are very attentive to the needs of their babies, they do not speak to them in the way the mother in Example 8.1 does. The Kaluli cultural norms hold that interactions with babies are minimal. The child is greeted but adults 'rarely address other utterances to them' (1994: 483). Nor do the Kaluli simplify their language with children. This is avoided as it is thought to inhibit language development (1994: 495). The Kaluli example demonstrates, again, that societal expectations for certain groups are reflected in language use.

With respect to language use during this life stage, much research has been conducted about how children acquire language and is too complex for us to detail here (e.g. Fletcher & MacWhinney 1996, Peccei 1999). In terms of social influences on their language, linguists have come to understand that children develop sociolinguistic competence from the earliest stages of speech (e.g. Romaine 1978, Labov 1989). In a child's early years, their caregiver is the most important model for language. When children begin to socialise independently of their caregivers, their most important models for language become their peers (Chambers 1992; Payne 1980; Roberts 2004). This is especially important in the adolescent life stage.

8.4 ADOLESCENT LIFE STAGE

Adolescence is a relatively new age group, historically speaking. Eckert observes that adolescence is the 'product of industrial society, its history closely tied to the development of universal institutionalized secondary education' (2003b: 112). Like most other social groups, it is not a homogenous group. What adolescents share is a kind of **liminal** status; they are neither children nor adults. They are also generally delegitimised (Eckert 2003b: 114). While adolescents have some rights and even some economic power, these are not the same as those acquired in adulthood. Adolescents are required to stay in education, abide by specific rules of behaviour, dress and activity. Because of their marginalised status, their development of individual taste, through clothing and leisure choices, is often derided (Eckert 2004).

Activity 8.2

Go to a search engine on the World Wide Web and type in 'why are teenagers so' allowing the auto fill function of the search engine to predict what word comes next in this question. What does it produce? What does this tell you about perceptions of teenagers?

8.4.1 What teenagers do

Eckert (1997) suggests that the transition from childhood to adulthood is a key feature of this life stage. This transition brings with it a number of obstacles that must be overcome. First, this is a time when young adults are often given certain levels of autonomy and freedom to develop their own identity. Second, adolescents are negotiating and navigating their marginalised status. Part of this development and negotiation may include a purposeful divergence from adult norms in order to assert an identity that is their own (Eckert 2005). This divergence may take the form of words or phonological forms that are different from their parents (deKlerk 2005; Eckert 1988). 'The development of adolescent social structure provides a major impetus for phonological change' (Eckert 1988:197).

What words or expressions have you noticed adolescents using? Do you understand what they mean? How do you think they are evaluated by other groups?

Activity 8.3

8.4.2 Multiple negation

Eisokovits' (2011) research in Sydney examined the speech of teenage boys and girls over two years to understand ways young men and women negotiate their marginalised status in different ways. Students (10 girls and 10 boys) from a working class area of inner city Sydney were interviewed in year 8 (at about age 13) and again in year 10 (at about age 15). One of the linguistic features of this group (among many others) is **multiple negation**. Multiple negation refers to the use of more than one negative morpheme or lexeme in an utterance. For example, instead of saying 'I *didn't* do anything', multiple negation is used by including another negative word as in 'I *didn't* do *nothing*'. Multiple negation is part of non-standard English and often stigmatised by prescriptivists.

Table 8.1 shows Eisokovits' results for the use of 'multiple negation' by age and sex. The first number shows how many times multiple negation was used compared with the number of times it could have been used.

Table 8.1 Percent of multiple negation, according to gender and age in Sydney (adapted from Eisokovits 2011: 41)

Younger girls	Older girls
56/115; 48.7%	42/192; 21.7%
Younger boys	Older boys
54/107; 50.5%	56/127; 44.1%

We can see that for the younger students, levels of multiple negation are roughly the same. The older students, however, demonstrate a difference in their pattern of use. Older girls use multiple negation less frequently than younger girls while older boys and younger boys use multiple negation at roughly the same rate.

In the case of other non-standard features Eisokovits examined, the older girls showed reduced use of other non-standard linguistic features while the boys did not. The boys increased their use of some non-standard variables. Example 8.2 from Eisokovits' interview data suggests a reason why this pattern is found among these Sydney adolescents. In this example, a female and a male respondent both correct their own usage. Both correct themselves, but in entirely different directions; the female repeats herself using a more prescriptively correct form but the male does so using a more prescriptively incorrect form.

Example 8.2

a. Female respondent: 'An me an Kerry – or should I say, Kerry and I – are the only ones who've done the project' (Eisokovits 2011: 45).
b. Male respondent: 'I didn't know what I did – what I done' (Eisokovits 2011: 46).

Eisokovits argues that these choices are related to perceptions of what it means to be an adult woman or man in their society. As we saw in Chapter 6, expectations about how women should speak relate to ideas about how women should behave (e.g. they should use 'correct' language). The same is of course true of men; it is simply that these expectations are rather different (e.g. they may use 'correct' language less frequently), resulting in different use of language. Eckert (2009) also investigated multiple negation use among adolescents in Detroit, Michigan, US and found similar results (see Chapter 9).

8.4.3 'Like' as a discourse marker

A common linguistic feature that people mention when they criticise young people's use of language is the discourse marker 'like' (D'Arcy 2007). A discourse marker structures utterances and provides important cues about the attitude of the speaker with regard to what they are saying or responding to. With regard to the meaning of this discourse marker Underhill (1988:234) explains that 'this discourse marker is neither random nor mindless. Instead, it functions with great reliability as a marker of new information and focus' (see also D'Arcy 2007, Laserna, Seih & Pennebaker 2014). Sali Tagliamonte (2005) studied how young Canadians use this discourse marker as shown in Examples 8.3 a–c (2005: 1897).

Example 8.3

    a.   I'm just like so there, you know?
    b.   Like, that's what I like told you.
    c.   I just decided and just went.

Tagliamonte found that, among the Canadians she studied, the youngest and oldest speakers in the sample used 'like' the least. There was a concentration of more usage of 'like' among the 15–16-year-olds. Figure 8.1 shows this distribution of use.

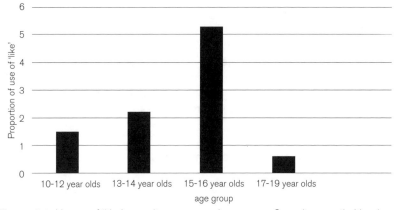

Figure 8.1 Usage of 'like' as a discourse marker among Canadian youth. Numbers reflect proportion of total words (adapted from Tagliamonte 2005: 1903)

> What characteristics of life stages might account for the difference in usage among these age groups?
>
> Activity 8.4

Tagliamonte suggests that the pattern of higher usage of 'like' among 15–16-year-olds reflects innovative use of language often found among adolescents, as described by Eckert (1999) (see also Wagner 2008). This is followed by a reduction in the 17–18-year-olds, reflecting 'linguistic change towards standard (mainstream) norms as adolescents enter young adulthood' (Tagliamonte 2005: 1910). This sort of pattern of change across the lifespan can be referred to as age grading, a change in the use of language that correlates with life stages and does not reflect change of community norms.

As Tagliamonte and other linguists have shown (e.g. D'Arcy 2007), 'like' used as a discourse marker is a strategic functional use of language. However, as we have already seen with regard to other non-standard features, this use is highly criticised.

> Many parents and teachers have become irritated to the point of distraction at the way the weed-style growth of 'like' has spread through the idiom of the young. And it's true that in some cases the term has become simultaneously a crutch and a tic, driving out the rest of the vocabulary as candy expels vegetables.
>
> (Hitchens 2010)

Hitchens' (2010) comments reflect the marginalised position of adolescents described previously.

The sociolinguistic competence that teenagers acquire and exploit depends very much on the environments in which they live and the identities they want to communicate. This development of identity is also connected to styles of dress, hairstyles and leisure activities.

8.4.4 Computer-mediated communication

Crispin Thurlow (2006) examined the representation of computer mediated communication (CMC) in the popular press. These representations are discussed in terms of Computer Mediated Discourse (CMD). CMD examines the public debates and discussion about the use of computer mediated language. This research examines metalanguage, that is, the language used to talk about language. This type of study reveals the attitudes that people have towards this language as well as what they think it is (Preston 1996). It also tells us what attitudes are held about the users of this language.

Thurlow examined newspaper representations of CMC and uncovered three major themes:

1. computer mediated language is a new form of language
2. statistical panic – CMC is being used too much
3. moral panic – use of CMC has negative effects on society.

The idea that CMC is new was common. Evidence for this can be found in the terms used to describe it (e.g. 'netlingo', 'weblish' and 'netspeak') (Thurlow 2006: 673). The claim that it is new is also made by comparing CMD with other language forms or by describing it in terms usually used about separate languages. For example, users of CMC are said to be 'fluent' and 'bilingual' and there is coverage of the inclusion of CMC items in dictionaries (2006: 673–4). Thurlow argues that the newness of CMC is promoted by those with an interest in the form being seen as new (2006: 674). Therefore, providers of technology are often quoted or refereed to when claims about the newness of CMC are being made.

The second theme Thurlow identifies relates to levels of use of CMC. Thurlow notes that 'the use of numerous, superlative numerical citations' about its use were found in the data set (2006: 675). The third theme is the most relevant to our discussion about life stages, as it relates to the moral panic surrounding the use of CMC. This 'new' kind of language is represented as a threat to the language, one specifically associated with young people (2006: 677) and one that older people don't understand.

> While it would be untrue to suggest that there were no positive claims made for the effects of CMD ... for the most part the nexus of popular discourses about language, about technology, and about young people generates an overwhelmingly pessimistic picture.
>
> (2006: 677)

Once CMC is established as a threat to the language, it can be represented as a threat to social order, to progress and to culture in general. This is one more example of the kinds of arguments used against language change (see Chapter 2) that have been common throughout history (Milroy & Milroy 1999). A part of this argument is the claim that CMC is being used by young people in their written exams (Thurlow 2006: 684). Such stories are used as evidence for the negative effect of CMC on literacy and language skills. Linguistic scholarship, however, does not support this claim (Thurlow 2006: 679).

In addition, further research conducted by Thurlow (2003) shows that what people think teenagers are doing with CMC is not necessarily what they are actually doing. In an effort to examine SMS text communication among university students and describe how young people are using this media, Thurlow (2003) collected text messages from 135 students at Cardiff University. He examined message length, the typographic and linguistic content (emoticons, abbreviations and letter homophones) and the primary purpose of the text. The average message length (14 words and 65 characters) seemed to be rather short, especially given the 140 character limit of texts. The linguistic forms used were also surprising. While the use of 'x' was high (443 of all instances of emoticon – 509), emoticon use was generally rather low. '!!' occurred 35 times and ☺ 17 times. These three are the most used, showing that other emoticons are only infrequently employed (only six times). Texters also used around three abbreviations in each message. There were some (73) homophones with letter/number play, for example 'u' for 'you' and 'b4' for 'before' and some use of onomatopoeia (e.g. 'ha ha').

When considering the function of the messages, Thurlow found that rather than conveying information, the young people use texting to build and maintain relationships, that is, to interact with their friends in much the same way as they might do face to face. Moreover, texting was also used to communicate when they were in the same location, in order to create a parallel communicative space.

Thurlow identifies three features of texting:

1.   brevity and speed
2.   paralinguistic restitution
3.   phonological approximation.

Brevity relates to the short message length. Paralinguistic restitution is the use of available forms to communicate paralinguistic information, information that is usually conveyed in addition to the actual content of the speech such as tone, volume or emotion. For example the use of capitals to indicate shouting or emphasis, and employing emoticons or punctuation (e.g. '!!!') to convey affect are ways to communicate paralinguistic features. The third feature, phonological approximation, refers to the way texters exploit the conventions of written language to convey features of spoken language. For example changes are made to conventional spelling (e.g. 'goin') to evoke spoken use. Thurlow concludes that text-messages of these students are on the one hand 'remarkable' in their use of creativity to project particular identities and 'unremarkable' in that they conform to sociolinguistic and communicative conventions (Thurlow 2003). We can see in Thurlow's examination of texting by young people that students are not, contrary to popular belief, losing the skills of either written or spoken communication.

8.5 MIDDLE LIFE STAGE

Much of the sociolinguistic research we have explored in many of the chapters in this book describes the language use of speakers in the middle life stage (e.g. Labov 1972a, Trudgill 1974). Research has focused on this age group for a few reasons. First, this age group is seen as the 'unmarked' age group; that is, childhood, adolescence and later life are frequently described in terms of how they are different from adulthood. Second, there is an assumption that the middle life stage is one where language use is stable and not expected to change, especially with regard to child language development (Roberts 2004). In addition, in practical terms, as subjects of research, adults are easier to access because they can give consent to participate, and they do not tend to have age-related cognitive or physical attributes that interfere with language research.

Because this life stage has been the subject of a good deal of research, a few generalisations can be reliably made about their language use. In addition to the gendered, socioeconomic and ethnicity-based variation previously discussed, people in this life stage are usually conservative in their language use. That means that they use standard language features more than the other age groups (Chambers 2009). Scholars suggest this is due to the need for linguistic capital in the labour force because most people in this age group have entered the labour force and are pursuing careers (Sankoff & Laberge 1978).

> Make a list of words we use to refer to people in the middle life stage. What does the list represent in terms of perceptions of this life stage?

8.6 LATER LIFE STAGE

As we noted above, because middle age is the unmarked life stage, the language use of older adults has been the subject of linguistic research much less than other age groups. Only recently have people in the later life stage been the focus of sociolinguistic research (e.g. Coupland 1997, Giles & Reid 2005, Ylänne-McEwan 1999). Sociolinguistic research on language use and older people takes as its primary focus the representation and performance of identity of people in the later life stage. This research has shown that people in this life stage, like children and adolescents, are frequently depicted in a negative way and therefore reflects prominent age-stereotyping, or ageism, in society.

This ageism can be prominent in terms referring to people in this life stage. While children and babies may be spoken about as cute, playful, mischievous and annoying, the terms and stereotypes associated with the elderly as not as varied or attractive. Research shows that while there are some more positive portrayals of older people such as 'kind, supportive, and wise' (Zhang, Harwood, Williams, Ylänne-McEwan, Wadleigh & Thimm 2007: 266), 'older people are perceived as incompetent, fragile, complaining, social unskilled, overly self-disclosive, and dominating' (Zhang et al. 2007: 266). Gerlinde Mautner (2007) examined a large collection of language (a corpus) in order explore the term 'elderly'. Charting the words that commonly occur together with (such word pairs are called **collocates**) 'elderly' makes the negative connotations of the term clear (as we saw with gendered terms in Chapter 6). Table 8.2 shows the most common collocates of 'elderly'.

Mautner's analysis shows that the elderly are associated with 'disability, illness, care, and vulnerability to crime' (2007: 63). Also significant is that one does not find evidence of 'independence, initiative, and empowerment' or of 'education, jobs, experience' (2007: 63). These perceptions suggest that citizens in the later life stage don't so much *do* things but rather have things done for them.

The term 'elderly' has come to be associated with being infirm, disabled, handicapped and sick (Mautner 2007). These results do not establish that elderly people are necessarily infirm or ill; rather, it demonstrates that these

Table 8.2 Lexical collocates of elderly with the highest joint frequencies among the top 50 collocates (adapted from Mautner 2007: 57)

Collocate	Joint frequency
people	255
woman	75
disabled	55
man	51
care	51
couple	41
children	41
lady	37
women	35
sick	32

are the ideas that people associated with the word 'elderly'. As Mautner points out, 'elderly' is a 'social' rather than a 'chronological' label (2007: 60), a perspective that is reflected in a 'lifespan' approach and other approaches to social categories that we've discussed such as gender (see chapter 6).

8.6.1 Representations of older people

The media we consume and are exposed to has an effect on our under-standing of the world. Because media, including advertising, has to commu-nicate with its audience, it draws on existing ideas about people. Even if an advertisement challenges the common conceptions of a product or a group of people, it nevertheless draws on these very conceptions. A good example of this is a campaign for a margarine made from olive oil (Zhang *et al.* 2007). The study of these printed advertisements shows that the ads began by providing information about the health benefits of olive oil but also linked these to portrayals of age. Specifically, older people are used in this context 'to symbolize longevity and healthy, active old age' (Zhang *et al.* 2007: 237). Using older people sends a message: consume this product and you too will live for a long time. The campaign continued to develop this theme in several stages, by portraying older people in a family context and partaking in particularly active pursuits. This includes positive visual portrayals of older people as well as using words normally associated with younger people to describe them. For example, an older man is featured in an ad with the caption 'babe magnet, the new name for handsome fellow' (Zhang *et al.* 2007: 273). This campaign provides positive representations of older people in terms of longevity, life fulfilment, and sexuality and perhaps even 'new ways of being old' (Zhang *et al.* 2007: 274). Further, 'These images and messages might reflect changing attitudes and stereotypes of old age, in turn affected by changes in the aging cohort group' (Zhang *et al.* 2007: 274).

8.6.2 Self-representation of older people

Considering Table 8.2, it's hardly surprising that older people would reject the term 'elderly' as a self-descriptor. At the same time, because we don't have complete control over our identity, the negative associations of 'elderly' are real and problematic. 'The labeling expressions, in turn, shape both people's identities and interpersonal relationships. In the process, both individuality and non age-related group identities are backgrounded or forfeited altogether' (Mautner 2007: 53).

The difficulty of managing the dominant discourses of age and ageing can be seen in the way older people construct themselves in dating advertisements. 'Dating ads are an ideal site in which to observe the constructive function of linguistic labelling and categorization' (Coupland, 2000: 11), especially as the advertiser is labelling her or himself.

Gather some dating ads. Look for patterns in how they are structured. How does age play a role in how people describe themselves or what type of partner they are looking for?

Activity 8.6

As people are now living longer, with better health and generally a better quality of life than in previous generations, new possibilities are available for older people. In this context, the effect of gender is important. The identities available to older men differ from those available to older women. Moreover, because of cultural norms around relationships and age, it has generally been easier for older men to behave, and be accepted, in ways that were not always thought to be appropriate for women (Sontag 1972). This can clearly be seen in the way age gaps between heterosexual partners are understood. Traditionally, it has been acceptable for an older man to be in a relationship with a younger woman (see Chapter 6), and while societal expectations are changing, older women dating much younger men contradicts societal conventions. This demonstrates the importance for identity markers like gender and age to be considered as acting together.

Activity 8.7

In the following table, write down the terms associated with each of the partners in the relationship. For example, in the top right hand box, write down the terms that might be used to describe a younger woman in a relationship with an older man and those used for the older man in a relationship with a younger woman. What kind of age difference would be required for the terms you identify? What do the terms say about society's views of these relationships and the people in them?

	Younger man	Older man
Younger woman	[unmarked]	Terms for a woman: Terms for a man:
Older woman	Terms for a woman: Terms for a man:	[unmarked]

Coupland studied older people's dating ads to explore how older people describe themselves and engage in 'age-identity negotiations' (2000: 9). She found that these ads have a fairly standard structure (2000: 22).

> F11786 Smart widow,
> mid 60's, non-smoker,
> seeks smart, tall, sincere
> gentleman, 60–68, for
> friendship and companionship,
> car owner preferred,
> share expenses,
> photo appreciated.
> W Sussex area.

The ads seem to demonstrate some recognition of older age, as older advertisers tend to 'articulate less ambitious, more modest, and certainly less sexual relationship goals' (Coupland 2000: 28). While the texts are positive, as dating ads generally have to be, there is less attention to physical traits than found among younger people. It is also common to resist chronological age through some kind of qualification, for example, 'young 60s' or 'active widower'. This 'is to claim that although the person is older, he or she is not "fully" or "normatively" so' (Coupland 2000: 28). This is not to say that all the ads are the same; but, they do tend to both 'acknowledge and resist ageist cultural norms' (Coupland 2000: 28). Exactly because of the strength of age related ideologies, acknowledging age is almost unavoidable, at least in certain contexts.

Different media have different norms for this genre of text. While Coupland's account of the structure of dating ads applies to the vast majority of venues for dating advertisements, there are exceptions. In a periodical called the *London Review of Books* (LRB), the entire genre of dating ads is subverted. Ads in this publication are typically unconventional. They are so unusual and amusing that collections of these ads have been published (e.g. Rose 2006, 2010). In the introduction to one such volume, the editors confirm what Coupland shows. Rose observes that dating ads 'throughout the world usually become fairly homogenous statements that often default to bland physical descriptions. Height, weight, eye and hair colour are all standard, but so too is every clichéd adjective that can be applied to them' (Rose 2006: 2). The ads in the LRB, however, are not always positive, about age or about any characteristic. Example 8.4 shows how LRB ads that explicitly mention age do so in an atypical way.

Example 8.4
a. Virtually complete male, 63, seeks woman with spares and shed (Rose 2006: 16).
b. Tonight, female LRB readers to 90, I am the hunter and you are my quarry. 117-year-old male Norfolk Viagra bootlegger finally in the mood for a bit of young totty. Which realistically could be any of you with working hip joints and a minimum of 20% lung capacity. Hopeful right through the Complan and Horlicks main course (Rose 2006: 18).
c. If you get a camcorder for Christmas, can you video-tape your love and send me a copy? If you don't get a camcorder for Christmas, still photos will do. If you don't own a camera, I'll accept donations of cash towards my therapy. Man, 98 (Rose 2006: 113).

Not all the personal ads in the LRB mention age. While these personal ads are unusual, they demonstrate how individuals completely subvert expectations about age and the genre of personal ads.

8.6.3 Language used to talk to older people

Because of the negative associations of people in the later life stage and because age is a characteristic assumed by looking at someone, older people sometimes find themselves being spoken to in entirely inappropriate ways. One of these ways of speaking is called 'elderspeak' (Kemper 1994: 18).

> [Elderspeak] refers to the use of a patronizing speech style resembling speech addressed to children; this patronizing speech style results from and reinforces (negative) stereotypes that older adults are cognitively impaired. Elderspeak also refers to the use of a simplified speech register which is assumed to enhance older adults' comprehension.
>
> (Kemper 1994: 18)

This kind of speech is used by some people when interacting with older people and appears to be driven by stereotypes rather than because it is necessary for communication to take place. The features of elderspeak are similar to those of child directed language, e.g. the simplification of language, shorter utterances, changes in pitch and particular forms of address (Sealey 2000). While speakers may use these features to communicate care and affection, they may also be heard as patronising or infantilising (Giles & Reid 2005; Sealey 2000).

Because of the negative terms in which aging is understood, it can be difficult to position oneself as an older person. This has consequences for the way people are able to construct their own identities. Example 8.5 is a transcript from a medical context in which a woman negotiates the stereotypes associated with age and aging (Coupland 1997: 37).

Example 8.5
A conversation between Doctor A (male) and Patient 10 (female, aged 88) (from Coupland 1997: 37):

After the physical examination, patient and doctor have been talking about Patient 10's recent hospital stay.

P 10: everything was done for me I was well looked after (.) you can't expect much at eighty eight can you? (chuckles at length) still I see some of them are flying across the world at ninety (.) true (laughs)

Dr A: [that's r that's right

P 10:   [laughs   ]

(more seriously) so I don't know (.) (coughs) as long as I can get this breathing (.) better (.) bit easier you see

Dr A: yeah

Coupland notes that the patient seems to endorse the idea that one becomes less able as one gets older but also rejects it when she mentions people flying round the world at 90. 'She thus acknowledges that the stereotype of poor health-in-aging is not invariable, and the light-hearted key offers a possible interpretation of her ageist claim as not being resolutely held' (Coupland 1997: 38). It's also clear that she hopes for some improvement, as she'd like to get her 'breathing better'. The key factor here may be the context. Speaking to a medical doctor one may adjust utterances according to the perceived beliefs of the doctor. Indeed, it has been found that 'older patients have relatively low expectations of the extent to which medical services can improve their lives' (Coupland 1997: 39). Other interactional contexts may allow for more negotiation of age and identity.

8.6.4 Construction of age in a travel agency

Research on interactions in a travel agency by Virpi Ylänne-McEwan (1999) shows how representations of age are brought into a conversation in a commercial interaction. In addition, she examines how brochures of holidays aimed at older customers are used to explain and illustrate the kinds of product on offer. Ylänne-McEwan points out that these brochures construct and rehearse stereotypes about travel and aging that may be received as patronising or reassuring.

Example 8.6 is a transcript of a conversation between customers and travel agents. Mrs and Mr Morgan are the customers, who have already disclosed they are in their seventies. The other participants are employees in the travel agency. Alun is 24, Emma is 25 and Mary is 40 (Ylänne-McEwan 1999: 424–5).

Example 8.6

```
 1   Mrs Morgan:    well er (.) what we want we as I [said]
 2   Alun:                                            [mm]
 3   Mrs Morgan:    we'd like to go to Portugal we only want
 4                  to go for seven days
 5   Mary:          yes
 6   Mrs Morgan:    we want to go with people (.) and [we
 7   Mary:                                            [do you
 8                  want something like a Young at Heart
 9                  type of holi[day?
10   Alun:                      [yes yes
11   Mary:          [something] like that
12   Mrs Morgan:    [well uh] (very hesitantly) (1.0)
13   Mary:          is do you wan do you want to be
14                  categorised (.) as one of [(.) one of =
15   Mrs Morgan:                              [(laughs)
16   Mary:          = the over fifty fives [or
17   Mrs Morgan:                           [oh yeah
18   Mr Morgan:                            [yeah
19   Mrs Morgan:    we're over one definitely over the fifty
20                  [fives (laughs)
21   Mr Morgan:     [(laughs)
22   Mary:          [(laughs) cos that's what they're [they
23   Mrs Morgan:                                      [yeah
24                  our own age group then [you know yes yeah
25   Emma:                                 [yeah not eighteen
26                  thir[ty
27   Mr Morgan:         [thirty two =
28   Mrs Morgan:    = oh no no no no [(laughs)
29   Emma:                          [you're sure?
30   Mrs Morgan:    positive (laughs)
```

Age is clearly made relevant in this conversation. There is a great deal of discussion not just about age in general terms, but about particular ages and the products (holidays) associated with them. Lines 13–14 are particularly interesting. Ylänne-McEwan points out that Mary's statement can be understood as request for age disclosure, something that can be very **face threatening** (1999: 425); in most contexts, it is thought to be rude to ask how old someone is. Mary's statement is an indirect request, however, which may reduce the face threat that the question poses (Ylänne-McEwan 1999: 426). It also invites the client to participate in the identification of their age: 'they are given the choice to comment on or to self-construct their contextual age' (1999: 426). The exchange is rather humorous in nature, especially in the discussion of the 18–30 age-group holidays (lines 24–30). Ylänne-McEwan argues that Mary's question is 'ironic'; as suggested by the fact that Mrs Morgan starts to laugh before the question is finished.

It is also possible to understand Mary's question in a slightly different way (without claiming that this is how Mary or the Morgans understood it). Mary's use of the word 'categorised' suggests a particular kind of treatment, a particular classification of people in terms of their age. Given the context of interaction, it may well be that Mary is trying to establish what kind of holiday the Morgans want; do they want a holiday that has been created for the 'category' of older people? While it has already been established that the Morgans would like something 'like a Young at Heart type of holiday', Mary's question may be seeking further confirmation of this. As Ylänne-McEwan explains, these holidays are aimed at older people who want to travel with other people of a similar age, be looked after by 'hosts' and engage in particular kinds of activities, such as ballroom dancing, bingo, walking tours and so on. These holiday products are aimed at a particular kind of older person, a particular 'category'. This category may be seen as ageist (assuming older people only want to play bingo and so on) or positive as 'promoting an active lifestyle for older people' (Ylänne-McEwan 1999: 437). It looks like the Morgans orient more to the second interpretation. There may be no way for a travel agent to be sure of this. This makes their job quite difficult. They need to ensure that clients know what kind of products are on offer without offending people by offering something that would be inappropriate. Offering a customer who appears to be older than 55 a holiday aimed at 'the over 55s' is risky because it reveals an assumption about the customer's age. However, one also can't assume that the customer would not be interested in these kinds of products, even if the products seem be ageist and patronising. As Ylänne-McEwan succinctly puts it, 'Moral issues … underlie the discourse strategies adopted by assistants who sell these holidays' (1999: 437).

In order to market products, certain assumptions are made about potential consumers in relation to their interests, and self-perception. In the case of the travel agency conversation age identity is prominent. Negotiation of personal identity takes place in all kinds of interactions whether they are commercial or personal and involve dealing with the expectations and assumptions of the interlocutor and society in general.

8.7 THE CREEP OF AGEISM

While most attention has focused on the ways older people are discriminated against, both in the way they are represented and the way they are spoken to, scholars make clear that ageism can affect many age groups. Ageism is not always explicit; one may be discriminated against on the basis of something that is not age as such, but rather, related to expectations of age. Considering someone 'too young' as well as 'too old' could be a result of ageism depending on the context. For example, a 28-year-old may be 'too old' for a new boy band while a 50-year-old may be considered 'too young' to be appointed as a senior member of the judiciary. Or, instead of someone being told they are 'too young' for a particular post, they may be told they don't have enough experience. Societal expectations associated with age can be used as a kind of 'cover' for age discrimination. It is a dominant cultural norm that youth and beauty go together (Palmore 1999: 22; Sontag 1972) thus sometimes this kind of discrimination is linked to appearance more generally: past a certain age (which differs for men and women), it becomes more difficult to be considered 'beautiful'.

These ideologies of age and beauty can be seen as informing the marketing of cosmetic surgery. The (often unstated) argument for cosmetic surgery is that looking younger means being more attractive and therefore brings with it positive benefits. While the discourses found in advertisements for cosmetic surgery (and cosmetics, face creams and so on) may focus on being more confident, or aligning your appearance with who you 'really are', they ultimately depend on the equation of youth, beauty and success (Ellison 2014). Image 8.1 is a constructed advertisement demonstrating how ageism underlies the argument for cosmetic surgery.

In order to succeed, being good is not enough. You have to look good too. Dr Mark has years of experience in facial rejuvenation and helping experienced businessmen outshine the competition. If you need help to look as top-notch as you are, call us for an appointment. It could be the most important meeting you'll ever have.

Image 8.1 Plastic surgery advertisement

This ad (Image 8.1) asserts, to an employment market audience, that to be successful you have to look the part. This connects directly to ideas about physical appearance and personal competence. Notice that age as such is never mentioned, and the professional expertise of the addressee is acknowledged through the use of business related lexis. A cosmetic procedure is recast as a meeting, invoking practices of networking and professional development rather than surgery. While the advertisement takes account of the positive aspects of age, it also stresses the importance of experience. Mautner notes that scepticism is warranted with regard to such characterisations of aging because '[i]deologies built on the pathologization of normal aging and the concomitant creation of pressures on individuals to "do something about it" – should not be allowed to become hegemonic either' (2007: 64).

Activity 8.8

What do Image 8.1 and words such as 'brotox' suggest about the performance of identity for men, especially in relation to age?

8.8 SUMMARY

Age plays an important role in social hierarchies. In this chapter we have seen how each life stage has unique challenges. Societal expectations of what certain life stages involve creates specific pressures on people in that life stage. These pressures can manifest themselves in the particular usage of language such as the avoidance of non-standard features or innovation of grammatical features. We have also seen that perceptions of life stages by society result in the use of certain forms of communication with people in a particular life stage (e.g. babytalk, elderspeak) and certain ways of referring to people associated with a particular life stage (e.g. 'elderly', 'tween', 'tearaway') that further limit and marginalise members of those groups.

FURTHER READING

Aldridge, M. (ed.) (1996) *Child Language*, Bristol: Multilingual Matters.
Eckert, P. (2004) 'Adolescent Language', in E. Finegan and J. Rickford (eds) *Language in the USA: Themes for the Twenty-first Century*, Cambridge: Cambridge University Press: 360–75.
Makoni, S. and Grainger, K. (2002) 'Comparative gerontolinguistics: Characterizing discourses in caring institutions in South Africa and the United Kingdom', *Journal of Social Issues*, 58 (4): 805–24.
Ylänne, V. (ed.) (2012) *Representing Ageing: Images and Identities*, Basingstoke: Palgrave Macmillan.

CHAPTER 9

Language, class and symbolic capital

9.1	**INTRODUCTION**	177
9.2	**WHAT IS SOCIAL CLASS?**	177
9.3	**ATTITUDES TO CLASS**	179
9.4	**LINGUISTIC VARIATION**	183
9.5	**SOCIAL NETWORKS**	190
9.6	**COMMUNITIES OF PRACTICE**	191
9.7	**SYMBOLIC CAPITAL**	193
9.8	**REVISING THE BRITISH SOCIAL CLASS MODEL**	194
9.9	**SUMMARY**	196

9.1 INTRODUCTION

In this chapter we explore social class and **symbolic capital**. The reason for taking both together is twofold. First, social class is notoriously difficult to define. Second, in order to fully understand the effects of social class and the power it may bring, it's important to engage with the notion of symbolic capital. Objective definitions of class don't always explain language variation. We begin by examining attitudes to social class before considering research on the correlation between language and class. We then consider social networks and communities of practice in order to see that language use and symbolic capital may be rather more local than traditional definitions of social class suggest. Finally, we examine a recent model of class that gives symbolic capital a central place.

9.2 WHAT IS SOCIAL CLASS?

Social class has long been associated with how much money a person has; the amount of money a person possesses or can earn places a person in a particular position in a social class hierarchy. However, this relationship has been complicated by the fact that the possession of money no longer relies on being born into a particular family or pursuing a particular profession. While personal wealth can still be considered one of the factors that contribute to the perception of 'class', other factors such as education, where someone lives and, of course, the language a person speaks play an important role in the perception of social class.

Many people think that social class is no longer relevant. However, even in societies presented as lacking social class distinctions, it can still be found. In Denmark, like other Scandinavian countries, there is a strong ideology of egalitarianism. As Ladegård puts it, 'Denmark … is often presented as a country in which social-class distinctions are virtually non-existent' (1998: 183). To investigate this, Ladegård recorded people using different regional varieties of Danish, as well as 'Standard Danish'. He then asked informants to listen to the voices and rate their intelligence, education, socio-economic status, reliability, friendliness, sense of humour and so on (1998: 187). Significant differences emerged across all categories. Standard Danish scored well across all domains as did a variety known as High Copenhagen. The distance between these two varieties and all others, however, across all domains, was significant. Ladegård observes:

> the Danish subjects do *not* perceive members from different social groups in their society as equal. They see, for example, the Northern suburban Copenhagener as intelligent, well-educated, rich, and with great leadership potential, as opposed to the inner-city Copenhagener, who is perceived as relatively unintelligent, poorly educated, and with low socioeconomic status and poor leadership potential.
>
> (1998: 188)

Even in a country with low objective inequality, social class and attitudes about social class can still be found, and linked to linguistic performance. While we may think we live in classless societies, the reality is rather different as we see in the linguistic research we cover in this chapter.

Activity 9.1

What other things might be associated with social class? Imagine a person from an upper class, middle class and lower class background. Where do they work, how do they spend their leisure time, how do they dress?

9.3 ATTITUDES TO CLASS

As we saw in Chapter 1, the idea that there is a 'correct' and 'standard' form of the language is widespread. This prescriptivist perspective has a number of components and consequences. First, any non-standard language variety will be viewed as somehow deficient in relation to the 'standard' (Milroy & Milroy 1999). Even though prescriptivists argue that standard language is more 'logical', more 'beautiful' and more 'correct', these are subjective judgements (see Labov 1972c; Milroy & Milroy 1999). The valuation of standard language over all other varieties is an arbitrary one. This view of the standard language is not just held by a few people, but rather forms the basis of a widely held and powerful ideology; that is, insisting that the standard variety is better than others is a way of expressing, claiming and maintaining power (Wolfram & Schilling-Estes 1998: 164). The consequences of negative attitudes to language varieties are a result of the link between access to power and language. Recall that the principle of linguistic subordination (see Chapter 7) states that the language of a marginalised group will also be marginalised. Therefore those in marginalised groups may be denied access to power because of their language use. In terms of social class, there are degrees of marginalisation. The lower on the social hierarchy a person is, the more marginalised in every respect they become.

The negative attitudes toward social class were apparent when the UK Chancellor of the Exchequer, George Osborne, addressed a group of employees in a supermarket warehouse in Kent. On this occasion, Osborne's language was characterised as non-standard although he typically uses a more standard variety. This kind of linguistic 'shifting' is called linguistic '**accommodation**' and is very common among speakers of any language. It is a strategy used by Osborne to perhaps gain some covert prestige, or at least reduce the perceived social distance between him and his audience. The media, however did not approve of Mr Osborne's linguistic accommodation. In fact, some labelled his language as 'mockney'. As one journalist put it, 'Mr Osborne was at pains to show his audience that he was on their side' (Deacon 2013).

In addition to the disapproval of Mr Osborne's linguistic accommodation, we also can see the very negative attitudes toward the working class language variety he was accommodating to. Deacon represented Osborne's speech in the following way:

> He spoke up for the Briddish, for people ooh wanna gedd on, for people ooh doan wanna be oudda work. It was iz job da make sure they be bedder off in work. Things ud be bedder fa business too, now he'd rejuiced corporation tax da twenny-three per cent.
>
> (Deacon 2013)

The way Deacon describes Osborne's speech as 'a swamp of slurring vowels, a tar pit of glottal stops' (Deacon 2013) demonstrates the negative views of working people's language. Moreover, it assumes that all people who work in a warehouse share a social class and a linguistic variety.

These sorts of negative comments about language are especially revealing. Remember that attitudes toward a group's language reflect attitudes toward a group. For example, expressing negative attitudes toward the language that working class people use is the same as expressing negative attitudes about the group. Culturally, it seems to be acceptable to criticise a language variety when it would not be acceptable to criticise the group in other ways. People know that labelling someone as 'white trash' is pejorative, but labelling their language in negative ways may be acceptable. This is true of all social identities. It applies in the realm of ethnicity, age, gender and social class.

Activity 9.2

What other language varieties are negatively assessed? How do these assessments carry over to the speakers of this variety?

9.3.1 Class as other

Very often, the 'hidden' ideologies we find in talk about social groups reveals the negative attitudes held about them. Just as we saw with other marginalised groups, social class creates a social hierarchy that marginalises and 'others' groups that are positioned lower in the hierarchy. The significance of social class in this respect is often overlooked because the terms used to refer to these groups are not obviously connected to social class. Nevertheless, close examination of the representation of social class demonstrates the negative attitudes held toward these groups by members of society. Because social class is salient everywhere, analogous terms that 'other' lower social classes exist in all English speaking countries such as 'bogan' in Australia, 'chav' in Great Britain (Hayward & Yar 2006) and 'white trash' in the US (Hartigan 1997). Note that these terms index social class and a set of characteristics including clothing, behaviour and language. Scholars have described the very negative attitudes that society has toward these groups (Gibson 2013; Hartigan 1997; Tyler 2008). The Australian term 'bogan' exemplifies how this 'othering' takes place.

> Bogans are stereotypically associated with crime, hard rock music, beer barns, customised old cars, and cheap clothing such as track suits, flannelette shirts, mullet haircuts, and the now iconic Australian sheepskin "ugg" boots.
>
> (Gibson 2013: 62)

While the term bogan is generally associated with low income, there is more to the designation than this. Bogans are also defined in terms of their consumption and leisure activities, both of which are perceived as unappealing by groups who are higher in the social hierarchy (Gibson 2013; Pini & Previte 2013). 'The use of bogan in some circles implies poor upbringing and bleak fortunes, a synonym for lack of wealth. But more deeply, bogan means an absence of cultivated aesthetics or tastes' (Gibson 2013: 64). In the case that someone who is labelled bogan acquires a certain amount of wealth (a 'cashed up bogan'), they are not considered 'middle class' and continue to be labelled bogan (Gibson 2013: 64). Gibson and others argue that this is part of middle class strategy to protect their power and hegemonic status. The clothing and habits attributed to bogans thus take on a greater significance for social class attribution than wealth or income.

9.3.2 'Chavspeak'

In the United Kingdom the term 'chav' refers to

> '(originally the south of England)' a young person of a type characterized by brash and loutish behaviour and the wearing of designer-style clothes (esp. sportswear); usually with connotations of a low social status.
>
> (OED)

Joe Bennett (2012) has explored representations of how chavs use language by examining books with titles such as *Chav!* and the *Chav Guide to Life*. These are meant to be humorous books and intended for a mass audience. Note that Bennett is not concerned with the actual language of chavs as described by linguists, but rather with the ways 'chavspeak' is defined by non-specialists. This type of sociolinguistic study is called 'folk linguistics'. Bennett finds in these books detailed accounts of the stereotypes and ideologies held about working class Britons.

Bennett observes that the linguistic features attributed to chavs are features that are actually widely used and reflect stereotypes of several marginalised varieties of English. For example, in order to speak like a chav, the reader is instructed on pronunciation such as using 'v' instead of 'th' (Example 9.1a), to drop h (Example 9.1b), include glottal stops (Example 9.1c), and avoid pronouncing 'ing' (Example 9.1d).

Example 9.1
a. muvaaa – mother
b. 'ave – have
c. aun'ie – auntie
d. aahyagaahndaahntaahnlayhtaah? – Are you going down town later?

(Bennett 2012: 10-11)

There is more than simply pronunciation to chavspeak, however. Bennett notes that chavspeak has a range of other conventions, including novel vocabulary items, specific topics of conversation and a communicative **style**. Features attributed to chavs seem to be stereotypical linguistic features found in many other varieties borrowed from other sociolects, including Black Englishes, West Indian English, rap and hip hop music. The books Bennett examined portray chavs as 'rude and incoherent: their language varies from a "mutated" form of English to "white noise"' (2012: 19). These books also show how 'language is available as a material on which to peg various social associations' (Bennett 2012: 20 following Hudson 1996: 211–16). That is to say, a range of negative characterisations about a group associated with a social class (or, other social groups) can be expressed simply by describing their language. Even wearing a particular piece of clothing may be enough to invoke these language ideologies and label a person as a 'chav'.

9.3.3 Pittsburghese

It is important to note that the stereotyping of non-standard Englishes can have positive functions too. Johnstone, Bhasin and Wittofski (2002) describe features of US working class English in Pittsburgh, Pennsylvania. In contrast to the negative perceptions of chavs, Johnstone notes that linguistic features in Pittsburgh seem to allow both positive and negative interpretations.

> In Pittsburgh, the same features that are in some situations, by some people, associated with uneducated, sloppy, or working-class speech can, in other situations and sometimes by other people, be associated with the city's identity, with local pride and authenticity.
>
> (Johnstone 2009: 160)

Local pride is evident in artefacts such as T-shirts, mugs and dictionaries containing local terms; these products are found in many parts of the English speaking world. Johnstone found that T-shirts from Pittsburgh display dialect words, local pronunciation and local values. These items are evidence of what people think of the English spoken there. One of the most salient features of Pittsburgh English is the word used for second person plural pronoun. While standard English does not have such a pronoun, several English varieties do have one (e.g. 'y'all' in southern US English). In Pittsburgh this pronoun is 'yinz'. Because 'yinz' is a non-standard feature, it is stigmatized. However, 'yinzer' has been positively embraced by some locals (Johnstone, Andrus & Danielson 2006: 97). The reproduction of words such as 'yinz' on t-shirts raises the profile of the pronoun by turning local linguistic variation into a product that can be bought. This is a signal of both identification of and even pride in the local language. Such reclamation has been found in other communities such as Corby, England and Kingston, Jamaica (Wassink & Dyer 2004).

The commodification of local language is found in many places. Have you noticed this in your region? Or, perhaps, a region you're familiar with? What does the linguistic variation that has been commodified represent? Where is it found? What does it mean?

9.4 LINGUISTIC VARIATION

9.4.1 New York City

Noticing that different department stores often cater to particular social classes, William Labov (1972a) investigated whether the use of a feature of New York City English (NYC) by store clerks varied according to the different store they worked in. In NYC, the pronunciation of 'r' has high prestige. Speakers who pronounce the 'r' in words such as 'card' and 'bar' are said to be 'rhotic'. It is important to note that although **rhoticity** is a prestigious feature in US English, it is not in many varieties of British English. This demonstrates the arbitrariness of value attributed to a linguistic feature (see Section 9.3).

Labov conducted his study in three department stores: Saks, Macy's and S. Klein. He determined their relative prestige on the basis of the location of the stores, the price of goods they sold, where they advertised and the general layout and aesthetics of the store itself. Saks was the most prestigious, Macy's was less prestigious than Saks and S. Klein the least prestigious of the three. In order to elicit the linguistic feature of rhoticity, in each department store he identified an item sold on the fourth floor and then asked clerks where he could find that item. Naturally, the person would respond 'fourth floor'. He would pretend not to have heard so that they would be required to repeat the answer. This provided up to four examples where rhoticity could be present. Figure 9.1 shows the results.

These results suggest that rhoticity is **socially stratified**, that is, it is used more by people associated with higher social class. It also appears to be used more when in word final position (in the word 'floor') and there is some increase when the response is repeated. Of course, not everyone who works in a store necessarily shares the same social class. Labov argues that salespeople 'borrow' prestige from the store in which they work (1972a: 45). The results certainly suggest that this is the case. A replication of this study in 2009 showed the same 'general pattern of social and stylistic stratification of [r]' although there were some differences, especially in relation to ethnicity and age (Mather 2011: 353).

Figure 9.1 Percentage of use of 'r' by clerks in three department stores (Saks, Macy's and S. Klein) (adapted from Labov 1972a: 52)

9.4.2 Norwich

Another classic study that reveals patterns in linguistic usage associated with social class was conducted in the United Kingdom. Peter Trudgill (1972) examined a number of pronunciations in the English spoken in Norwich. In order to allocate his informants to a social class, he considered their occupation, father's occupation, income, education, where they lived and in what kind of house. Each characteristic was given a score and then these scores were taken together in order to allocate people to a class. This resulted in five classes:

- LWC – Lower Working Class
- MWC – Middle Working Class
- UWC – Upper Working Class
- LMC – Lower Middle Class
- UMC – Upper Middle Class (Trudgill 1972:181).

In addition to examining the effect of class on linguistic variables, Trudgill also examined the changes in language use that occur in different speaking contexts. He elicited a number of styles:

- WLS –Word List Style (informants read a word list)
- RS – Reading Style (informants read a passage of text)
- FS – Formal Style (during the 'interview' itself)
- CS – Casual Style (other talk, usually before or after the interview)

The linguistic variable that we consider here is the pronunciation of 'ing' at the end of a word (e.g. fishing, swimming). In formal English 'ing' is usually pronounced fully. In other varieties 'ing' is often pronounced only with 'n'. In lay terms, this is referred to as 'dropping gs'. For our purposes, we'll refer to 'dropping gs' as the 'non-standard' variable, however, this variable is used by most speakers of English in informal contexts. Results of Trudgill's study can be seen in Table 9.1 and Figure 9.2.

Table 9.1 Percentage use of non-standard (ng) by Norwich speakers according to social class (adapted from Trudgill 1972: 91)

Class	Word list	Reading passage	Formal speech	Casual speech
Middle middle class	0	0	3	28
Lower middle class	0	10	15	42
Upper working class	5	15	74	87
Middle working class	23	44	88	95
Lower working class	29	66	98	100

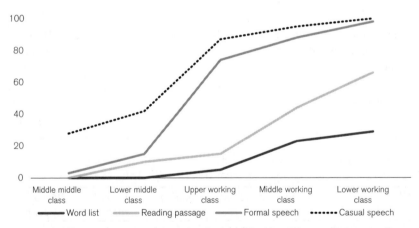

Figure 9.2 Percentage use of non-standard (ng) by Norwich speakers according to social class (adapted from Trudgill 1972: 91)

In these results, note that a score of 100 indicates consistent use of the non-standard variable. There are two important features of the results. First, each group uses the variable in varying amounts overall. Notice that none of the lines in Figure 9.1 overlap, showing that each class group uses the variable at a different proportion. The LWC uses the highest proportion of 'g dropping' of all the social groups, regardless of the speech context: they use it 100 percent of the time in the Casual setting and 29 percent in the most formal setting.

Second, each group's percentage of use changes according to speech context. That is, all groups use the non-standard variable less in the most formal context and vice versa. This type of change according to speech context is called **style shifting.** Even more interesting, with regard to style shifting, is how the lines/numbers in Figure 9.2 diverge. The lines representing (ng) use by the LWC and MWC run more or less parallel to each other, as do the LMC and MMC. The percentage for (ng) among the UWC shifts abruptly from the reading passage style to formal style. Trudgill observes that UWC speakers appear to have a 'greater awareness' of 'the social significance of linguistic variables', which can be 'explained by the "borderline" nature of their social position' (1974: 91). Trudgill describes this in terms of Labov's concept of '**linguistic insecurity**' (1974). Linguistic insecurity refers to a speaker's perception that their own (variety of) language is inferior to others. In the case of Norwich, this means that the LWC speakers believe their English isn't as 'good' as that of the MMC and UWC speakers.

While this pattern of usage of non-standard features in different contexts has been found in other groups, it's also important to remember the other variables we have considered in previous chapters that may interact with and influence language use. Trudgill's Norwich study provides a good example of this. Table 9.2 adds the variable of sex to Table 9.1 (Trudgill 1972: 182).

<table>
<tr><td>Activity 9.4</td><td>Draw a graph using the data in Table 9.2 (like the graph in Figure 9.2). How would you interpret the usage of non-standard (ng) by men and women?</td></tr>
</table>

Table 9.2 Percentage of use of non-standard (ng) by female and male Norwich speakers in four contexts (adapted from Trudgill 1972: 182)

Class	Sex	Word list	Reading passage	Formal speech	Casual speech
Middle middle class	M	0	0	4	31
	F	0	0	0	0
Lower middle class	M	0	20	27	17
	F	0	0	3	67
Upper working class	M	0	18	81	95
	F	11	13	68	77
Middle working class	M	24	43	91	97
	F	20	46	81	88
Lower working class	M	60	100	100	100
	F	17	54	97	100

Drawing a graph of the data from Table 9.2 will show you that in each class, men use more of the non-standard variant than women. There is one exception: the men in the LMC in the casual context use less than the women. Trudgill explains that the low score of men in this group, which would suggest they are using the prestige variant, is 'due to the fact that only a very small number of instances of this variable happened to be obtained for this group in CS' (1974: 93 n 1).

There are a number of explanations for this difference between women and men. Trudgill (1972:182) suggested women need to choose their linguistic variables carefully because of the lower social status they have in relation to men and because women are often evaluated not by their occupations but by how they behave. It is also possible to explain the difference by considering men's language. Trudgill argues that the men's linguistic behaviour may be explained by the '**covert prestige**' associated with this variety. Working class speech has 'connotations of masculinity, since it is associated with the roughness and toughness supposedly characteristic of WC [Working Class] life, which are, to a certain extent, considered to be desirable masculine attributes' (1974: 94).

9.4.3 Glasgow

We have seen that rhoticity is a prestige variable in New York. In the United Kingdom, however, it is associated with a variety of non-standard Englishes including Scottish English. Because this is a non-standard accent we might expect it to be stigmatised, and thus not used by the middle classes. Research undertaken in Glasgow, however, shows that this is not the case.

Stuart-Smith, Timmins and Tweedie (2007) undertook research on teenagers from both working class and middle class speakers in neighbourhoods of Glasgow. Of particular interest here is the fact that the neighbourhoods border each other. Bearsden, the middle class neighbourhood, lies to the north of the working class neighbourhood, Maryhill. A number of linguistic variables were investigated. Here, we discuss two: rhoticity (see Section 9.4.1) and a sound called a voiceless velar fricative, represented as /x/. The /x/ sound is found at the end of words like 'loch'. While a standard English speaker would pronounce 'loch' in the same way as 'lock', many Scottish speakers use a different sound. Rather than using a /k/, some use a sound more like 'kh' pronounced in the back of the throat, like the final sound in the name of the German composer 'Bach'.

The results of Stuart-Smith et al.'s research show that working class teenagers in Maryhill do not use /x/ nor are they rhotic. That is, for these two features, working class Maryhill teenagers use the same variants a speaker of standard English does. The Bearsden teenagers, however, use the Scottish variants of rhoticity and /x/.

As we have shown, typically we find working class speakers using more non-standard linguistic features than social classes above them. Among Glasgow teenagers, this is not what Stuart-Smith et al. found. In order to explain the use of these features, we need to consider what these features mean in the contemporary Glasgow context. Stuart-Smith and colleagues suggest that if we consider 'the language ideologies which speakers construct to make sense of social and linguistic practices in Glasgow' we may be better placed to understand what these features mean for the speakers using them (Stuart-Smith, Timmins & Tweedie 2007: 248).

Stuart-Smith *et al.* argue that working class teenagers are positioning themselves in opposition to the middle class teenagers (2007: 243). What the working class teenagers understand to be 'standard' is informed by the speech they hear middle class peers using. Working class teenagers 'are innovating and changing their form of Scots, as they polarise themselves linguistically and ideologically from middle-class speakers' (Stuart-Smith, Timmins & Tweedie 2007: 254). Working class teenagers abandon rhoticity and /x/ not because they want to align with 'standard English' but because they want to disassociate from the middle class teenagers. This shows that language and class can interact in various ways, with speakers' perceptions and attitudes having an effect on the meaning attributed to particular features. What seems to inform these changes is not class as such, but rather 'class based language ideologies' (Stuart-Smith, Timmins & Tweedie 2007: 224). Example 9.2 is a transcript of an interaction between a researcher and Maryhill teenagers.

Example 9.2

CT: (shows card with loch)
All: loch [k]
CT: You know how it's really meant to sound?
All: loch [x]
CT: And so why don't you say it that way?
All at once: that's pure gay
                       you need to be poofs
                       cos we're not poofs
                       pure Bearsden
                       pure daft
                       [and other similar comments for several seconds]
(Stuart-Smith *et al.* 2007: 253)

The Maryhill teenagers' comments suggest that there is nothing about the variant itself that they object to. Rather, they object to the people who they perceive to be using it: posh people. 'Being in opposition is the point' (MacFarlane & Stuart-Smith 2013: 768).

9.4.5 London

Young people in London are also drawing on the associations of particular codes to express their identities and also their attitude to specific events. Rampton (2011a) shows that his subjects at Central High in London clearly understand the difference between 'posh' and Cockney English and use linguistic features from those varieties to express different stances to topics and to other speakers. Example 9.3 is a transcript of speech from one student that took place in a drama class as students were about to make presentations.

Example 9.3

1.	Ninnette:	((calling out to the teacher, loudly:))
2.		MISS
3.		(.)
4.		MISS
5.		WE AINT EVEN DONE NU-IN
6.		(.)
7.		((even louder:)) MISS WE AIN'T DONE NOTHING
8.		(2)
9.		((not so loud, as if Miss is in closer range:))
10.		miss we aven't done anything.

(Rampton 2011a: 1240–1)

> In Example 9.3, look at the different ways Ninnette says the same thing in line 5, 7 and 10. What differences are there? How might you explain it?
>
> Activity 9.5

As line 7 shows, Ninnette clearly 'knows' the standard English form – 'haven't don't anything'. Even though 'have' is produced as 'ave', there is a progressive difference between her utterances in line 5, 7 and 10. Ninnette appears to know both the 'posh' and the Cockney variants and uses them in her normal speech (Rampton 2011a: 1241). It is possible to argue that she uses the non-standard form to attract attention (line 5), but once attention of the teacher is secured, she shifts to a more 'correct' variant (line 10). Ninnette seems to be aware of the prestige of standard English and the working class associations of Cockney. In this school, Cockney 'evoked solidarity, vigour, passion and bodily laxity, while posh conjured social distance, superiority, constraint, physical weakness and sexual inhibition' (Rampton 2011a: 1239). Ninnette understands that the world in which she lives in contains these class ideologies, and that these are associated with particular values and codes.

The examples of research in this section demonstrate that there is an association between language features and social class. Linguistic features can be used to index social class, attitudes to topics and other speakers, or perform different kinds of action. How the associations between language and social class are exploited depends on the context.

9.5 SOCIAL NETWORKS

Because of the complex relationship between language features and social class, models that don't rely on income or occupation to define social class have also been developed. One way to do this is to represent and quantify the relationships among people in a community. These relationships are called **social networks**. In this context, social network does not refer to online communities of people. Rather, it describes the type and frequency of interactions people have with one another. A social networks model allows us to focus on an individual while taking account of their relationship with other people.

Research undertaken in Belfast, Northern Ireland by Milroy (1987) examined the social networks of the individuals in three neighbourhoods. They developed a Network Strength Score (NSS) in order to quantify the strength of ties of individuals to the local area. Informants received 'points' for the following:

a.   'Membership of a high-density, territorially based cluster'
b.   Kinship ties with other households in the neighbourhood
c.   Works in the same place as at least two other people from the neighbourhood
d.   Works at the same place as at least two other people of the same sex
e.   Voluntarily associates with workmates outside of work

(Milroy 1987: 141)

A person with stronger ties with the local area would receive a high NSS while a person who is less connected to their neighbourhood would receive a lower NSS. These social networks can be described in terms of **density** and **plexity**. Density accounts for the *number* of other people they interact with. Plexity accounts for the different *kinds* of ties people have with others. For example, if a woman both works and socialises with her sister, this would be a multiplex (rather than uniplex) relationship. Dense, multiplex social networks are more common in traditional working class neighbourhoods (Milroy 1987: 137). Milroy and Milroy also found that dense, multiplex social networks compel conformity to local linguistic norms (1987).

Activity 9.6

Using Milroy and Milroy's Network Strength Scale, calculate your own network strength score. What do you think your score says about your social network?

Some linguistic variables showed the same patterns found by Labov and Trudgill, that women used more of the prestige variant than their male counterparts; however, not all of the women followed this pattern. For one linguistic variable (the pronunciation of /a/), young women in the neighbourhood called the Clonard used more of the non-standard variant than their male counterparts and more than women in the other two neighbourhoods. The NSS provides a way to interpret this result. In the Clonard, women had to find employment outside the neighbourhood, changing the nature of their social network. They had a high NSS as they were part of dense, multiplex social networks. What explains the difference between young men and young women in the Clonard is not their sex, but their social networks. The fact that these women are working outside their local neighbourhood is also important, as this provides access to new linguistic variables. The Belfast study shows that the 'traditional' working class neighbourhood was already changing.

9.6 COMMUNITIES OF PRACTICE

Penelope Eckert's Belten high study (1989a, 2009) provides a different way of thinking about the intersection of class and gender. Eckert did not classify informants according to where they lived or their parents' occupations. Instead, she spent time at the high school observing the behaviour, interaction and social practice of the students. It became apparent that there were two main groups in this high school; the 'jocks' and the 'burnouts'. Jocks are very much focused on academic achievement and success in school-sanctioned activity. Burnouts are less interested in school and orient to urban culture. The two different orientations of these groups with regard to school reflect class-based cultural norms, yet Eckert found that social class groupings did not account for the linguistic variation she found. Eckert notes that these two groups define the extreme poles of social positions available in the school, and that the majority of students belong to neither group and refer to themselves as 'in-between'.

Eckert argues that the jocks and burnouts should be thought about in terms of 'communities of practice' rather than representations of social class groups. A community of practice (CoP) is a group of people who have a shared common goal or activity. Because of the nature of the interaction in a CoP, they may develop their own linguistic norms. The individual CoP's norms are not pre-determined; rather, they evolve and are developed collaboratively by members of the group.

One of the linguistic variables Eckert investigated was **multiple negation**. This linguistic feature involves using more than one negation in a sentence such as in 'I didn't do nothing'. Multiple negation, negative concord, is considered non-standard in English and is often stigmatised. Figure 9.3 shows the use of this feature by jocks and burnouts.

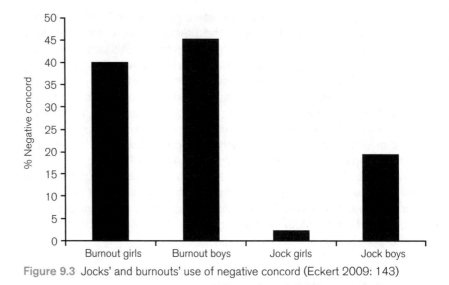

Figure 9.3 Jocks' and burnouts' use of negative concord (Eckert 2009: 143)

Figure 9.3 displays some striking contrasts. While the jock girls hardly use multiple negation, the burnout girls use it a great deal. In addition, the jock group overall uses multiple negation less than the burnouts. Figure 9.3 seems to bear out the predictions one would make, based on other research we have examined so far. However, if we examine the groups more closely, and abandon the notion that jocks burnouts are homogenous CoPs, we find

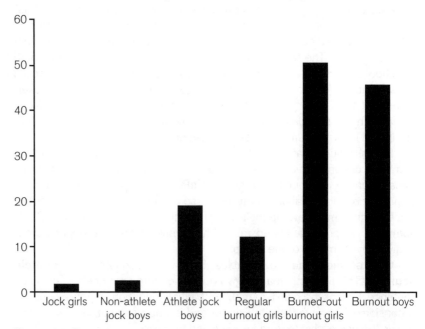

Figure 9.4 Percent use of negative concord by six subcategories of jocks and burnouts (Eckert 2009: 146)

that within the groups there are some finer distinctions. For example, especially for males, membership in the jock group does not require being on a school sports team. Therefore there are members of the jock group who are non-athletes. The women in the burnout group also distinguish themselves with more or less extreme burnout behaviour. Females who engage in the most extreme burnout behaviour are labelled 'burned-out burnouts'. Figure 9.4, shows the usage of multiple negation by subgroups of each CoP.

Figure 9.4 shows that the burned-out burnout girls use more multiple negation than any other group and that jock girls use it the least. Thus young women at Belten high are found at both extremes for usage of this variable. Neither social class nor communities of practice fully explain the results in Figure 9.4. To understand this, we need some new perspectives.

9.7 SYMBOLIC CAPITAL

According to Eckert (1989b), **symbolic capital** refers to intangible attributes a person can 'accumulate' in order to establish or improve their position in a group including society in general. Such attributes might include, a degree from a well-regarded university, an uncle who is a judge, mastery of a prestigious language and so on (Bourdieu 1984, 1991).

In Section 9.4.2, we saw that Trudgill observes that men are often identified by their profession, what they do. Women, on the other hand, may be more likely to be judged by their appearance, including how they speak and what they wear. As Eckert states,

> women are thrown into the accumulation of symbolic capital. This is not to say that men are not also dependent on the accumulation of symbolic capital, but that symbolic capital is the *only* kind that women can accumulate with impunity.
>
> (1989b: 256 italics in original)

Thus, the male jocks and burnouts can establish their jock or burnout status through their activities (e.g. sports, fights) while the female jocks and burnouts have to develop their jock or burnout image through symbolic means such as demeanour, clothes and language (1989b: 259). Eckert explains that 'Status is not only defined hierarchically: an individual's status is his or her place, however defined, in the group or society. It is this broader status that women must assert by symbolic means' (1989b: 256). The adolescents orient not to the 'standards' of broader society, but to their own local symbolic markets.

With regard to language, conforming to standard language practices is a key feature for being identified as a jock because jock activities are directed towards mainstream definitions of success: good grades in school, being an athlete and so on. What has symbolic capital for a jock (getting high grades in school) has very little value for a burnout. Non-standard language is valued in the burnout group; it has covert prestige. Members of both communities of practice want to accumulate prestige in their groups; precisely how to do this depends on what is valued by the particular community of practice. Figure 9.4, then, reflects the value that multiple negation has as symbolic capital for the burned-out burnout girls. For the burnout girls to display and perform their chosen identity, within their community of practice, the choice of the otherwise stigmatised multiple negation is logical. The same processes operate in other contexts and communities. Eckert's research demonstrates the importance of symbolic capital in understanding the performance of identity, especially for adolescents and women.

9.8 REVISING THE BRITISH SOCIAL CLASS MODEL

In the previous examples, we considered some models of identifying social class that focused on income and occupation and noted that these models are sometimes unsatisfactory for accounting for linguistic patterns we find. Savage *et al.* observe, 'this occupationally based class schema does not effectively capture the role of social and cultural processes in generating class divisions' (Savage *et al.* 2013: 220). That is, there is more to class than simply occupation or income. Savage, a sociologist, and his colleagues propose a new model of identifying a person's position in the social class hierarchy. Their model draws on the work of Pierre Bourdieu (1984), a French sociologist, who argued that there are three kinds of capital. First, economic capital refers to wealth and income. Second, social capital describes the social connections an individual can profit from. This kind of capital is recognised in the aphorism, 'it's not *what* you know but *who* you know'. Finally, cultural capital includes education, whether formal or related to other social practices. For example, a university degree enables you to apply for particular jobs. A recognised qualification in a foreign language may give you access to careers that were otherwise unavailable. Cultural capital gives you access to opportunities, people and lifestyles. It is a very durable kind of capital. A university degree doesn't diminish when a person 'spends' it, in the way that money does. Competence in particular forms of language is a form of cultural capital; being able to speak standard English may give a person opportunities they might not otherwise have.

In order to arrive at a more comprehensive social class model for Britain, they conducted a survey called the Great British Class Survey (GBCS). They asked over 160,000 Britons about aspects of their economic, social and cultural capital.

Table 9.3 Question categories for Great British Class Survey

Economic capital	Social capital	Cultural capital
Income, savings and value of home	The professions of social contacts	Leisure activities, including musical taste, hobbies and social activities

In the GBCS, cultural capital was assessed by asking about preferences in relation to food, clothes and leisure activities (Table 9.3). In Activity 9.1, you might have decided that while upper class people attend the opera and listen to classical music, working class people aren't so interested in these pursuits. These kinds of activities are often discussed in terms of 'taste' and include things such as the kind of food you like to eat (foie gras or pizza), the kinds of clothes you wear (haute couture or mass produced) and the kinds of places you like to visit (museums or casinos). These different preferences are not a reflection of which preferences are inherently better than others. The theory of social and cultural capital simply recognises that some attributes give people power in the social hierarchy in which they exist. While cultural capital may be durable, it is not always portable. Standard English may be worth very little in some contexts.

Savage and his colleagues assessed the GBCS results, together with an additional representative survey, and suggested seven social class groupings (Table 9.4).

Table 9.4 Summary of social classes (adapted from Savage *et al.* 2013: 230)

Social class	Description
Elite	Very high economic capital (especially savings), high social capital, very high highbrow cultural capital
Established middle class	High economic capital, high status of mean contacts, high highbrow and emerging cultural capital
Technical middle class	High economic capital, very high mean social contacts, but relatively few contacts reported, moderate cultural capital
New affluent workers	Moderately good economic capital, moderately poor mean score of social contacts, though high range, moderate highbrow but good emerging cultural capital
Traditional working class	Moderately poor economic capital, though with reasonable house price, few social contacts, low highbrow and emerging cultural capital
Emergent service workers	Moderately poor economic capital, though with reasonable household income, moderate social contacts, high emerging (but low highbrow) cultural capital
Precariat	Poor economic capital, and the lowest scores on every other criterion

The class groupings in Table 9.4 are a very different picture to the traditional high, middle and low class hierarchy. In particular, the new model identifies a new group they call 'precariat'. Further, this new system reflects changes in employment opportunities and also allows for different combinations of different kinds of capital (economic, social and cultural) to be recognised as distinct classes (e.g. new affluent workers, emergent service workers).

9.8.1 Power and access to symbolic capital

Sometimes groups do not have access to typical types of **symbolic capital**. Access to social capital depends on the position of the individual, but also on the ideologies that structure society. The most dominant ideologies can structure the world in concrete ways that prevent some members from acquiring symbolic capital. For example, many societies believe that deafness is a disability. This belief is called 'audism'. Because of audism, the deaf community does not have access to the same cultural and symbolic capital. Sutton-Spence and Woll observe that, in Great Britain, 'Social class does not have the same linguistic defining features for the British deaf community as for British hearing people. Deaf people are more likely to have unskilled and semi-skilled jobs than hearing people' (2004: 170). The fact that deaf people are more likely to have lower paid jobs demonstrates that the opportunities for claiming economic capital are limited. This is indicative of the marginalised position that the deaf community occupies in society. That is, because the hearing world privileges speech and hearing, accessing kinds of capital that rely on speech and hearing will also be difficult.

Activity 9.7

What other groups of people have difficulty accessing typical symbolic and cultural capital?

Sutton-Spence and Woll show that income is not a good way of defining class among the British deaf community (2004: 170). That is not to say that there is no social class system in the British deaf community. In fact, social class in deaf communities (in Great Britain) is linked to one's family. British deaf children born to deaf parents are more likely to 'have had early exposure to a good model of adult BSL [British Sign Language]' (2004: 170) and therefore are more likely to become members of a 'linguistic elite' in the British deaf community. Sutton-Spence and Woll argue that in the US deaf community, members of the 'recognized elite social class' (2004: 170) are those who attended the only university for deaf people in the world, Gallaudet University (an example of cultural capital) (Gesser 2007). Gesser's account shows that what counts as symbolic capital is local and depends on what the members consider to be valuable.

9.9 SUMMARY

Social class is difficult to define yet it is nevertheless a concept with social reality. In spite of this reality, many people do not recognise classism when it is present. We have also seen that there is some correlation between social class (variously defined) and linguistic features. The associations with particular linguistic features may be locally managed and what is esteemed in one community may be irrelevant in another. Therefore, models such as social networks and communities of practice illuminate what social roles are available and what is valuable symbolic capital in a community. Finally, we described a new model of social class developed in the UK. This model takes account of the different kinds of capital (economic, social and cultural) and provides a nuanced picture of what comprises social class in contemporary Britain.

FURTHER READING

Ash, S. (2004) 'Social Class', in J. K Chambers, P. Trudgill and E. Schilling (eds) *The Handbook of Language Variation and Change*, London: Blackwell: 402–22.
Block, D. (2013) *Social Class in Applied Linguistics*, London: Routledge.
Gesser, A. (2007) 'Learning about hearing people in the land of the deaf: An ethnographic account', *Sign Language Studies*, 7(3): 269–83.
Kerswill, P. (2001) 'Mobility, Meritocracy and Dialect Levelling: The Fading (and Phasing) out of Received Pronunciation', in P. Rajamäe and K. Vogelberg (eds) *British Studies in the New Millennium: The Challenge of the Grassroots*. Tartu: University of Tartu: 45–58. http://www.teachit.co.uk/armoore/lang/dialect. PDF
Loughnan, S., Haslam, N., Sutton, R. M. and Spencer, B. (2013) 'Dehumanization and social class: Animality in the stereotypes of "white trash", "chavs," and "bogans"', *Social Psychology*, 45 (1): 54–61.

CHAPTER 10

Global Englishes

10.1	INTRODUCTION	198
10.2	WHAT DOES GLOBAL ENGLISH MEAN?	199
10.3	LEARNING ENGLISH	202
10.4	INSIDE THE INNER CIRCLE	207
10.5	'SINGLISH'	208
10.6	INDIAN ENGLISH	210
10.7	PIDGINS AND CREOLES	211
10.8	LINGUISTIC MARKETPLACE	213
10.9	LINGUISTIC IMPERIALISM	214
10.10	WHAT DO LANGUAGE VARIETIES MEAN IN THE GLOBAL CONTEXT?	217
10.11	SUMMARY	219

10.1 INTRODUCTION

This chapter explores language and power by considering the use of Englishes around the world. It is important to note that we use the term in the plural form (English**es**, not English). While there have been some efforts to identify a single variety of English, which would be known as 'global English' and capable of functioning as an international 'lingua franca', linguists don't believe there is one variety of English that could or should be labelled as 'global English'. There are, nevertheless, strong opinions among non-linguists about which variety of English used around the world should be called 'global English' or a 'lingua franca'. This chapter explores what different perceptions of global English mean and how society negotiates these ideologies.

We begin by considering how 'global English' might be defined and the issues and ideologies that play a role in that definition. Different models for describing the multiple Englishes around the world are explored and the ramifications of these models, especially with regard to teaching and learning, are considered. Examples of UK, 'Singlish' and Indian English are presented to illustrate differences that exist among them. We then explore how different varieties of English play a role in social capital in the global linguistic marketplace and how perspectives on the position of English as a global language as active **linguistic imperialism** are presented. Finally we consider variation and subjectivity in the meaning of English by considering how it is used in linguistic landscapes around the world.

10.2 WHAT DOES GLOBAL ENGLISH MEAN?

In the first chapter of this book, we examined the question 'what is language?' To that end, we considered how language is a structured system that speakers inherently understand and learn along with linguistic and communicative competence. We also raised the topic of politics and power in relation to how languages are defined; that is, whether a variety counts as 'language' rather than simply a variety of another language is more a question of power and other ideologies than it is a question of linguistic structure or fact. These are key issues to keep in mind as we consider global Englishes.

In order to understand what global Englishes means, we begin with Kachru's model of 'World Englishes' (1985), which considers the different kinds of English around the world and provides a visual representation of these varieties that can be interpreted in different ways.

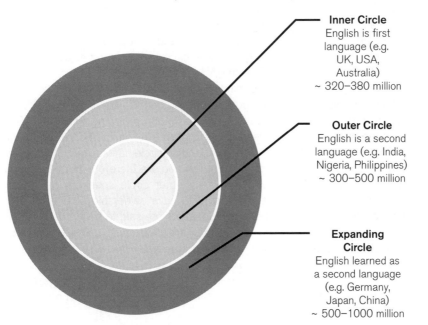

Inner Circle
English is first language (e.g. UK, USA, Australia)
~ 320–380 million

Outer Circle
English is a second language (e.g. India, Nigeria, Philippines)
~ 300–500 million

Expanding Circle
English learned as a second language (e.g. Germany, Japan, China)
~ 500–1000 million

Figure 10.1 Kachru's Circles of English

The concentric circles in Figure 10.1 outline the distinction that Kachru makes between inner, outer and expanding circle nations in the World Englishes context. Inner circle nations are countries where English is spoken as a first language ('mother tongue' or **L1**). They are very often nations to which very large numbers of people migrated from the UK. For example, the US and Australia are inner circle nations. Outer circle nations are countries where English is often one of the official languages and may even be an L1 for a section of the population, but it isn't the only official language. Outer circle nations are often countries that have previously been colonised by the UK and the relatively smaller number of migrants brought with them the English language. The expanding circle includes countries where English is used in addition to other languages. English may well be widely taught and learnt in the expanding circle, but it tends to be neither official nor the L1 of a majority of the population.

Whether a country is in the inner, outer or expanding circle, then, has little to do with geography but more to do with history, migration patterns and language policy. The circles in Figure 10.1 may nevertheless suggest a transmission from one circle to the other. Seeing the image in this way suggests that inner circle nations are the 'origin' of English and the language reaches other countries through a kind of diffusion, like ripples in a pond of water. Such a reading implies a one directional relationship between these nations with inner circle nations at the centre. This might suggest to some that inner circle nations are the originators of English. However, as Kirkpatrick observes, while Kachru's model does not suggest that one variety is better than any other (2007: 28), inner circle nations are, in fact, perceived as having greater ownership over the language, in that they have inherited English as their L1. Even among inner circle nations, not all nations can claim authenticity of the English language. The UK is widely perceived as being the 'origin' of the English language and is seen as the authority on what counts as 'standard' English; inner circle nations tend to be regarded as 'authentic' speakers of English (Evans 2005). However, as we will show, the English used even in inner circle nations is not homogenous.

Nevertheless, the ideologies about 'authentic' language are strong. Kachru describes inner circle Englishes as 'norm providing' (Kachru 1992: 5): inner-circle varieties, especially UK English, are considered the model for all Englishes to emulate. Therefore, expanding circle nations are not afforded permission to change the form of English and are therefore 'norm dependent' (Kachru 1992: 5). Even the many outer circle speakers for whom English is their L1 are not considered to have ownership of English that inner circle users have. Outer circle speakers are said to be 'norm developing' (Kachru 1992: 5). The norms they are developing come together in distinctive varieties of English that differ in a systematic way from those of inner circle nations.

So far, we've been discussing the 'origin' and ownership of English as it is connected to the inner circle. This raises serious issues about power and hierarchy. Before we consider these in more depth, it's worth considering Figure 10.1 again. Even though it is possible to understand this image as presenting inner circle nations as the originators of English, there is at least one other way to interpret it.

The number of speakers in each group indicates that there are far more expanding circle speakers of English than inner and outer circle speakers (Crystal 2003: 61). The numbers could be interpreted as representing sets of speakers, where inner circle speakers are − numerically speaking − a subset of both outer and expanding circle speakers.

Acknowledging both the number of speakers outside the inner circle and the prejudice that can attach to outer and expanding circle varieties of English, Jennifer Jenkins (2009) suggests that we should cease making a distinction between speakers of English. Jenkins uses the term 'World Englishes' for any English − irrespective of which 'circle' it fits into: 'In other words, my interpretation does not draw distinctions in terms of linguistic legitimacy between say, Canadian, Indian, or Japanese English in the way that governments, prescriptive grammarians, and the general public tend to do' (2009: 200).

The power and prevalence of attitudes about different varieties of English are captured by Jenkins' inclusion of governments, prescriptivists and the general public; and while Jenkins' position is very attractive as it acknowledges that all these varieties of English count as 'English', it is nevertheless important to pay some attention to the attitudes to English that are so prevalent.

If all varieties of English are included in a visual model of World Englishes, the possible 'circles' can be redrawn (see Figure 10.2).

Figure 10.2 seems to support Jenkins' interpretation of 'World Englishes' by including all varieties. Significantly, what this representation calls into question is the possibility of talking about 'English' as unspecified. At best, 'English' is a convenient abstraction that hides a great deal of variation in terms of phonology, syntax, lexis and also in terms of domain and power.

What these two different representations suggest is that we can approach World Englishes from a number of perspectives. The perspective chosen depends very much on the argument one wants to make.

The idea that there is a global English that is the same all over the world is unfounded. If it could be developed, it is unlikely that it would remain unchanged. As Mufwene remarks: 'If WSSE [World Standard Spoken English] were to arise spontaneously, or could do so at all, it would be the first such evolution toward linguistic uniformity in the history of language spread and contact' (2010: 46). In a sense, there is no such language as English − at least, it exists only in the most abstract of conceptions.

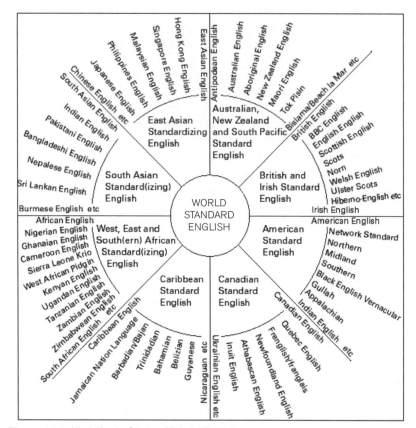

Figure 10.2 McArthur's Circle of World English

10.3 LEARNING ENGLISH

Learning English or any language as a second or additional language will usually mean that speakers will be found wanting when compared to the L1 standard. As we will discuss, linguists have argued that to use inner circle English norms as the 'standard' that all speakers should aim for is to create a goal that is both impossible (see Image 10.1) and stigmatising.

10.3.1 Two models

In the case of English around the world, then, there are at least two competing models. One is the English as a lingua franca model and the other a World Englishes model. Both have consequences for the kind of English that is taught.

Quirk argues for the importance of English teachers having English as their L1 (1990). Further, he argues that valuing regional ethnic and social varieties results in insufficient attention being given to the importance of

Image 10.1 Learning English

teaching a standard variety (1990: 7). Despite the existence of other varieties of English, such as Indian English, Quirk argues that students should
also aspire to and be instructed in standard English. 'It is neither liberal nor
liberating to permit learners to settle for lower standards than the best, and
it is travesty of liberalism to tolerate low standards which will lock the least
fortunate into the least rewarding careers' (1990: 9). Quirk's argument may
seem unappealing in the sense that it values local varieties of English less
than standard varieties. Kachru argues that Quirk's position is essentially
'deficit linguistics' (1991: 4) that portrays varieties that are not standard as
deficient in some way.

Lay people rate some varieties of English more highly than others (e.g.
Bayard, Weatherall, Gallois & Pittam 2001, Cowie 2007, Deuber 2013,
Evans 2005/2010, Ladegård & Sachdev 2006, Zhang 2013); however, the
context and the prevailing linguistic market (see Chapter 6) play important
roles in the esteem of the variety:

> Certainly, if I were a foreign student paying good money in Tokyo or
> Madrid to be taught English, I would feel cheated by such tolerant
> pluralism [of language varieties]. My goal would be to acquire English
> precisely because of its power as an instrument of international
> communication.
>
> (Quirk 1990: 10)

Indeed, students are aware of the hierarchy of Englishes. Marr (2005) describes the attitudes of Chinese students studying English in London. He found that they had chosen to study in the UK because they believed it was a place where they could learn 'standard' English. One student stated that the 'English language in England is the pure and original' (Marr 2005: 243). If the goal is a high power job in an inner circle nation, then standard English is precisely what is required. Until negative attitudes to outer and expanding varieties of English change, a local variety of English will not be as valuable as Standard English. However, Kachru argues that we 'cannot develop a language policy merely on attitudes' (1991: 9). Moreover, the particular linguistic market in which Quirk assumes speakers to be using language is not that in which many speakers live. Most outer and expanding circle speakers are using English to interact locally rather than to compete for jobs with the global elite. Kachru notes that 'English has become the main vehicle for interaction among its non-native users, with distinct linguistic and cultural backgrounds – Indians interacting with Nigerians, Japanese, Sri Lankans, Germans with Singaporeans and so on' (1991: 10).

As such, English is not simply used to interact with native speakers nor to understand British and American values, nor with any goal of 'nativeness' in mind. Kachru urges a full consideration of language use, in its social and cultural context, while also attending to the dimensions of power that the deficit model at least implicitly condones. There is no reason why there cannot be more than one standard (see also Jenkins 2009). The idea that there is, or should be, only one standard is an ideological exercise of power in which only those who 'own' the standard benefit. These benefits are both personal (in terms of what the variety gives speakers access to in the linguistic market) and also financial for those who produce materials using these standards for instruction.

Those who argue for more democratic standards acknowledge the current benefits of standard English. In order for a system of multiple standard Englishes to be accepted, however, there needs to be a paradigm shift (Kachru 1991: 11) that takes seriously the social, cultural and linguistic context in which many speakers of English actually live and work. The linguist Suresh Canagarajah argues that the teaching of English (or any language) must take into account the social, linguistic, and cultural context in which it takes place. Rather than inner and outer circle, he refers to the 'core' or 'centre' and 'periphery'. This highlights the power differential among language varieties.

> My position, then, is that while we must recognize the contextual appropriacy of different Englishes and teach students as many variants as possible ... it is equally important to teach students that any dialect has to be personally and communally appropriated to varying degrees in order to be meaningful and relevant for its users.
>
> (Canagarajah 1999: 181)

Canagarajah's position emphasises the importance of developing learners' use of many varieties. However, if the paradigm of hierarchies of English is to be changed, it also needs to be addressed in the inner circle community.

Referring to varieties of English as 'better' or 'worse' is − of course − vexing and technically inaccurate. This is exactly what Jenkins' concept of 'World Englishes' aims to remedy. For Jenkins, 'World Englishes' 'refers to *all* local English varieties regardless of which of Kachru's three circles they come from' (Jenkins 2009: 200). All these varieties are 'bona fide varieties of English regardless of whether or not they are considered to be "standard", "educated", and the like, or who their speakers are' (Jenkins 2009: 200). She is particularly interested in the use of English as a lingua franca, 'the common language of choice, among speakers who come from different linguacultural backgrounds' (Jenkins 2009: 200).

Consider the following statement from then Prime Minister of Singapore, Goh Chok Tong.

> Singlish is not English. It is English corrupted by Singaporeans and has become a Singapore dialect. . . . Singlish is broken, ungrammatical English sprinkled with words and phrases from local dialects and Malay which English speakers outside Singapore have difficulties in understanding. . . . Let me emphasise that my message that we must speak Standard English is targeted primarily at the younger generation . . . we should ensure that the next generation does not speak Singlish.
>
> (*The Straits Times* 29 August 1999; cited in Wee 2005: 58)

Do you think inner circle varieties would ever be described in this way?

Activity 10.1

It is often the case that speakers of outer and expanding circle varieties accept the negative attitudes toward their English as accurate. This belief is referred to as **linguistic insecurity** (Labov 1966). Lippi-Green (1997) suggests that by accepting their own variety as inferior, speakers contribute to the marginalisation of their variety: 'When persons who speak languages which are devalued and stigmatized consent to the standard language ideology, they become complicit in its propagation against themselves, their own interests, and identities' (Lippi-Green 1997: 66).

Wee (2005) argues that the defence of varieties of languages (like Singlish) is often forgotten in arguments about the protection of languages. While there are many who support the protection of endangered and indigenous languages, he argues that we also need to pay attention to intra-language variation and the maintenance of these varieties. Wee reports that views like those espoused by MP Chok Tong in Activity 10.1 led to the Speak Good English Movement (SGEM) in 2000, which endorsed inner circle varieties as 'good' while arguing that Singlish was not (Wee 2005: 58).

While the denigration of Singlish is common, there is evidence that speakers of varieties such as Singlish want to protect these languages because of the way they express both culture and identity for Singaporeans (Chye 2000; TalkingCock website; Wee 2005).

> Before teachers are likely to promote L2 inter-speaker variation in the classroom, they will need to experience a change of attitude towards it and, in turn, be equipped with the means of changing their students' attitudes (and this includes L1 students, possibly at secondary school level).
>
> (Jenkins 1998: 125)

For the purposes of English language instruction or teaching in the English language medium, the most important thing is probably to interrogate and investigate attitudes. Only then can learners make informed choices and – more importantly – perhaps start to shift the perceived value on different varieties.

> To prevent language attitudes from serving as false prophecies, or worse yet becoming themselves self-fulfilled prophecies, teachers should be trained to be sensitive to the variations in social dialects and the variations in performance. Language evaluation, which incorporates the attitudinal side of the social dialect coin, should be included as part of the teacher training process.
>
> (Williams, Whitehead & Miller 1972: 276)

Williams, Whitehead and Miller (1972) show that debates about attitudes to language and their impact on teaching have been around for some time.

10.3.2 'Lingua franca core'

The question remains, then, what variety of English should be taught to L2 learners? We have seen that Jenkins' concept of World Englishes seeks to remove the prejudice that attaches to some varieties. Jenkins also proposes a model for teaching that takes account of the linguistic difficulties of learning English as an L2 and which seeks to create equality among dialects of English. Jenkins points out that British and American English can be very difficult to acquire as second languages (L2). Part of this is due to the sound systems of the varieties. For example, the pronunciation of 'th' by L2 speakers of English frequently creates misunderstanding. Jenkins therefore argues that pronunciation of English could be more achievable for those learning English (Jenkins 1998: 119) if 'standard' pronunciation were ignored and more natural, simplified forms were taught. Jenkins argues that 'Any neutral, universal forms of English pronunciation, simplified or otherwise, will therefore probably have to be unplanned, emerging naturally from "below" rather than being imposed from "above"' (1998: 120). Nevertheless, Jenkins has proposed a 'lingua franca core' (LFC) in relation to pronunciation models of English for learners.

This model prioritises intelligibility over sounding like a native speaker of an inner circle variety. Features of the LFC are drawn from empirical examination of Non Native Speakers (NNS) and the variants that impeded intelligibility. In the case of 'th', substitution of 'v' or 'f' is acceptable in the LFC. We can't provide all details here (see Jenkins 2002: 96 ff); rather we simply note that the LFC, by promoting intelligibility over prestige, provides a practical model for teaching EIL (English as an International Language) and therefore makes an important contribution to eroding the power differential among varieties of global Englishes.

Likewise, Canagarajah points out that in English Language teaching contexts, especially in outer circle nations, learners should be permitted to develop a functional command of English (e.g. Canagarajah 1999). Thus, instead of judging learners on how well they can command a legitimated construct of an inner circle variety, the focus is successful communication.

10.4 INSIDE THE INNER CIRCLE

As indicated in Figure 10.2, there is a great deal of variation in the forms of English used around the world. Despite the arguments that appeal to some 'pure' or 'original' form of the language, identifying a 'standard' form is not straightforward. This is clear when one considers variation in inner circle nations. Here we consider an example from British English. Although McArthur's circle (Figure 10.2) acknowledges various 'British' Englishes, his representation is hardly the full picture. Just as English in outer and expanding circle nations is characterised by hybridity, contact and 'interference', so too is 'British English' (whatever that might mean).

As we noted earlier, there is a perception that British English is somehow more correct, more logical and more beautiful than other varieties of English. We can question at least the first two of these claims by considering the stigmatised use of 'ain't'. According to prescriptive rules, 'I ain't' is not 'grammatical' (see Section 1.4). This form may be interpreted as indicating a lack of education or lower social class. However, if we consider the linguistic 'job' that 'ain't' is doing, this form doesn't seem illogical at all. Table 10.1 presents a paradigm for the English verb 'to be' in the negative.

Table 10.1 'To be' in the negative with contraction options

	Singular subject	Plural subject	Singular subject Pronoun & are contracted	Plural subject Pronoun & are contracted	Singular subject are & negation contracted	Plural subject are & negation contracted
1st person	I am not	We are not	I'm not	We're not	I'm not	We aren't
2nd person	You are not	You are not	You're not	You're not	You aren't	You aren't
3rd person	She/he is not	They are not	She/he's not	They're not	She/he isn't	They aren't

What verb form would fill the gap in the first person singular contracted with the negation in Table 10.1.? Would your suggestion be accepted by prescriptivists?

The gap in Table 10.1 is known as the *amn't gap (Broadbent 2009). The * indicates that the form is 'ungrammatical' in the linguistic sense. Following the paradigm, the form 'amn't' is logically what should fill this gap. Why do you suppose 'amn't' has not filled the gap?

Try saying 'I amn't' repeatedly and quickly. What happens?

Having gathered and analysed data from Yorkshire in England, Judith Broadbent (2009) argues that 'ain't', having undergone a process of sound change, is actually a realisation of 'amn't' and thus fills the gap in Table 10.1 (but see Liberman 2014). This suggests that 'ain't' is, contrary to popular perception, in fact a logical solution to a gap in the English verb paradigm. This is more evidence of the arbitrariness of preferred prescriptive forms of so-called standard English ('ain't' is not a 'legitimate' verb form).

10.5 'SINGLISH'

Singaporean English (SgE) is comprised of several varieties. There are a number of different Englishes spoken in Singapore because of the number of L1s that are used there. These include Mandarin, Malay, Tamil and a range of other languages (Leimgruber 2012: 2). Most Singaporeans are multilingual and English is encouraged because 'from an official perspective, [it] is solely meant to strengthen international competitiveness' (Leimgruber 2012: 2). English is a medium of education and has become more common as the primary language used in the home (Leimgruber 2012: 3). However, there is also anxiety that learning English may bring with it particular cultural values, such as individualism, that are considered undesirable (ibid).

Standard English is advocated in education and by official language policy (Gupta 2004). Singlish, then, functions as a local variety of English in the same way as regional dialects in English-speaking countries such as the UK and the US. In places where standard English and Singlish exist, it is possible to say that it is a **diglossic** speech community. In a diglossic speech community, one language is considered the H (or High) variety and the other the L (or Low) variety (Ferguson 1959). Standard English, then, is the H while Singlish and other regional varieties of English are L. H and L varieties are used in different domains and for different purposes. Education, dealings with government and formal interactions take place in H while talk between friends and family is likely to take place in L. The belief that the L variety is not a language at all but rather a 'corruption' of the standard (Chapter 2) is common in diglossic communities.

Here we explore a feature of the outer circle variety of English known as Colloquial Singaporean English (CSE), also referred to as Singlish. We focus on **discourse markers**. A discourse marker structures utterances, especially longer ones, but also provides important cues about the attitude of the speaker towards what they are saying or responding to. It should be understood, though, that there are other ways CSE varies when compared to standard English.

One of the many discourse markers found in Singlish is 'ah'. Deterding (2007) shows that this is used to mark the topic of an utterance. In addition to the discourse marker 'ah', topic marking is also accomplished by putting the topic at the beginning of the sentence. The Example 10.1 shows how both of these strategies are used together.

Example 10.1
a.   Reading, ah, I guess, erm … fictions (Deterding 2007: 72)
b.   Magazines, ah, magazines … er … mmm … all sorts lah, I guess I would try to read … also kinds of magazines (Deterding 2007: 72)

Note that examples in 10.1 put the topics ('reading' and 'magazines') first, then followed by 'ah'. The rest of the information follows after this topic marking. As Deterding points out, something generally follows 'ah' (2007: 74). Leimgruber notes that 'ah' seems to be a discourse marker that is very frequently used. The second discourse marker we examine, 'lah', may be less commonly used but it is closely associated with the idea of Singlish and is often used to index this language and the identity it conveys. 'Perhaps the one word that is most emblematic of Singapore English is the discourse particle lah' (Deterding 2007: 66). Examples 10.2 a–c demonstrate how the particle is used as a discourse marker in Singlish.

Example 10.2
a.   shopping-wise, nothing much to buy there lah, basically (Deterding 2007: 63)
b.   a lot of things to do lah, so didn't really enjoy the three weeks there (Deterding 2007: 66)
c.   I do enjoy talking to them at times lah, yah, er yup but … OK lah I guess (Deterding 2007: 68)

In these examples, note that 'lah' comes at the end of clauses. Deterding notes that the particle 'serves to soften the tone of an utterance and build solidarity between speakers' (2007: 74). Given this function, and the meanings of Singlish itself, it is not surprising that this is considered its emblematic discourse marker. Leimgruber argues that CSE and standard English in Singapore signal very different meanings. While Singlish is associated with localism, informality, closeness and community, standard English is linked to authority, formality, distance and educational attainment (2012: 56, following Alsagoff 2007: 39). The different forms of these varieties are connected to very different functions. The distinction between these varieties is not only *when* they *should* be used but also *what they communicate*, over and above content.

10.6 INDIAN ENGLISH

According to the models outlined previously, Indian English is another outer circle variety, which arose from a history of colonisation by the UK. While we have pointed out that some people in India use English as their L1, it is not the case that all people in India speak English. Sailaja notes that while few people report English as their 'mother tongue', over 64 million people use English (2009: 3).

Nevertheless, it is generally accepted that there is a variety of English called 'Indian English', which bears traces of contact with other languages used in India, especially Hindi. Some of the syntactic and lexical features in Table 10.2 are found in Indian English (Sailaja 2009, 2012).

While we can identify some unique features of Indian English, it is not a variety that lends itself easily to description. Nor does Indian English fit easily into first/second/additional language divisions. As Sailaja notes, 'while it is a second language to most of its speakers, many users, especially those who are displaced from their regions, claim it as their first language. It remains alien to many others' (2012: 360). Further, given the particular link of region, language and identity in India, it is not easy to get reliable self-reported figures of language use. People may still report their 'mother tongue' as the regional language regardless of their own proficiency (Sailaja 2012: 360).

Sailaja also cautions against describing Indian English with feature lists (as in Table 10.2) as they have 'the danger of creating the impression of homogeneity, uniformity and universality' (2012: 366). She argues that more research and documentation of this variety is needed. Indian English demonstrates the complexity and difficulty in attempting to define global Englishes.

Table 10.2 Examples of Indian English

Syntactic features	
'No' as interrogative tag	You will come, no? (Sailaja 2009: 59)
Wh- questions no inversion	When you will begin? (Sailaja 2009: 57)
Use of progressive tense	I am having three books with me. (Sailaja 2009: 49)
Additional prepositions	To accompany with, to combat against (Trudgill & Hannah 2002:132)
'Itself' and 'only' as emphatic	We arrived today only; We will be required to have our classes here itself (Trudgill &Hannah 2002:132)
Lexical features	
Compound formation	key bunch (Sailaja 2012: 362), time pass (a relaxing leisure activity Behera and Behera 2012), good name (first name Behera and Behera 2012)
Pluralization of mass nouns	furnitures, aircrafts (Trudgill & Hannah 2002: 130)
Borrowings from Hindi	'thali' – plate; 'bandh' – strike (Sailaja 2012: 362)
Semantic variation from Standard English	'drama' – play; 'stir' – agitation (Sailaja 2012: 362)
Hybrid constructions	Police-wallah; paper wallah – where 'whallah' means 'occupation' (Sailaja 2012: 362)

10.7 PIDGINS AND CREOLES

In discussion of global or world Englishes, attention is often given to varieties not found in the inner circle. When turning to other circles, the question of what counts as a language and what might be considered a variety of English becomes even more complicated. The wide range of **pidgins** and **creoles** that are used throughout the world contribute to this issue. Pidgins are used as lingua francas largely for trade or other practical interaction. A pidgin will draw on the languages of the interlocutors in order to bring together the linguistic resources necessary for these tasks but is not the L1 of speakers in the community. Because of the specific uses of pidgins, they may be 'little more than strings of nouns, verbs and adjectives, often arranged to place old, shared information first and new information later in the sentence' (Bickerton 1983). The language providing vocabulary is called the **lexifier,** while the language that provides the syntactic structure is called the **substrate** language. After an extended period of use of a pidgin in a community, it becomes more fully developed, and serves as an L1 for the community. The language at this stage is called a creole. Note that the term 'Pidgin (with capital P)' is sometimes used to refer to a variety that is actually a creole. Activity 10.4 is a text in Hawai'i Creole English (HCE).

The following text in Hawai'i Creole English (HCE) is from the Bible (http://www.pidginbible.org/Concindex.html). Can you identify features that vary with respect to standard English?

Day Numba One
[3]Den God say, 'I like light fo shine!' an da light start fo shine. [4]God see how good da light. Den he put da light on one side, an da dark on da odda side. [5]Da light time, he give um da name 'Day time.' Da dark time, he give um da name 'Nite time.' So, had da nite time an da day time, az day numba one.

Vocabulary items in Activity 10.4 are identifiable as English, demonstrating that English is the lexifier language although the written form suggests that there are phonological differences. There are significant differences in syntax due to the number of languages (including Cantonese, Portuguese and Japanese) that contribute to the form of HCE (Siegel 2000). A translation of the Bible into HCE serves as evidence that HCE has a full range of functions and is in every sense a language. Table 10.3 demonstrates a few of the differences between HCE and English.

Table 10.3 Some features of Hawai'i Creole English (HCE)

Feature	HCE	English
'Get' means both 'has/have' and 'there is/there are' (Sakoda & Tamura 2008)	'They get three sons'	'They have three sons'
	'Get one student he bright'	'There is a student who's bright'
Like in many other languages, no verb is required in some sentences (Hargrove, Sakoda & Siegel)	Mai sista skini	'My sister's skinny'
'Wen' is used before a verb to indicate past tense (Sakoda & Tamura 2008)	Ai wen si om	'I saw him'

Although creoles may draw on English as either a **lexifier** or **substrate** language, they are not simply varieties of English but fully functional languages. The distinction is not easy to draw and there may even be a continuum in a speech community between an English-based Creole and a local variety of English. As we have seen, both will be stigmatised in relation to a standard variety and this is the case with HCE (Drager 2012; Ohama, Gotay, Pagani, Boles & Craven 2000, and see Wassink 1999 for Jamaican Creole).

10.8 LINGUISTIC MARKETPLACE

We have already encountered the concept of 'social capital' as developed by sociologist Pierre Bourdieu (Chapters 1 and 6). In relation to global Englishes, social capital is also relevant. The difference is the context, that it is a global linguistic marketplace rather than a local one. Local markets in the global context do not, however, cease to be important. Rather, these local markets need to be understood as situated in a broader linguistic economy. We have already discussed the importance of different attitudes towards varieties of English (Chapter 1), but it makes sense to consider attitudes to varieties in terms of social capital and global linguistic markets as this highlights the power that accrues to speakers of esteemed varieties.

The metaphor of linguistic market is particularly useful in the context of global Englishes. There is a great deal of research into language attitudes and what kind of capital one accrues on the basis of particular varieties of English (see Section 10.3.1). What people think about a variety will have an influence on what context they think it is appropriate for. Knowing the value of a variety of English on the linguistic market is crucial in understanding and deploying the linguistic resources a person has. Some argue that the linguistic market is controlled by global elites and that their 'elite' variety of English becomes important as a symbolic resource (Bourdieu 1977).

Which variety of global English do you think has the most value in the global linguistic marketplace?

Activity 10.5

In Activity 10.5, you probably guessed that inner circle Englishes, particularly UK English, are the most highly valued in the global linguistic marketplace because of the complicated interaction of language ideologies and the global political landscape we described above. This means that people who wish to enter the international job market cannot compete for jobs if they do not have a suitable level of fluency in the 'right' form of English (although it should be noted that this is also true on the local level; see Chapter 9).

Such attitudes, especially when linked to access to the labour market, can be understood in terms of changes in the labour market that are being brought by the globalization of all types of markets.

10.8.1 Call centres and English

Many businesses rely on 'call centres' for a variety of services that they provide to their customers. In a call centre, employees of a company provide service to customers over the phone. Because the service to the customers is provided over the phone, the call centre may be located in a place that is not near the customers or the company headquarters. Sometimes, companies will 'outsource' such labour to save money. That means that a call centre may even be located in a foreign country. In order to get hired in a call centre that serves English-speaking customers, an employee must have an excellent command of English.

Claire Cowie's (2007) research documents the demand from companies for employees working in call centres in India who have or can learn 'neutral' English accents. Cowie notes that it is difficult to know what 'neutral' means in this context, but she suggests it may refer to an 'unmarked' variety, a variety that is not easily identified in terms of place or status. As we have already seen, in the context of global English, whether an accent is marked or not is completely relative to the context in which the language is used, and the individuals using it. Other research on call centres also documents the importance of employees having the 'right' type of accented English (Friginal 2009; Rahman 2009). Rahman studied the linguistic capital of a 'neutral accent' in the Pakistani call centre labour market: 'This accent is the scarce good, the salable commodity, which enables the [customer service representatives] to cross linguistic boundaries and, if successfully deployed, even pass as native speakers of English' (2009: 238). Further, Rahman notes, 'Call centre workers consider their acquired accent not only a business necessity but also "normal," thus implying the deficiency of all other accents and, hence, the desirability of changing them' (Rahman 2009: 250). This demonstrates the deeply rooted ideology of hierarchical organisation of varieties of English in Pakistan.

Heller (2003) describes the commodification of language in Francophone Canada to highlight the many tensions created by this commodification in the global economy. Such tensions may arise between the authenticity of L1 speakers and standardised varieties or hybridity versus a stable corporate image. All these tensions have ramifications for the global labour market.

10.9 LINGUISTIC IMPERIALISM

Some scholars focus on the **hegemonic** nature of English around the world; that is, because of the political and economic dominance of English speaking countries, the English language is seen as dominant (Phillipson 2003). While most scholars attribute the position of English to 'the particular history of the English-speaking nations' (de Swann 2010: 72), others are more specific than this, linking this history to a conscious project of expansion and acquisition of power. Phillipson and Skutnabb-Kangas argue that the spread of English is indicative of a more general neo-imperial project, one that seeks to encourage the growth and dominance of neo-liberal values, including freedom of trade, freedom of action for corporations and free movement of money. 'English can be seen as the *capitalist neo-imperial language* that serves the interests of the corporate world and the governments it influences' (Skutnabb-Kangas & Phillipson 2010: 82). This perspective highlights the power, maintenance and spread of English. Evidence for this view can be found in a range of places, including the institutional infrastructure of the EU (European Union). There are 23 official languages in the EU (de Swaan 2010: 69). While all of these are used informally, for official documents and public events, English is used most of all (de Swaan 2010: 70).

In addition to an active project of expansion, some label English as a 'killer language' (e.g. Phillipson 2003): one could interpret the number of speakers of English and the way English is used around the world as correlated with the well-established death of many minority languages.

de Swaan characterises English as a 'hypercentral' language, 'the hub of the linguistic galaxy – like a black hole devouring all languages that come within its reach' (2010: 57).

What are the underlying assumptions in this quotation?

Activity 10.6

Calling English a 'black hole' or even a 'killer language' suggests that there is something about English itself that is a danger to other languages. However, as de Swaan points out, the present status of English 'has nothing to do with the intrinsic characteristics of the English language; on the contrary, its orthography and pronunciation make it quite unsuitable as a world language' (2010: 72). Attributing human attributes to a language overlooks the impact of activities of governments, corporations and other bodies as well as the language attitudes associated with that language.

Mufwene (2010) describes the reasons people acquire English, largely for professional advantage, and notes that such acquisition does not necessarily lead to abandoning one's first language. Language death, he argues,

occurs insidiously, when the socioeconomic structure of the relevant populations forces them to communicate more often in a dominant language other than their ancestral one, without them realising what the long-term effect of their communicative practice is, namely loss of capacity to use their respective heritage languages.

(2010: 50)

Socioeconomic structure is the most relevant issue and it is impossible to disentangle the global economic structure from the status and future of languages. While it may make logical and economic sense for speakers to abandon their languages in particular contexts, how these conditions came about is also worth exploring.

Activity 10.7

Table 10.4 presents details on the language used at home for Chinese people in Singapore. What trends can you see? What might the trends suggest about language policy and the economic context?

Table 10.4 Language most frequently spoken at home among Chinese resident population in Singapore aged five and over (adapted from Lee Eu Fah (n.d))

Home language	1990 (%)	2000 (%)	2010 (%)
English	19.3	23.9	32.6
Mandarin	30.1	45.1	47.7
Chinese dialects	50.3	30.7	19.2
Others	0.3	0.4	0.4

Table 10.4 shows that Mandarin use at home among Chinese residents in Singapore is increasing (Lee Eu Fah nd). Silver (2005) describes evolving language policy in Singapore, noting that while English has always been seen as important for global economic competitiveness, there is now also recognition of the importance of Mandarin in this context. It is perhaps not surprising then that there is a 'Speak Good Mandarin' campaign (Silver 2005: 58) that is parallel to the 'Speak Good English' campaign (see Section 10.3.1) and thus confirms the importance of Mandarin in this community.

The connection between economic power and language works in many ways. It is not simply that a language provides economic and symbolic capital once it has been acquired. As Mufwene notes, gaining a language 'comes at a cost ... the expense and effort of language learning itself' (2010: 66). If resources are limited, it makes sense to acquire only one language. Ammon notes, 'sets of competing languages function to some extent, like zero sum games: the rise of one can entail the fall of the other' (2010: 118). The relevant resources include not only those of the individual concerned but also of the nation in which they live. It is possible, for example, to produce multilingual individuals if the education system is set up to do so. Of course, this relies on education being affordable, accessible and well provided for in terms of teaching staff and materials. Under good conditions, the acquisition of another language can result in additive multilingualism.

There are many viewpoints on **linguistic imperialism** and the positive or negative effects of the position of English as a global language. The arguments made depend very much on the goal of the author. Some may want to highlight injustice, lack of power and language death. This position highlights linguistic and other inequalities in the world. While accepting that there are inequalities, others seek to change this state of affairs, drawing attention to the relationship between language, trade, economics and language policy.

10.10 WHAT DO LANGUAGE VARIETIES MEAN IN THE GLOBAL CONTEXT?

As we have seen, there is no such thing as a singular global English, and we've discussed in this chapter and others the impact of language ideologies and how they lead to consistent perceptions of language variation. At the same time, it is important to be careful about making generalisations. In the global context, we must consider how English is transported around the world, how it is modified in local contexts and what it means to those who use it. Blommaert points out that it shouldn't be assumed that varieties will have the same effect when they are used outside their local context. In other words, if a local variety of a language is used outside of that local context, the audience may or may not notice the relative meaning associated with that variety. According to Blommaert,

> Values and functions of resources are attributed locally, and people construct meanings on the basis of codes, conventions, hierarchies and scales available to them … but the values and functions thus attributed to resources … are not necessarily transferrable to other environments.
>
> (Blommaert 2003: 44)

Further, because language is an important aspect of how people construct their identities, the different meanings of a variety have consequences for the identity a person is able to construct. For example, Singlish is an important marker of local Singaporean cultural identity. The government programme of encouraging 'standard English' indicates that Singlish is valued in informal contexts but not in formal contexts such as education and government. In terms of linguistic markets, Singlish provides a great deal of cultural capital for Singaporean identity, but may provide very little in other English speaking contexts. Singlish is very valuable in some contexts but in others doesn't count as a legitimate language (Blommaert 2009: 565).

Blommaert notes that we can make sense of these different values, these different markets and contexts, in terms of Dell Hymes' 'second linguistic relativity' (2009: 565 ff). In Chapter 2 we outlined linguistic relativity, the idea that the language a person speaks has an effect on how they interpret the world. Second linguistic relativity takes into account what language is used for, the social context in which it is used. The associations that a listener has with a language depend on the variety used. Therefore it is not possible for English to have a single affective association because the associations a listener or speaker makes with it depends on where it is used, in what form and by whom. This is second linguistic relativity; what the language denotes is relative to the form it takes and the context in which it is used.

> Whenever discourses travel across the globe, what is carried with them is their shape, but their value, meaning or function do not always travel along. They are a matter of uptake, they have to be *granted* by others, on the basis of the dominant [values].
>
> (Blommaert 2009: 567)

In other words, not all varieties are equal. This inequality has consequences for the people who use these languages. As Blommaert notes, '*differences* in the use of language are quickly, and quite systematically, translated into *inequalities* between speakers' (Blommaert 2009: 567; see also Mufwene 2010).

10.10.1 Discourse in advertising and linguistic landscapes

As we have seen, English is widely used around the world. In fact English can be found in contexts even where a consumer is not expected to know English. Discourse in advertising and linguistic landscapes in transnational contexts demonstrates the ideology of valorisation of English. For example Androutsopoulos (2013) describes how English is used in Germany in marketing brochures, commercials, webpages and magazines. He calls this usage 'a framing device that establishes, symbolically or indexically, frames of interpretation for the adjacent national-language content' (2013: 234). Piller (2001: 180) argues that in Germany 'English has become thoroughly associated with a certain segment of German society as it appears through advertising discourse: the young, cosmopolitan business elite'. This means that the use of English in commercial contexts points the audience to a particular way of understanding a text. For example, the use of an English expression such as 'hip-hop' in a heading for a story in a music magazine immediately evokes a set of meanings and representations of hip-hop musical culture for the readers. This set of meanings can only be evoked by an expression like this; thus, using English in this way may be a means for indexing a variety of meanings that help sell, persuade and inform. 'This leaves English to do mainly symbolic work, to work through stereotypical associations with the language, its speakers, and the cultures where it is spoken' (Piller 2001:180). This type of usage of English has also been studied in other countries. For example, Troyer (2012: 110) found that in Thai online newspapers

English is used to associate products and services (especially those related to media and technology) with concepts of modernity, globalization, mass communication and media, commerce, and wealth while Thai is used to initiate a closer connection between sponsor and audience in advertisements for organizations and events.

This type of symbolic meaning is found even in expanding circle nations such as the D R Congo (Kasanga 2012a) and Cambodia (Kasanga 2012b). The symbolic usage of English around the world demonstrates the power and influence that English has. Nevertheless, it is important to remember that, as discussed, the meanings that English may evoke are variable according to the locale and audience.

10.11 SUMMARY

In this chapter we have explored why global English cannot be considered a single way of speaking. It refers to many different varieties of English and each has their own value and meaning associated with them depending on the speaker and the context. Language ideologies play a very important role in these meanings and therefore afford certain varieties a great deal of power and influence in the local and global linguistic marketplace.

FURTHER READING

Chew, P. G. (2007) 'Remaking Singapore: Language, Culture and Identity in a Globalized World', in A. B. M. Tsui and J. W. Tollefson (eds) *Language Policy, Culture, and Identity in Asian Contexts*, Mahwah: Lawrence Erlbaum: 73–93.

Evans, B. (2010) 'English as Official State Language in Ohio: Market Forces Trump Ideology', in H. Kelly-Holmes and G. Mautner (eds) *Language and the Market*, London: Palgrave.

Gupta, A. F. (2004) 'Singlish on the Web', in A. Hashim and N. Hassan (eds) *Varieties of English in South East Asia and Beyond*, University of Malaya Press: Kuala Lumpur: 19–38.

Jenkins, J. (2009) 'English as a lingua franca: Interpretations and attitudes', *World Englishes*, 28(2): 200–207.

Seidlhofer, B. (2009) 'Common ground and different realities: World Englishes and English as a lingua franca', *World Englishes*, 28(2): 236–45.

CHAPTER 11

Projects

11.1	**INTRODUCTION**	**220**
11.2	**THINGS TO BEAR IN MIND WITH DATA COLLECTION**	**221**
11.3	**PROJECTS**	**223**
11.4	**RESEARCH RESOURCES**	**230**

11.1 INTRODUCTION

In this chapter, we provide some ideas about projects you could do to explore the topics introduced in this book. The best way to find out about what language is and what it means is to go and see how the language around you is being used. In the chapters so far, you have read about some of the research that sociolinguists do. The important thing to remember is that every language community, every text, every utterance can tell us something new. The way that you use language, the way that communication occurs with your friends or in your family is all valuable sociolinguistic data. But as you may have realised already, a lot of this data passes us by. We're so accustomed to using language to do things, that we don't normally pay much attention to how we do this. We seem to know instinctively what works and what is appropriate; but think about how difficult it would be to explain these rules to someone new to the language situations that you know.

The projects will give you some idea of what sociolinguists do when they conduct research. It should give you an understanding of the kind of work involved, how long particular kinds of investigations take and what kinds of questions we can ask. Most importantly, we hope that in doing some of these projects (or designing your own) you'll realise that the language that you use or observe is just as interesting, and complex, and worthy of consideration, as the examples that have been given throughout the text.

Some of these projects are based on particular topics that have been covered. However, more often than not, it will be helpful to consider topics and approaches from a variety of perspectives rather than just those suggested by a particular chapter in the book. For example, transitivity analysis (Chapter 2) is useful in all kinds of contexts. Likewise, recording and transcribing conversation is an excellent way to examine the tiny details that we're not generally aware of when participating in, or even listening to, conversations.

11.2 THINGS TO BEAR IN MIND WITH DATA COLLECTION

11.2.1 What is data?

Data can be found everywhere in many forms. Sociolinguists work with spoken and written data. Obviously, written data can be easier to work with as you don't need to transcribe it. You need to consider data as any language that is used by people, in all kinds of situations.

One easy way of collecting spoken data is to record the people you know. There are two advantages to this. First, it will be easy for you to obtain permission from the people you record. It is imperative to inform your respondents that they are being recorded and obtain their permission to do so (see BAAL guidelines). Linguists never record anyone without their knowledge, as this is unethical.

Second, people you know will feel more comfortable being recorded by you. If people are self-conscious about being recorded, they're more likely to 'perform'. The problem raised by the presence of the researcher and the desire to get natural speech is usually spoken about in terms of the 'observer's paradox'. The paradox is that you want to observe, to be present, but exactly this presence may change the way people speak. There are a number of ways to minimise the effects of the paradox. One strategy Jennifer Coates used was to have respondents record themselves when she wasn't there (2002). William Labov suggests asking respondents to tell a story about an emotional event. Such an emotional story may reduce the amount of attention people pay to being recorded and to their speech performance. There might not be a good way, or even any way, of overcoming the observer's paradox. When you're analysing your data you must remember the observer's paradox, especially in terms of what you can claim about the way your respondents use language. Sometimes it is clear in the data that respondents are thinking about being recorded. There may be evidence that the speakers are or are not aware of being recorded. Do they constantly refer to the fact of being recorded? It's impossible to be inside someone's head and know for certain whether they are aware of being observed. This doesn't mean that you can't trust your data. It just means you have to think carefully about *what* you can trust it to tell you.

11.2.2 Transcribing

If you are working with recorded data, you need to transcribe it: you need to construct a written representation of the spoken data. You can see some examples of transcription in Chapters 6, 7 and 8. You may have noticed that some details of the talk are indicated with symbols and other typographic conventions. These details are explained in a 'transcription key'. There is a transcription key provided at the start of the book.

Transcription is a very time consuming process. As a rule of thumb, it takes at least four hours to transcribe one hour of clearly recorded speech. Transcription time will increase if there is more than one speaker or if the quality of the recording is poor, but it is important to construct a good, detailed transcription. It is not possible to make claims about characteristics of a conversation without this level of detail. It can take a few times of listening to figure out what people are saying; so you need to be patient and listen to your data more than once.

11.2.3 Data analysis

Analysing data requires spending time looking at and thinking about the material. Everyone has their own methods for working with data and these projects should help you research and develop your own methods by trying out different methods to see what works for you. Ideally, when you collect your data you will have a clear question in mind, or a particular feature you want to examine.

If you're not sure about what you expect to find, one way to begin is to look for surprising characteristics; sometimes things 'jump out at you'. Think about and speculate on why you noticed it. Is the characteristic something very unusual (for the speaker or the situation?), is it something you don't understand, or is it something that appears in more than one place in the text or the conversation?

If this doesn't work, consider the kinds of variation we find in language that we have discussed in earlier chapters. For example, transitivity analysis (Chapter 2) is a good feature to consider when looking at written texts, particularly persuasive texts. With patience, and attention to detail, you can discover and describe the data. Further, when you're working with data it will usually be impossible to say *everything* about it. If you're going to say anything meaningful about what the patterns are, you have to focus on a small number of features. If you've spent enough time with your data, the analysis will always provide more than you can write up in a paper of reasonable length.

Different types of text will require you to look for different features, but the same general approaches that we have described will still be useful to get you started.

The following projects are suggestions for research to help you practice the skills and understand the theories in the previous chapters. The projects suggest features that you might look for and questions that you might ask about your data. It's important to remember that the data you have limits the questions you can ask about it. Your conclusions must be supported by sufficient evidence in your data. For example, if you have conversational data from men in their 20s, you obviously won't be able to say anything about how women behave in conversations, or about how older or younger men might behave. You also won't be able to say anything about what these same men might do in the presence of different people (women, older men, and so on). Every data set has specific limitations. The goal of this kind of research is not to come to conclusions about the whole of the human race. You will learn something about how *these people* use language in *this situation*. Therefore, you must choose your data set carefully.

11.3 PROJECTS

Project 1 – Mini-dictionary

Your task is to compile a mini-dictionary of novel linguistic terms in your speech community. Language changes all the time. While lexicographers constantly update dictionaries, the process is slow. In any case, some words or expressions don't stay around for very long. Over the course of at least a week, keep a notebook with you and write down all the words and expressions you suspect you wouldn't find in a dictionary. It may be the case that the word is common, but the particular meaning is not. Think about what the words on your list mean (their definition) and how they can be used. You might need to sit down with friends and test their intuitions about how terms can be used. If it's an adjective, can it be used only about people or also about things? If it's a verb, what kind of subject can it take? Does it need an object? Choose at least six words and write as full an entry as you can for each one. Look it up in a good dictionary (like a full version of the Oxford English Dictionary). Does it appear there? Does it have the same meaning? Try and see if other people also use the terms you found in your speech community. Can you find anything out about the history and origins of these terms or how long they have been in use? Some words are used in very limited contexts or in a particular way. For example, in British English, 'bang' can be used in specific collocations as an intensifier, e.g. 'bang on time', meaning exactly on time; 'bang up to date', meaning completely up to date. When the first author encountered this term she tried it out as an intensifier in all kinds of situations. To express the shaggy nature of a toothbrush, she said, 'bang old toothbrush'. A competent member of the speech community informed her that this was not how the intensifier is used.[1] 'Bang' can only be used as an intensifier in a very limited set of circumstances. Documenting the details of use and meaning of new may require more thought than you would expect.

Project 2 – Political speech

In this project, the task is to examine political speech in detail in order to uncover strategies of persuasion, self-representation and conveying information. Choose a recent speech by a politician from your country or region, then choose another speech, either from the same politician to a different kind of audience or on a different topic. You might also choose a speech from a different politician to compare to; but pick a speech that is similar in some way to the first. You'll need the audio from each speech. Transcribe them, including pauses, stress on particular words, hesitations and 'mistakes'. You might also find it useful to make a note of speed if this varies through-out the speech. It's a good idea to transcribe any laughter or applause from the audience too. For national politicians, you can often find transcripts of speeches on a government website. Don't assume their transcripts will be accurate or include the information you need, but you can use it as a starting point to save some transcription time.

Examine each speech carefully. What is the goal of each speech? Is it intended to inform or persuade? Is it an emotional or a rational speech? How is the argument constructed? You will need to provide evidence from the specific linguistic choices made to justify your conclusions about the speech. For example, if you think that it is an emotive speech, you will probably look for particular word choices (recall the paradigmatic axis in Chapter 2). What register is used? Is it formal or informal? There are any number of tools and concepts you can use for this project, but it's a good idea to look at Chapters 2, 3 and 4 for an idea of what might be appropriate. Compare the similarities and differences between the two speeches.

Project 3 – Your own many voices

This project explores how your own use of language changes in different situations. Sociolinguists call this change 'style shifting'. Over the course of a week, record yourself in different situations. You may not be able to analyse all the data, but you should have a good selection of your speech in different contexts. Remember to be aware of sections of the data where you're aware of the recording. You'll need to focus on analysing only the natural, spontane-ous data. It can be very difficult to be objective when analysing yourself so you might try to team up with a colleague and exchange data.

You will probably have conversations with friends, conversations with family, talk in a work context, talk in a service encounter. Choose a small amount from each of the different contexts, about a minute, and transcribe them. Are there any differences in the way you talk? Do you address people differently? Do you use different words? Do you speak in a more standard way in some contexts? Thinking about the different kinds of variables examined in the book (age, gender, ethnicity and so on), which are relevant in the way your language changes?

Project 4 – Conversational politics

This project explores conversation in groups to find whether some participants have more power than others in the conversation. There is always a structure in conversations that all participants contribute to, to a greater or lesser extent. Very often each person plays a particular role in a conversation. For example, who seems to be directing the conversation? Sometimes the most powerful participant in a conversation is a child or baby (or even the television). Record a conversation that involves a group of people. You might choose your family or a group of friends. Is there someone who interrupts more than other people? Who asks questions? Who chooses topics of conversations? Whose contributions are responded to or laughed at? Ochs and Taylor (1992) may be useful as a model for analysing your conversations.

Project 5 – Expertise in the media

This project explores representations of expertise in the media (see Chapter 4). Choose a media report on a scientific issue. This may be about scientific research, a health risk of some kind or even unusual weather. Gather other reports on the same issue from a number of different outlets. Analyse the use and representation of expertise. Are experts quoted? What is their expertise? How are they identified? Is there more than one expert identified? How much emphasis are their views given?

Project 6 – Representation of women/men

This project explores the representation of women or men and involves written data. Narrow your data by choosing an issue and medium to focus on in the data. For example, you might want to look at news stories where a woman/man is involved, how a female/male politician or celebrity is written about, or how health and fashion features aimed at women/men are constructed. You can collect data from newspapers, magazines, television, radio and/or the internet. What words are used to address and describe women/men? What adjectives are used? What values and ideologies underlie the representations you are working with?

Project 7 – Titles around the world

The titles *Miss* and *Mrs*, because they are always followed by the family name of a father or husband, are historical reminders of a time when women were regarded as the responsibility, or indeed the property, of their fathers and husbands. While women's political and economic rights have changed considerably in many countries, the English language still allows us to mark the marital status of women in ways that do not exist for men. Is women's marital status marked in other languages? If so, how? It's important to examine a language you know well or to have a consultant who speaks that language natively. Do people try to avoid title and surname conventions when they get married? How can they do this with their language? You might investigate the use of titles and surnames in same-sex civil partnerships, which are frequently referred to as 'marriages'. One resource might be wedding announcements in newspapers or coverage of celebrity same-sex partners to gather the data here. How might labels for these new types of partnerships affect the language system?

Project 8 – Identity

These days, when you apply for a job or a course of study, you are usually required to fill in a form about your ethnicity, age, nationality and disability status. Find as many of these types of forms as you can. What terms are used for indicating a person's identity? What categories are included? From the categories and the labels and language used, is it possible to tell what is considered 'normal' or unmarked? What does this indicate about this society? Are the forms for different purposes the same? Are there identities that aren't represented? A local careers office or job centre or national census survey would be a good place to find some.

Project 9 – Friendly talk

This project is an analysis of both the conversational style and the different types of discourses in an extract of talk between young girls. The extract captures conversation between Ardiana, Hennah, Rahima and Varda, four 15-year-old Bangladeshi girls from London (Pichler 2009). In this extract, these girls align themselves with a modified version of a discourse of arranged marriage, that is, they very much accept that their families will play a role in finding their future spouse. However, the girls object to certain forms of arranged marriage, in particular to being married to boys from Bangladesh. In addition, as with all groups, there is always a certain amount of negotiation of different positions and discourses that takes place before a consensus can be found. Some things to consider in your analysis are if and how the conversation contributes to the girls' construction of (gender) identities within their friendship group. Complement your analysis of the extract with some data from your friends talking about what they think about marriage, whether arranged or not. Record and transcribe some of their conversation. Analyse it in the same way as you analyse the extract. Are the discourses the same?

(1)
Ardiana   EXCUSE ME I LOVE MY BOYFRIEND here right I don't wanna

(2)
Ardiana   get married to somebody else I don't /**know**
Hennah   (-)   [(inn]it) (.)
Rahima   (-) innit ma[n]
Varda   (-) {- - - laughs - - -}

(3)
Ardiana   [but then
Hennah   {amused}he may be gorgeous but then again he mig[ht have a

(4)
Ardiana   again (a] ha-)
Hennah   (a)]   personality like a (.) **ape** or **some**thing=

(5)
Ardiana   =YEAH:: [that's] true (.)
Dilshana   [yeah]   (.) yeah when they come to England

(6)
Ardiana   they just wanna get
Hennah   [(they just]xxx-)
Dilshana yeah they just lea[ve you man]

(7)
Ardiana   married to girls from London [because like they are Londoni]
Varda   [yeah because of the passport]

(8)
Ardiana   (.) **yeah**   [they are from London they are British] they are British
Varda   (.)   [they want their passport inn]it
Dilshana   (ah[::){agreeing}

(9)
Ardiana   and they wanna come to this country as well
Varda   (-) {swallows} they want

(11)
?Varda   the passports (the British) passport

Project 10 – Little bits of data

Personal ads in a magazine or newspaper constitute what Michael Hoey
identified as a 'discourse colony'. The discourse colony is a particular kind of
text 'whose component parts do not derive their meaning from the sequence
in which they are placed' (Hoey 1986: 4). Because the colonies have small
component chunks, they provide a ready-made set of small texts that can be
compared and contrasted. First, identify the discourse colony you want to
examine (personal advertisements, job advertisements etc.); then, think
about what features are interesting in the texts that could be compared to

each other. For example, you might want to compare job advertisements from the public and private sector. Alternatively, you might want to compare the same kind of discourse colony from different publications, perhaps comparing letters to the editor from magazines read by women to those in magazines read by men. You'll need to analyse the texts closely, paying attention to their syntax, lexical choices and structure. What do you find, and why do you think the texts are structured in the way they are?

Project 11 – Children's television

At certain times of the day, usually morning and afternoon, television channels broadcast programmes for children. These programmes are often composed of different segments joined together. In between segments hosts of the programme conduct competitions, interview celebrities and so on. Focusing on the hosted sections, transcribe parts that are addressed directly to the audience (the camera/children). Is there anything distinctive about the way the audience is addressed? Is a specific vocabulary or tone used? Does language speed up or slow down? Are there any features of Child Directed Language (see Chapter 8)?

Project 12 – Data in plain sight

Sometimes the most interesting data to analyse is that which you probably never considered worthy of examination. In 2009, Veronika Koller examined the Christmas catalogue of a major British retailer, Boots the chemist (2009). She examined the difference in written text between sections aimed at men and those aimed at women. Her results demonstrate a clear gendering of products and audience. Gather some examples of marketing for different brands of the same product. The junk mail that comes to your home might be a good source for this. For example, brochures from mobile phones, internet and television providers, charity appeals and local services might be interesting resources. Gather data from a range of companies providing the same service. Look at the language used to describe the products and to address the reader. Pay attention to the other representational choices that are made. What kinds of colours are used in the material? What do the photographs show? Working with such data lends itself to quantitative research. Choose about six very specific features and conduct quantitative and qualitative analysis on them. You might find van Leeuwen (2004) useful to look at.

Project 13 – Email and texting

This project examines text messages. Many people now have mobile phones and use them to text (SMS). Save all your incoming and outgoing texts for a period of time. How long this should be depends on how active you and your friends are in terms of texting (so that you'll have enough data for an analysis). How does text language differ from other kinds of written language? Are there differences in syntax, spelling and lexical choices? Are other symbols used? Finally, do text conversations share any features with face-to-face conversations? You can think about this by writing out an exchange of text messages as though it were a face-to-face conversation (using transcription conventions). Does this look like a 'real' conversation?

You might like to add a second component to this project. Once you have analysed your data and thought about why the use of language may be the same or different, interview some of your texters. You could ask them why they text (instead of phoning); do they use language differently when texting; have they noticed texting conventions; has their language use in other areas changed because of texting? You might like to take notes when interviewing, but it's also very helpful to record the interview. You may not need to transcribe all of it; but transcribing some of the interview conversation with texters will give you very useful comparative material for deciding whether 'real' conversations and text conversations are similar or different.

Project 14 – Email spam

This project explores communication strategies used in spam. Spam mail is the junk mail of the virtual world. But it is useful for something. Blommaert and Omoniyi (2006) argue that spam can tell us important things about globalisation. Gather some spam from your email account (make sure it's not something dangerous for your computer or so offensive you don't want to spend time with it). Try and gather a few examples of the same kind of text, and choose examples with more written language than pictures. Through detailed analysis of the language, try and identify features that could signal its identity as spam. What kind of features these will be will depend on the kind of text you're looking at (and how good the spammers are).

Project 15 – Blogs and vlogs

This project examines blogging and vlogging in order to explore the conventions of written and spoken language in an emerging genre. Blogs are a reasonably recent genre of online interaction. Brown (2008) argues that they are a place where we find linguistic innovation. Identify a blog to analyse. You might like to choose comparable material (about the same subject) from different bloggers, or you might like to follow an individual blogger over time (there are usually archives on their sites). Alternatively, you could choose a vlog (video blogging). Examine the structure of the texts and identify new lexemes or syntax. Are these features linked to the purpose of the blog? Do they succeed in portraying a particular identity? Are some forms of blogs more successful than others? To answer this last question, you'll have to think about what blogs are for.

Project 16 – Linguistic landscapes

Many scholars have studied the significance of public signs, their legal significance and their linguistic force. Signs that detail legal rules are every-where, from parking signs to conditions of entry to shopping centres. Collect as many examples of regulatory signs as you can. What you will find depends on your local area, though parking lots are excellent places, as the contrac-tual terms are often detailed near the entry for the car park. Look at the kinds of syntactic choices that are made. Pay attention to pronouns and modal verbs. What kinds of transitivity choices are made? Are the notices clear? Would you say they constitute information, requests or warnings?

11.4 RESEARCH RESOURCES

11.4.1 Where to find published research

You might like to look at research being published in specialist journals. Your school or university may have access to these, but there are often some articles and issues that are freely accessible. Even reading the abstracts will give you a good idea of the kind of work that researchers are doing.

> *Communication and Medicine*
> *Critical Discourse Studies*
> *Discourse and Society*
> *International Journal of Speech Language and the Law*
> *Journal of Language and Politics*
> *Journal of Sociolinguistics*
> *Language in Society*
> *Language Variation and Change*
> *Text & Talk*

11.4.2 Other resources

There are a great many resources available online which may be useful for your own research or project work. Some of them have been mentioned already.

> *Ethics* – BAAL (British Association of Applied Linguistics) Recommendations on Good Practice: Student Project Version (http://www.baal.org.uk/about_goodpractice_stud.pdf)

Blogging linguist – Language log (http://languagelog.ldc.upenn.edu/
  nll/) This is a blog that a number of linguists contribute to. It is an
  interesting and often amusing insight into the concerns of linguists,
  especially in relation to language in the real world.

Transcription resource: www.transcribe.com

Computers and language – Sociolinguistics and Computer Mediated
  Conversation (http://sociocmc.blogspot.com/)

Dialects – American Dialect Society (http://www.americandialect.org/)
  BBC Voices (http://www.bbc.co.uk/voices/): hear samples of
  different accents and dialects.
  International Dialects of English Archive (http://web.ku.edu/idea/)
  While this is a resource for actors, the international perspective is
  very useful.
  Language Varieties (http://www.une.edu.au/langnet/) A site from
  Australia with language varieties you might not find elsewhere.
  Languages in Ireland website (http://www.uni-due.de/IERC/) A
  great deal of information including an aural map.
  'Sounds Familiar? Accents and Dialects of the UK' (http://www.
  bl.uk/learning/langlit/sounds/index.html) Multimedia pages at the
  British Library
  The Speech Accent Archive (http://accent.gmu.edu/) English
  accents from around the world.

Dictionaries – links to a variety of different dictionaries (http://
  linguistlist.org/sp/Dict.html)
  (http://www.singlishdictionary.com/)
  Dictionary of American Regional English (http://dare.wisc.edu/)
  Macquarie Dictionary of (Australian) English (www.macquariedic-
  tionary.com.au)

Law and language – Forensic Linguistics Institute (http://www.thetext.
  co.uk/index.htm) A site with texts that you can analyse and information about what forensic linguists do.

Lists of and for linguists – (www.linguistlist.org) This website has a
  number of different areas which you may find useful, from dictionaries to information about current research projects.

It is becoming more usual for large research projects to have websites that
detail the work they're doing. For a whole list of and links to ongoing research
projects, which gets updated: http://linguistlist.org/sp/Projects.html

FURTHER READING

Cameron, D. (2001) *Working with Spoken Discourse*, London: Routledge.
Carter, R., Goddard, A., Reah, D., Sanger, K. and Swift, N. (2007) *Working with Texts:
  A Core Introduction to Language Analysis*, Adrian Beard (ed.), London:
  Routledge
Cukor-Avila, P. (2000) 'Revisiting the Observer's Paradox', *American Speech*, 75(3):
  253–4.

Hillier, H. (2004) *Analysing Real Texts: Research Studies in Modern English Language*, Basingstoke: Palgrave.

Mallinson, C., Childs, B. and van Herk, G. (2013) *Data Collection in Sociolinguistics: Methods and Applications*, London: Routledge.

van Leeuwen, T. (2004) *Introducing Social Semiotics*, London: Routledge.

Wray, A. and Bloomer, A. (2012) *Projects in Linguistics and Language Studies*, 3rd edn, London: Routledge.

NOTE

1. Thanks to Isobel Scott-John for her expertise and patience in inducting Mooney into the British speech community.

Glossary

AAE – African American English.

accent – a way of describing the set of features that characterise a speaker's language. Accent is usually used to refer to pronunciation and may provide social or regional information. See also **dialect**.

accommodation – adjusting the way one speaks to be more like a real or imagined interlocutor.

active and passive – verbs can be in the active or passive form. This changes the location of the agent of the verb. In active constructions, the agent is first; in passive constructions the agent is last and can be deleted. 'Fido ate the biscuit' is active; 'The biscuit was eaten by Fido' is passive.

address forms – a word or phrase used when speaking to a person in order to identify them. The form used depends on the context and the relationship between the two people. Address forms include titles such as 'Mr' and 'Ma'am' and also less formal terms such as 'darling' or 'mate'.

adjective – words used to modify a noun or provide further information about it. For example, the italicised terms are adjectives: 'the *hungry* dog' or 'the *intelligent* woman'.

affective – related to affect, that is, emotion. For example, tag questions may have an affective function, to signal concern for another speaker or invite them to participate in a conversation.

agency/agentive – agency can describe the role of the agent in a sentence (see active/passive). It can also be used to describe the power people have over particular actions, events or processes.

arbitrariness of the sign – this is Saussure's theory of the sign, specifically that there is no necessary connection between the signifer and the signified.

asymmetry/asymmetrical see **symmetry**.

asynchronous communication – communication that takes place when interlocutors are not present in the same temporal location. In asynchronous communication there is a lag between turns. Letter writing and email are asynchronous. See also **synchronous communication**.

audience design – a model that attempts to explain why speakers adjust their speech for the audience/interlocutor they are speaking to. See **accommodation**.

auxiliary verb see **modal auxiliary verb**.

back channel support – the practices that listeners engage in to display they are paying attention to a speaker. This includes nodding, facial expressions and **minimal responses**.

bilingual – strictly, having two (bi-) languages; but also used for someone who speaks more than one language.

binomial – a noun phrase that consists of two nouns placed together, usually separated by 'and'. For example, 'fish and chips' is a binomial.

child directed language (CDL) – language used by adults to speak to children. CDL is characterised by slower and more explicit language that is perceived to facilitate language acquisition.

citizen journalism – a type of user generated content, where people who are not professional journalists provide material for broadcast or publication in news outlets.

code – a general term that may refer to a language (linguistic code) or any other semiotic code, including colour, typeface, dress and so on.

code switching – when a speaker changes from one language or variety to another. This may occur in a variety of linguistic contexts such a word, phrase or a longer stretch of talk.

collocation/collocate – combinations of words that frequently appear together such as 'salt and pepper', often in a noun phrase. Frequent collocations can indicate the connotations of a word, and other associations.

communicative competence – in contrast to **competence and performance**, communicative competence is the knowledge a speaker uses to construct utterances that are appropriate for a particular speech community.

community of practice – a group of people who come together for a common aim or activity. Communities of practice often develop their own ways of using language. Sociolinguistics has taken up this model of interaction to examine local language use.

competence and performance – competence is knowledge of the rules of a language, its syntax, semantics and so on. Performance is actual use of the language, how competence is exploited. See also **communicative competence**.

conative – one of Jakobson's six functions of language. The conative function of language is relevant when the focus of the message is the addressee, or the speaker's attitude to the addressee.

connotations – the associations of word, over and above its denotative meaning.

covert prestige – the assignment of positive value to a language or variety that exists only within a particular group. A variety that has covert prestige is valued within the community it is used but not the wider community. See also **overt prestige**.

creole – a language that has emerged from two or more languages in contact. In contrast to a pidgin, a creole functions as a first language for its speakers.

crossing – the use of a language variety by a person who is not a member of that variety's speech community in order to express a particular attitude stance.

cultural capital see **symbolic capital**.

deictic – a word that depends on context in order to communicate meaning. Common deictics include 'here' and 'there'. A physical sign may also perform deictic functions by pointing to something. This relies on spatial context.

denotation – the literal meaning of something, that is, what a term refers to. See also **connotation**.

density see **social networks**.

descriptive/description – the approach to language that seeks to describe the features of language as it is used by speakers rather than to prescribe the form that should be used. See **prescriptivist**.

diachronic – examining a situation as it changes over time. See also **synchronic**.

dialect – a way of describing the varying features (e.g. syntactic, phonological, lexical) of a language. Dialects may be linked to region, social group or other identity. See also **variety**.

dialectologists – those who study and document language varieties.

discourse – a term used in linguistics with a range of meanings. First, it refers to various forms of communication such as conversation among people, written texts, and the like. Second, it refers to the ideology that underpins a text. For example, 'the discourse of romantic love' refers to a set of ideas about behaviour and conduct relating to love. Further, it refers to even larger ideological structures that are referred to as 'dominant' discourses.

discourse marker – a word whose function is to structure speech rather than provide meaning. 'So', 'well', 'now', 'really' and the like are all discourse markers.

dominant discourse see **discourse**.

dysphemism see **euphemism**.

epistemic modal forms – a form of modal auxiliary verb that expresses levels of certainty.

ethnographic – a research methodology that seeks to describe a particular society or event through such methods as participant observation and interviews, usually over a long period of time.

ethos – one of three persuasive strategies. Ethos involves appealing to or relying on the credibility, status or reliability of the speaker. See also **pathos** and **logos**.

euphemism – a word to refer to something unpleasant or offensive in a more appealing or positive way. Dysphemism does the opposite, making something pleasant seem unappealing.

face threat – an action or utterance that either impedes a person's desire to do something or impedes their own self-image. Face threatening acts (like requests) may be mitigated in some way (for example, with 'please') to reduce the face threat.

first person pronoun, see **pronoun**.

foreground – to draw attention to something; this is a visual metaphor, something that is put in the foreground is made more prominent. This can also be done linguistically, through the use of marked terms, stress in speech or other modes of emphasis.

given information – in contrast to new information, given information has already been explicitly introduced in a text or is assumed by other structures. See also **presupposition**.

hedges – linguistic devices or forms that minimise at utterance in some way. This may take the form of epistemic modals, tag questions or other discourse markers. For example, one might say 'I *think* she arrived' to hedge the claim that she did in fact arrive.

hegemonic (adj) /hegemony (n) – refers to the social, political or cultural dominance of one group or **ideology**.

ideology – an organised collection of values or beliefs.

imperative – a verb form, which is a command. 'Come!' or 'Speak!' are both imperative forms.

imply, to – a way of communicating something without directly saying it. This is very similar to **pragmatic presupposition**.

in-group – refers to the relationship of members to a group. The in-group is a group to which a person belongs. In contrast, an out-group is a group to which a person does not belong.

interlocutor – another way of describing an addressee.

interpellation – describes the way people are addressed and positioned by ideologies (Althusser 1971).

interruption – variously defined as simultaneous speech and an utterance that stops the interrupted person speaking.

intertextuality – generally used to refer to the referencing of or allusion to one text by another. This may be done by obvious quotation, parody or borrowing a textual feature readily associated with another text.

L1 and L2 – an abbreviation for Language 1 and Language 2: a person's first language (L1) and their second language (L2).

langue – the language system or building codes, according to Saussure. The language people actually produce depends on langue, but is called parole.

lexical item – a term used by linguists to refer to 'a word'.

lexicographer – a person who documents the changing meaning of works in a language and writes dictionaries.

lexifier – the language which serves as a lexical base for a **pidgin** or **creole**.

life stage perspective – this perspective considers age as defined by the various periods that people pass through as they get older rather than as determined by how old a person is in years.

lingua franca – a language that is not native to either speaker or listener but is used for communication.

linguistic determinism/relativism – also known as the Sapir-Whorf hypothesis, this is the idea that language influences thought. The strong version, linguistic determinism, holds that a person cannot conceive of things that are not expressed by their language. The weaker, and more accepted version, suggests that people are influenced by things that are expressed by their language.

linguistic imperialism – is the imposition of one culture's language upon another culture.

linguistic insecurity – refers to the belief that one's own language variety is somehow inferior to others, especially to standard varieties.

linguistic market – the linguistic market can be understood as a metaphoric 'market' where people can 'spend and trade' their social/cultural capital. Integral to this metaphor is the metaphoric value of a particular language variety that is allocated according to the social/cultural capital that the variety is associated with.

linguistic variable – a linguistic feature (phoneme, morpheme, lexeme, and so on), which has an identifiable alternative form that means the same thing but is associated with varying non-linguistic meaning. Negation in English, for example, can be expressed in different ways and these differences convey meanings to the interlocutor in addition to the denotative meaning (e.g. *I have no money* and *I ain't got no money*).

linguistic variation – refers to the inevitable differences across and within languages and dialects.

literacy – usually used to refer to the ability to read and write but can also be used to describe the ability to interpret and produce different kinds of texts and semiotic codes.

logos – one of three persuasive strategies. Logos involves appealing to or relying on the logic of an argument, including the use of verifiable facts. See also **ethos** and **pathos**.

marked – generally speaking, 'marked' means noticeably unusual. More specifically, linguistic forms that are marked reflect a deviation from what is perceived as the norm. This deviation can be signalled in a variety of ways (e.g. morphemically, lexically). Unmarked linguistic forms are neutral in so far as they represent the perceived 'norm'. For example, the unmarked form *nurse* is often assumed to refer to a woman. To refer to a nurse who is a man, the additional term *male* is often added: *male nurse* (the marked form).

metalingual – literally, above the linguistic, thus, the metalingual function of language describes how language can be used to talk about language. It is common when dealing with comprehension issues. This is one of Jakobson's six functions of language.

metaphor/metaphorical – a metaphor is a type of figurative way of describing something by comparing it to something else. It may be compared to something abstract or concrete. Unlike a simile, metaphorical expressions make an implicit comparison. Metaphors have the structure 'x is y' as in 'John is a bear'. It should be noted that metaphors in Lakoff and Johnson's model (1980) are slightly different as it refers to metaphors that exist at a cognitive level and result in metaphorical expressions in language. For example, the metaphor used in the phrase 'Bob attacked Jane's statement' is understood because of the existence of an unspoken cognitive metaphor 'ARGUMENT IS WAR'.

minimal responses – in conversations, the contributions that speakers make to show that they agree or that they are listening; for example, 'mm hm', 'yeah' and so on. See also **back channel support**.

modal auxiliary verb – the modal auxiliary verbs of English include 'will', 'shall', 'can', 'may' and so on. Modal auxiliaries have several meaning functions, including the indication of certainty or uncertainty (epistemic modality). For example, compare '*I will be coming*' and '*I may be coming*'. Tag questions ('isn't it?') may also have a modal function, and express uncertainty.

modality – this refers to the different possible modes of communication, including speech, writing and visual modes including sign language. The term is also used to discuss texts that combine modalities in 'mutli-modal' texts which are common in Computer Mediated Communication.

morphology – refers to the function and forms of morphemes, the smallest meaningful parts of language.

multimodal – see **modality**.

multiple negation – refers to the use of more than one form of negation in an expression in English. For example, the phrase *I didn't eat anything* has one negative form (*didn't*) while the phrase *I didn't eat nothing* has two (*didn't* and *nothing*). Multiple negation is also referred to as 'double negatives'. Prescriptivists argue that multiple negation is non-standard.

narrative – 'narrative' may be used in different ways. In sociolinguistics, it generally refers to a text (written or spoken) that relates events, in the past tense, with a temporal relationship between them. For example, 'Tom went out. Tom came back' is a minimal narrative. Both clauses are in the past tense, and the ordering suggests he first went out and then came back. Narrative can also be used as a partial synonym for **discourse**.

new information – something used for the first time in a text. See also **given information**.

nominalisation – the process of making a noun from another kind of word. Nominalisations may have the suffix '-tion' or '-ness'. For example, 'facilitation' is a nominalisation of the verb 'to facilitate'; and 'cleverness' nominalises the adjective 'clever'.

noun phrase – a term that linguists use to refer to a noun. A noun phrase may consist of a noun and other words such as *the* and *blue* in *the blue book*, or it may be 'bare' such as *book*.

out-group – see **in-group**.

overlap – an overlap is an instance of simultaneous talk that does not result in a speaker stopping what they were saying; it is distinct from **interruption**.

overt prestige – the positive value overtly associated with linguistic forms of language through the public acknowledgement of them as 'correct' by users. See also **covert prestige**.

paradigmatic – the paradigmatic axis of language refers to the notion that words that are used are chosen from among all possible choices and such choices can be said to be meaningful. For example, to call a woman a 'girl' rather than a 'lady' depicts her as young. This is part of the structuralist view of language. See also **syntagmatic**.

parallelism – when there is the same or similar syntactic structure in two or more parts of a text. This similarity asks the reader to understand the two parts in relation to each other. This is a stylistic choice common in persuasive speech.

parole – the language we actually produce, according to Saussure. Parole acts depend on **langue**.

passive voice see **active voice**.

pathos – one of three persuasive strategies. Pathos involves appealing to or relying on emotion. See also **ethos** and **logos**.

performance – see **competence**.

personification – to describe an entity that is not a person as though it is a person. For example, the weather may be described as 'angry' attributing it human emotions and thus personifying the weather.

phatic – one of Jakobson's six functions of language. The phatic function involves building or sustaining relationships. 'Small talk' is an example of the phatic function of language.

phonetics/phonetic – the study of individual speech sounds. This includes attention to how these sounds are made as well as to variation among speakers with respect to these sounds.

phonology/phonological – phonology is the study of the organisation of sounds, or sound systems, of languages.

pidgin – a simplified language that arises in a situation where speakers who do not know each other's language are in long-term contact. A pidgin borrows from a **lexifier** for words and a **substrate** language for syntactic structure. A pidgin is not the L1 for any speaker. A **creole** may develop from a pidgin, when it becomes the L1 for speakers in the community.

plexity see **social networks**.

pragmatic presupposition see **presupposition**.

prescription/prescriptivist – the belief/people that believe that there is a 'correct' form of the language, including specific syntactic and semantic rules that should be followed.

presupposition – there are two kinds of presupposition. Semantic presupposition is embedded in an utterance or phrase and remains true even if the utterance is negated. For example, 'My mother is coming to the party' presupposes that I have a mother and there is a party. Pragmatic presupposition is something that is implied by the utterance. For example, 'I forgot my umbrella' implies that it is raining.

pronoun – a class of words that can replace a noun or noun phrase in a sentence. Pronouns in English include 'I', 'me', 'she', 'her' and so on.

referential – one of Jakobson's six functions of language. The referential function of language is what we might normally think of as information, or the **denotative** function of language, but also includes the ideas, objects and conventions which speakers share knowledge of.

repetition – a particular kind of **parallelism** where content is repeated.

rhoticity – refers to the 'r' sound in language. For example, in the English language, the word *fourth* has an 'r' after a vowel sound. This linguistic variable is relevant to the concept of language variety because some varieties of English pronounce this 'r' (e.g. US English) while others don't (e.g. UK English). Thus a rhotic variety pronounces the 'r' while a non-rhotic variety does not. In addition, this linguistic variable is associated with language ideology because it has different values associated with it.

semantic derogation – process in which, over time, a word can take on a second or new meaning and/or connotations which are negative or demeaning. For example, the word *spinster* in English referred to a profession, spinning yarn, in the 14th century. In modern English, it is a negative word that refers to an older woman who is not married.

semantic presupposition see **presupposition**.

semantics – the study of the meaning of words.

semiotic – something that is meaningful as a sign; semiotics is the study of signs. Language is a semiotic, but so too are colours, typefaces, layout and so on.

sexism – the unequal treatment of people on the basis of their sex.

shared floor – in conversations, if more than one person is allowed to speak at a time it an be described as a shared (conversational) floor. The norm is generally considered to be the one-at-a-time floor where only one speaker has speaking rights at any given moment.

sign – the combination of the **signifer** and the **signifed**. The relationship between the signifier and the signified is arbitrary.

signified – the concept represented by the **sign**.

signifier – the form representing the **sign**.

simile – an explicit comparison made between two things usually employing the word 'like'. For example, 'her eyes are like stars' is a simile. In contrast, 'her eyes are stars' is a metaphor.

social network – a way of describing a person's social connections in a community in terms of the type and frequency of interactions they have with other members. Relations can be described in terms of plexity (uniplex or multiplex) and density (dense or loose). For example, if A is a work associate and cousin of B, their relationship is multiplex because they know each other in more than one capacity. If they only know each other in one context, their relationship is uniplex. Density refers to the relationships between members of a particular person's network. If many members of A's network know one another, A's network is dense. If very few people in A's network know one another, A's network is loose.

standard language – refers to the variety of language that is perceived to be the most correct version of that community's language. The definition of 'correct' varies according to the community, thus, there is not a single standard variety of a language.

stratified/stratification – division into layers, where a layer can be 'above' or 'below' another layer. In terms of social stratification, people in any one layer share certain social characteristics and are 'equals' but differ from and are not 'equal' to people in other layers. One example of social stratification by social class is: upper, middle and lower or 'working' class.

structuralism – for linguistics, the idea that the system of signs is structured, and that the meaning of signs depends on their position relative to other signs.

style – a particular meaning conveyed by the use of a set of linguistic forms that are associated with that meaning.

style-shifting – changing the way a person speaks according to context, topic and addressee. For example, people can change language use on a continuum from casual to formal according to the norms of their community.

substrate language – see **pidgin**.

symbolic capital – symbolic (or cultural) capital refers to intangible assets that individuals accumulate or inherit, which, like real capital (money), can be used to procure things. Such intangible assets might take the form of self-presentation, language, relationships, education and so on. In this book, we use 'symbolic capital' to include cultural and social capital. See also **linguistic market**.

symmetry – as used in linguistics, symmetry refers to a balanced distribution of related expressions. For example, standard English shows symmetry between the first person singular and plural pronouns *I/we*, that is, there is a different pronoun for singular and plural. However, the relationship of second person singular and plural pronouns is not symmetrical. There is only one second person pronoun, *you*, and it has a singular meaning. There is no second person plural pronoun in 'standard' English (note that many varieties of English have resolved this asymmetry with forms such as *y'all* and *youse*). Asymmetry can be seen in lexical relationships as well. For example, address forms for women *Mrs*, *Miss* and *Ms* while there is only *Mr* for men.

synchronic – to examine something at a particular point in time. See also **diachronic**.

synchronous communication – communication that happens when both interlocutors are in the same time frame. A face-to-face conversation is synchronous communication. See also **asynchronous communication**.

syntagmatic – as opposed to **paradigmatic**. The syntagmatic axis of language describes the way words are ordered in relation to each other, from left to right.

syntax – describes the rules and structures of a language at the level of clauses, phrases and sentences (i.e. word order). Different languages have different syntactic 'rules'. In English, for example, the typical word order is Subject-Verb-Object.

tag questions – a question that is added to the end of a declarative statement that turns the statement into a question. For example, the addition of *isn't it?* to the end of the statement *the weather is nice* results in the question *the weather is nice, isn't it?*.

three part list – a common feature of persuasive language. This is a particular form of parallelism involving three components. For example, 'ready, willing and able' is a three part list.

transitive/intransitive – a type of verb. A transitive verb requires a direct object in order to make sense, whereas an intransitive verb does not. For example, the verb *to buy* does not make sense without an object; *Frank bought* is meaningless but *Frank bought a book* is meaningful. An intransitive verb such as *vote* does not need a direct object to make sense: *Sarah voted.*

transitivity (model) – a way of analysing the structure of sentences that includes semantics as well as syntactic structure. It considers the actors, their actions, and the objects of their actions rather than just the positions of nouns, verbs and other parts of speech.

turn/turn taking – a turn is a contribution to a conversation; turn taking describes the way these conversational contributions are ordered, that is, who is allowed to speak and when.

unmarked see **marked**.

user-generated content – material contributed by audience and viewers to media outlets.

variety – a form of language used by a group of speakers; although similar to the term 'dialect' 'variety' is preferred because it avoids the negative associations of 'dialect'.

vlogger – a video blogger. Video bloggers produce online videos to express their opinions and ideas. Vlogs and vloggers are found on sites such as YouTube.

vocative – The vocative case is a grammaticalisation of socially directed speech. It is a special marker that tells the named person they are being searched for or spoken to.

References

ABC (2012) 'Fiji Gossip Warning "Dangerous"' *ABC Radio* www.radioaustralia.net. au/international/2012-03-21/fiji-gossip-warning-dangerous/473120 [accessed 26 September 2013].

Aldridge, M. (ed.) (1996) *Child Language*, Bristol: Multilingual Matters.

Althusser, L. (1971) 'Ideology and Ideological State Apparatuses (Notes Towards an Investigation)', in *Lenin and Philosophy and Other Essays*, Ben Brewster (trans.), London: Monthly Review Press: 127–86. www.marx2mao.com/Other/ LPOE70ii.html [accessed 12 December 2013].

Ammon, U. (2010) 'World Languages: Trends and Futures', in N. Coupland (ed.) *The Handbook of Language and Globalization*, Oxford: Blackwell: 101–22.

Androutsopoulos, J. (2013) 'English "on top": Discourse functions of English resources in the German mediascape', *Sociolinguistic Studies* 6(2): 209–38.

Aristotle (1991) *The Art of Rhetoric*, H. C Lawson-Tancred (trans.), London: Penguin.

Arora, K. (2014) 'Penguin to Destroy Copies of Wendy Doniger's book "The Hindus"', *The Times of India*, 11 February www.timesofindia.indiatimes.com [accessed 12 June 2014].

Attwood, F. (2007) 'Sluts and riot grrrls: Female identity and sexual agency', *Journal of Gender Studies* 16(3): 233–47.

Bailey, G., Baugh, J., Mufwene, S. S. and Rickford, J. R. (eds) (2013) *African-American English: Structure, history and use*, London: Routledge.

Bajak, F. and Rueda, J. (2014) 'Venezuelan leaders scramble to discuss crime as outrage spreads over slaying of beauty queen', *Montreal Gazette*, 8 January www.montrealgazette.com/news/Outrage+over+beauty+queens+slay ing+call+action+crimewracked/9363518/story.html [accessed 9 January 2014].

Baranowski, M. (2002) 'Current usage of the epicene pronoun in written English', *Journal of Sociolinguistics* 6(3): 378–97.

Baron, D. (1981) 'The epicene pronoun: The word that failed', *American Speech* 56: 83–97.

Barrett, D. (2013) 'Edward Snowden leaks could help paedophiles escape police, says government', *The Telegraph*, 6 November www.telegraph.co.uk/news/ uknews/terrorism-in-the-uk/10431337/Edward-Snowden-leaks-could-help- paedophiles-escape-police-says-government.html [accessed 12 June 2014].

Bateman, J. A., Delin, J. and Henschel, R. (2006) 'Mapping the Multimodal Genres of Traditional and Electronic Newspapers', in T. D. Royce and W. L. Bowcher (eds) *New Directions in the Analysis of Multimodal Discourse*, Mahwah: Lawrence Erlbaum Associates: 147–72.

Bauer, L. and Trudgill, P. (eds) (1998) *Language Myths*, Harmondsworth: Penguin.

Bayard, D., Weatherall, A., Gallois, C. and Pittam, J. (2001) 'Pax Americana? Accent attitudinal evaluations in New Zealand, Australia and America', *Journal of Sociolinguistics* 5(1): 22–49.

BBC News (2012) 'Caution on Twitter urged as tourists barred from US', 31 January www.bbc.co.uk/news/technology-16810312 [accessed 12 June 2014].

BBC News (2013) 'Godfrey Bloom quits as UKIP MEP after "sluts" joke row', 24 September www.bbc.co.uk/news/uk-politics-24222992 [accessed 9 January 2014].

Behera, A. K. and Behera, R. (2012) 'Indian English: Linguistics and social characteristics', *International Journal of English and Education* 1(1): 53–60.

Bell, A. (1991) *The Language of News Media*, Oxford: Blackwell.

Bell, A. (2014) *The Guidebook to Sociolinguistics*, Oxford: Wiley Blackwell.

Bennett, J. (2012) 'And what comes out may be a kind of screeching': The stylisation of chavspeak in contemporary Britain', *Journal of Sociolinguistics* 16(1): 5–27.

Ben-Rafael, E., Shohamy, E., Mara, M. H. and Trumper-Hecht, N. (2006) 'Linguistic landscape as symbolic construction of the public space: The case of Israel', *International Journal of Multilingualism* 3(1): 7–30.

Berlin, B. and Kay, P. (1969) *Basic Color Terms*, Berkeley and Los Angeles: University of California Press.

Bevans, A. and Streeter, M. (1996) 'Nelson Mandela: From 'terrorist' to tea with the Queen', *The Independent*, 9 July www.independent.co.uk/news/world/from-terrorist-to-tea-with-the-queen-1327902.html [accessed 12 June 2014].

Bickerton, D. (1983) 'Creole languages'. www.ohio.edu/people/thompsoc/Creole.html [accessed 11 August 2014].

Block, D. (2013) *Social Class in Applied Linguistics*, London: Routledge.

Blommaert, J. (2003) 'Orthopraxy, writing and identity: Shaping lives through borrowed genres in Congo', in James R. Martin and Ruth Wodak (eds) *Re/reading the Past: Critical and Functional Perspectives on Time and Value, Vol. 8*, Amsterdam: John Benjamins: 177–94.

Blommaert, J. (2009) 'A Sociolinguistics of Globalization', in N. Coupland and A. Jaworski (eds) *The New Sociolinguistics Reader*, Basingstoke: Palgrave: 560–73.

Blommaert, J. (2013) *Ethnography, Superdiversity and Linguistic Landscapes: Chronicles of Complexity, Critical Language and Literacy Studies*, Bristol: Multilingual Matters.

Blommaert, J. and Omoniyi, T. (2006) 'Email fraud: Language, technology and the indexicals of globalization', *Social Semiotics* 16(4): 573–605.

Bloxam, A. (2010) 'Students vow to continue rioting over fees', *The Telegraph*, 11 November www.telegraph.co.uk/education/universityeducation/8125050/Students-vow-to-continue-rioting-over-fees.html [accessed 12 June 2014].

Bodine, A. (1975) 'Androcentrism in prescriptive grammar: Singular "they", sex-indefinite "he", and "he or she"', *Language in Society* 4(2): 129–46.

Boletta, W. L. (1992) 'Prescriptivism, politics, and lexicography: A reply to Jane Barnes Mack', *ILT NEWS*, (October): 103–111.

Bonilla-Silva, E. and Forman, T. A. (2000) '"I am not a racist but … ": Mapping White college students' racial ideology in the USA', *Discourse and Society* 11(1): 50–85.

Boroditsky, L. (2001) 'Does language shape thought?: Mandarin and English speakers' conceptions of time', *Cognitive Psychology*, 43: 1–22.

Bourdieu, P. (1977) *Outline of the Theory of Practice*, R. Nice (trans.), Cambridge: Cambridge University Press.

Bourdieu, P. (1984) *Social Critique of the Judgement of Taste*, London: Routledge.

Bourdieu, P. (1991) *Language and Symbolic Power*, Cambridge: Polity Press.

Bourdieu, P. and Boltanski, L. (1975) 'Le fétichisme de la langue', *Actes de la recherché en sciences sociales* 2: 95–107.

Boyce, T. (2006) 'Journalism and expertise', *Journalism Studies* 7(6): 889–906.

Boyd, D., Golder, S. and Lotan, G. (2010) 'Tweet, tweet, retweet: Conversational aspects of retweeting on twitter', *System Sciences (HICSS), 2010 43rd Hawaii International Conference on IEEE*, 1–10.

Boyle, S. (2013) 'Barbies for girls, cars for boys? Let toys be toys and get them gender neutral presents this Christmas', *The Independent*, 17 December www.

independent.co.uk/voices/comment/barbies-for-girls-cars-for-boys-let-toys-be-toys-and-get-them-gender-neutral-presents-this-christmas-9011155.html [accessed 12th June 2014].

Briant, E., Watson, N. and Philo, G. (2013) 'Reporting disability in the age of austerity: The changing face of media representation of disability and disabled people in the United Kingdom and the creation of new "folk devils", *Disability & Society* 28(6): 874–89.

British APCO (2007) 'Police radio communications standard begins roll-out', *British APCO*, 14 July, www.bapcojournal.com/news/fullstory.php/aid/707/Police_radio_communications_standard_begins_roll-out_.html [accessed 5 June 2014].

Broadbent, J. M. (2009) 'The* amn't gap: The view from West Yorkshire', *Journal of Linguistics* 45(2): 251–84.

Brown, D. W. (2008) 'Paris Hilton, Brenda Frazier, blogs, and the proliferation of celebu-' , *American Speech* 83(3): 312–25.

Bucktin, C. (2013) 'Miss Venezuela and British husband shot five times by robbers as car was loaded onto recovery truck', *The Mirror*, 8 January www.mirror.co.uk/news/world-news/miss-venezuela-monica-spear-british-2999678 [accessed 9 January 2014].

Burridge, K. (1996) 'Political correctness: Euphemism with attitude', *English Today* 12(3): 42–3.

Cameron, D. (1995) *Verbal Hygiene*, London: Routledge.

Cameron, D. (2001) *Working with Spoken Discourse*, London: Routledge.

Cameron, D. (2007) *The Myth of Mars and Venus*, Oxford: Oxford University Press.

Cameron, D. (2011 [1997]) 'Performing Gender Identity: Young Men's Talk and the Construction of Heterosexual Masculinity', in *Language Society and Power: A Reader*, first published in S. Johnson and U. Meinhof (eds) (1997) *Language and Masculinity*, Oxford: Blackwell: 179–91.

Cameron, D. (2014 [1990]) 'Demythologising Sociolinguistics: Why Language Does not Reflect Society', in J. E. Joseph and T. J. Taylor (eds) *Ideologies of Language*, London: Routledge: 79–93.

Cameron, D. and Kulick, D. (2003) *Language and Sexuality*, Cambridge: Cambridge University Press

Canagarajah, A. S. (1999) *Resisting Linguistic Imperialism in English Teaching*, Oxford: Oxford University Press.

Canagarajah, A. S. (2012) 'Migrant ethnic identities, mobile language resources: Identification practices of Sri Lankan Tamil youth', *Applied Linguistics Review* 3(2): 251–72.

Carlson, H. K. and McHenry, M. A. (2006) 'Effect of accent and dialect on employability', *Journal of Employment Counseling* 43(2): 70–83.

Carrington, V. (2009) 'I write, therefore I am: texts in the city', *Visual Communication* 8(4): 409–25.

Carter, R., Goddard, A., Reah, D., Sanger, K. and Swift, N. (2007) *Working with Texts: A Core Introduction to Language Analysis*, Adrian Beard (ed.), London: Routledge.

Chambers, J. K. (1992) 'Dialect acquisition', *Language* 68(4): 673–705.

Chambers, J. K. (2009) *Sociolinguistic Theory*. rev. edn, Oxford: Blackwell.

Cheshire, J., Kerswill, P., Fox, S. and Torgensen, E. (2011) 'Contact, the feature pool and the speech community: The emergence of Multicultural London English', *Journal of Sociolinguistics* 15(2): 151–96.

Chew, P. G. (2007) 'Remaking Singapore: Language, Culture and Identity in a Globalized World', in A. B. M. Tsui and J. W. Tollefson (eds) *Language Policy, Culture, and Identity in Asian Contexts*, Mahwah: Lawrence Erlbaum: 73–93.

Chilton, P. (1982) 'Nukespeak: Nuclear Language, Culture and Propaganda', in C. Aubrey (ed.) *Nukespeak: The Media and the Bomb*, Comedia Publishing Group, London: 94–112.

Chomsky, N. and Herman, E. S. (1988) *Manufacturing Consent: The Political Economy of the Mass Media*, New York: Pantheon.

Chye, D. Y. S. (2000) 'Standard English and Singlish: The Clash of Language values in Contemporary Singapore', in Y. Treis and R. de Busser (eds) *Selected Papers from the 2009 Conference of the Australian Linguistic Society* www.als.asn.au/proceedings/als2009.html [accessed 11 August 2014].

Coates, J. (1996) *Women Talk. Conversation between Women Friends*, Oxford: Blackwell.

Coates, J. (2002) *Men Talk. Stories in the Making of Masculinities*, Oxford: Blackwell.

Coates, J. (2004) *Women, Men and Language: A Sociolinguistic Account of Gender Differences in Language*, 3rd edn., London: Routledge.

Coates, J. (2011) 'Gossip Revisited: Language in All-Female Groups', in J. Coates and P. Pichler (eds) *Language and Gender: A Reader*, 2nd edn, Oxford: Blackwell: 199–223.

Coates, J. (2013) *Women, Men and Everyday Talk*, Basingstoke: Palgrave.

Cohn, C. (1987) 'Slick'ems, Glick'ems, Christmas Trees, and Cookie Cutters: Nuclear Language and how we learned to pat the bomb', *Bulletin of the Atomic Scientists* 43(5): 17–24.

Conley, J. M., O'Barr, W. M. and Lind, E. A. (1978) 'The power of language: Presentational style in the courtroom', *Duke Law Journal* 6: 1375–99.

Coughlan, S. (2011) 'Is the Student Customer Always Right?' *BBC News* 28 June www.bbc.co.uk/news/education-13942401 [accessed 17 January 2014].

Coupland, J. (2000) '"Past the "perfect kind of age"? Styling selves and relationships in over-50s dating advertisements', *Journal of Communication* 50(3): 9–30.

Coupland, N., Bishop, H., Evans, B. and Garrett, P. (2006) 'Imagining Wales and the Welsh language: Ethnolinguistic subjectivities and demographic flow', *Journal of Language and Social Psychology* 25(4): 351–76.

Coupland, N. (1997) 'Language, Ageing and Ageism: a project for applied linguistics' *International Journal of Applied Linguistics* 7(1): 26–48.

Cowie, C. (2007) 'The accents of outsourcing: The meanings of "neutral" in the Indian Call Centre Industry', *World Englishes* 26(3): 316–30.

Croom, A. M. (2014) 'Slurs, stereotypes, and in-equality: A critical review of "How Epithets and Stereotypes are Racially Unequal"', *Language Sciences* in press DOI: 10.1016/j.langsci.2014.03.001

Crowley, T. (2003) *Standard English and the Politics of Language*, 2nd edn, Basingstoke: Palgrave.

Crystal, D. (2003) *English as a Global Language*, Cambridge: Cambridge University Press.

Crystal, D. (2007a) *The Fight for English: How Language Pundits Ate, Shot, and Left*, Oxford: Oxford University Press.

Crystal, D. (2007b) *Words, Words, Words*, Oxford: Oxford University Press.

Cukor-Avila, P. (2000) 'Revisiting the Observer's Paradox', *American Speech* 75(3): 253–4.

Cutler, Cecilia A. (1999) 'Yorkville Crossing: White teens, hip-hop and African American English', *Journal of Sociolinguistics* 3(4): 428–42.

Dailey O'Cain, J. (2000) 'The sociolinguistic distribution of and attitudes toward focuser like and quotative like', *Journal of Sociolinguistics* 4(1): 60–80.

Danet, B. (1980) '"Baby" or "fetus"? Language and the construction of reality in a manslaughter trial', *Semiotica* 32: 187–219.

D'Arcy, A. (2007) 'Like and language ideology: Disentangling fact from fiction', *American Speech* 82(4): 386–419.

de Saussure, F. (1966) *Course in General Linguistics*, C. Bally and A. Sechehaye (eds) with A. Reidlinger and W. Baskin (trans.), London: McGraw Hill.

de Swaan, A. (2010) 'Language Systems', in N. Coupland (ed.) *The Handbook of Language and Globalization*, Oxford: Blackwell: 56–76.

Deacon, M. (2013) 'Sketch: Mockney George Osborne plans a bedder Briddain', *The Telegraph*, 2 April www.telegraph.ac.uk [accessed 27 September 2013].

Dearden, L. (2014) 'Monica Spear: Teenagers among suspects arrested for murder of former Miss Venezuela and British ex-husband', *The Independent*, 7 January www.independent.co.uk/news/world/americas/former-miss-venezuela-monica-spear-and-british-exhusband-shot-dead-by-robbers-9045050.html [accessed 9 January 2014].

DeFrancisco, V. L. (1991) 'The sounds of silence: How men silence women in marital relations', *Discourse and Society* 2(4): 413–24.

deKlerk, V. (2005) 'Slang and swearing as markers of inclusion and exclusion in adolescence', in A. Williams and C. Thurlow (eds) *Talking Adolescence: Perspectives on Communication in the Teenage Years* (Vol. 3), Oxford: Peter Lang: 111–27.

Denis, J. and Pontille, D. (2010) 'Placing subway signs: Practical properties of signs at work', *Visual Communication* 9(4): 441–62.

Deterding, D. (2007) *Singapore English: Dialects of English*, Edinburgh: Edinburgh University Press.

Deuber, D. (2013) 'Towards endonormative standards of English in the Caribbean: A study of students' beliefs and school curricula', *Language, Culture and Curriculum* 26(2): 109–27.

Dixon, R. M. W. (2002) *Australian Languages: Their Nature and Development*, Cambridge: Cambridge University Press.

Dorothy, D. (2000) 'Evaluations of Hawaii Creole English and standard English', *Journal of Language and Social Psychology* 19(3): 357–77.

Drager, K. (2012) 'Pidgin and Hawai'i English: An overview', *Journal of Language, Translation, and Intercultural Communication* 1(1): 61–73.

Dubois, B. L. and Crouch, I. (1975) 'The question of tag questions in women's speech: They don't really use more of them, do they?', *Language in society* 4(3): 289–94.

Eades, D. (1996) 'Legal recognition in cultural differences in communication: The case of Robyn Kina', *Language & Communication* 16(3): 215–27.

Eades, D. (2000) 'I don't think it's an answer to the question: Silencing Aboriginal witnesses in court', *Language in Society* 29: 161–95.

Eades, D. (2003) 'The politics of misunderstanding in the legal system', in J. House, G. Kasper and S. Ross (eds) *Misunderstanding in Social Life: Discourse Approaches to Problematic Talk*, London: Longman: 199–226.

Eckert, P. (1988) 'Adolescent social structure and the spread of linguistic change', *Language in Society* 17(3): 183-207.

Eckert, P. (1989a) *Jocks and Burnouts: Social categories and identity in the high school.* London: Teachers College Press, Columbia University.

Eckert, P. (1989b) 'The whole woman: Sex and gender differences in variation', *Language Variation and Change* 1(1): 245–67.

Eckert, P. (1997) 'Age as a Sociolinguistic Variable', in F. Coulmas (ed.) *The Handbook of Sociolinguistics*, Oxford: Blackwell: 151–67.

Eckert, P. (1998) 'Gender and sociolinguistic variation', in J. Coates (ed.) *Language and Gender: A Reader*, Oxford: Blackwell: 151–67.

Eckert, P. (1999) *Language Variation as Social Practice: The Linguistic Construction of Identity in Belten High*, Oxford: Blackwell.

Eckert, P. (2003a) 'The meaning of style', *Texas Linguistic Forum* 47: 41–53.

Eckert, P. (2003b) 'Language and adolescent peer groups', *Journal of Language and Social Psychology* 22(1): 112–18.

Eckert, P. (2004) 'Adolescent Language', in E. Finegan and J. R. Rickford (eds) *Language in the USA: Themes for the Twenty-First Century*: 360–75.

Eckert, P. (2005) 'Stylistic Practice in the Adolescent Social Order', in A. Williams and C. Thurlow (eds) *Talking Adolescence: Perspectives on Communication in the Teenage Years* (Vol. 3). Oxford: Peter Lang: 93–110.

Eckert, P. (2009) 'Ethnography and the Study of Variation', in N. Coupland and A. Jaworksi (eds) *The New Sociolinguistics Reader*, Basingstoke: Palgrave: 136–51.

Edwards, W. F. (1992) 'Sociolinguistic behavior in a Detroit inner-city black neighborhood', *Language in Society* 21(1): 93–115.

Eisenstein, S. (2013) *Give Us Bread But Give Us Roses: Working Women's Consciousness in the United States, 1890 to the First World War*, London: Routledge.

Eisokovits, E. (2011) 'Girl-Talk/Boy-Talk: Sex Differences in Adolescent Speech', in J. Coates and P. Pichler (eds) *Language and Gender: A Reader*, Oxford: Blackwell: 38–48.

Ellison, K. L. (2014) 'Age transcended: A semiotic and rhetorical analysis of the discourse of agelessness in North American anti-aging skin care advertisements', *Journal of Aging Studies* 29: 20–31.

Evans, B. E. (2005) '"The Grand Daddy of English": US, UK, New Zealand and Australian Students' Attitudes toward Varieties of English', in N. Langer and W. Davies (eds) *Linguistic Purism in the Germanic Languages. Studia Linguistica Germanica*, Berlin: De Gruyter: 240–51.

Evans, B. E. (2010) 'English as Official State Language in Ohio: Market Forces Trump Ideology', in H. Kelly-Holmes and G. Mautner (eds) *Language and the Market*, London: Palgrave.

Fairclough, N. (1995) *Critical Discourse Analysis: The Critical Study of Language*, London: Longman.

Fairclough, N. (1999) 'Global capitalism and critical awareness of language', *Language Awareness* 8(2): 71–83.

Fairclough, N. (2001) *Language and Power*, 2nd edn, London: Longman.

Ferguson, C. (1959) 'Diglossia', *Word*, 15: 325–40.

Fernández Fontecha, A. and Jiménez Catalán, M. (2003) 'Semantic derogation in animal metaphor: A contrastive-cognitive analysis of two male/female examples in English and Spanish', *Journal of Pragmatics* 35(5): 771–97.

Fishman, P. M. (1980) 'Interactional shitwork', *Heresies* 2: 99–101.

Fletcher, P. and MacWhinney, B. (eds) (1996) *The Handbook of Child Language*, Oxford: Blackwell.

Flynn, B. (2013) 'Cheeky Beggars', *The Sun*, 31 December www.thesun.co.uk/sol/homepage/news/5350243/first-coachload-romanian-migrants-head-to-britain.html [accessed 13 June 2014].

Fontecha, A. F. and Rosa Maria Jimenez Catalan (2003) 'Semantic derogation in animal metaphor: a Contrastive–Cognitive analysis of two male/female examples in English and Spanish', *Journal of Pragmatics* 35(5): 771-97.

Fowler, R. (1991) *Language in the News: Discourse and Ideology in the Press*, London: Routledge.

Frable, D. (1989) 'Sex typing and gender ideology: Two facets of the individual's gender psychology that go together', *Journal of Personality and Social Psychology* 56(1): 95–108.

Friginal, E. (2009) 'Threat to the sustainability of the outsourced call center industry in the Philippines: Implications for language policy', *Language Policy* 8: 51–68.

Gawne, L. and Vaughan, J. (2011) 'I Can Haz Language Play: The Construction of Language and Identity in LOLspeak', in M. Ponsonnet, L. Dao and M. Bowler (eds) *Proceedings of the 42nd Australian Linguistic Society Conference* 97-122; ANU Research Repository – http://hdl.handle.net/1885/9398

Geek is Good www.geekisgood.org/ [accessed 26th September 2013].

Gesser, A. (2007) 'Learning about hearing people in the land of the deaf: An ethnographic account', *Sign Language Studies* 7(3): 269–83.

Gibson, C. (2013) 'Welcome to Bogan-ville: Reframing class and place through humour', *Journal of Australian Studies* 37(1): 62–75.

Giles, H. and Reid, S. A. (2005) 'Ageism across the lifespan: Towards a self-categorization model of ageing', *Journal of Social Issues* 61(2): 389–404.

Gill, C. (2010) 'Hijacking of a very middle class protest: Anarchists cause chaos as 50,000 students take to streets over fees', *Daily Mail*, 11 November www.dailymail.co.uk/news/article-1328385/TUITION-FEES-PROTEST-Anarchists-cause-chaos-50k-students-streets.html [accessed 10 July 2014].

Gillen, J. and Merchant, G. (2013) 'Contact Calls: Twitter as dialogic social and linguistic practice', *Language Sciences* 25: 47–58.

Guardian (2013) 'HSBC "Demises" Jobs – Another Absurd Business Euphemism', *The Guardian*, 23 April www.theguardian.com/business/nils-pratley-on-finance/2013/apr/23/hsbc-demise-job-cuts-euphemism [accessed 9 January 2014].

Gumperz, J. J. (2003) 'Cross Cultural Communication', in R. Harris and B. Rampton (eds) *The Language, Ethnicity and Race Reader*, London: Routledge: 267–75.

Gupta, A. F. (2004) 'Singlish on the Web', in A. Hashim and N. Hassan (eds) *Varieties of English in South East Asia and Beyond*, Kuala Lumpur: University of Malaya Press: 19–38.

Hamblin, J. (2013) 'Some Americans Say They Support the Affordable Care Act but Not Obamacare', *The Atlantic*, 1 October www.theatlantic.com/health/archive/2013/10/some-americans-say-they-support-the-affordable-care-act-but-not-obamacare/280165/ [accessed 3 January 2014].

Hargrove, E., Sakoda, K. and Siegel, J. (n.d) Hawai'i Creole. www.hawaii.edu/satocenter/langnet/definitions/hce.html#grammar-hce [accessed 13 June 2014].

Harris, R. and Rampton, B. (2003) 'Introduction', in *The Language, Race and Ethnicity Reader*, London: Routledge: 1–14.

Hartigan, J. (1997) 'Unpopular culture: The case of "white trash"', *Cultural Studies* 11(2): 316–43.

Hartley, J. (2010) 'Silly citizenship', *Critical Discourse Studies* 7(4): 233–48.

Hastie, B. and Cosh, S. (2013) '"What's wrong with that?" Legitimating and contesting gender inequality', *Journal of Language and Social Psychology* 32: 369–89.

Hayward, K. J. and Yar, M. (2006) 'The "chav" phenomenon: Consumption, media and the construction of a new underclass', *Crime Media Culture* 2(1): 9–28.

Heller, M. (2003) 'Globalization, the new economy, and the commodification of language and identity', *Journal of Sociolinguistics* 7(4): 473–92.

Heller, M. (2006) *Linguistic Minorities and Modernity: A Sociolinguistic Ethnography* 2nd edn, London: Continuum.

Herbert, J. (2000) *Journalism in the Digital Age: Theory and Practice for Broadcast, Print and On-Line Media*, London: Taylor and Francis.

Hermida, A. (2012) 'Tweets and truth', *Journalism Practice* 6(5–6): 659–68.

Herring, S. C., Johnson, D. A. and DiBenedetto, T. (1998) 'Participation in Electronic Discourse in a "Feminist" Field', in J. Coates, *Language and Gender: A Reader*, Oxford: Blackwell: 197–210.

Hillier, H. (2004) *Analysing Real Texts: Research Studies in Modern English Language*, Basingstoke: Palgrave.

Hines, C. (1999) '"Let Me Call You Sweetheart": The WOMAN AS DESSERT Metaphor', in M. Bucholtz, A. Laing and L. Sutton (eds) *Cultural Performances: Proceedings of the Third Berkeley Women and Language Conference*, Berkeley: Berkeley Women and Language Group.

Hitchens, C. (2010) 'The Other L-Word. On Language', *Vanity Fair*, 13 January www.vanityfair.com/culture/features/2010/01/hitchens-like-201001 [accessed 16 June 2014].

Hoey, M. (1986) 'The Discourse Colony: A Preliminary Study of a Neglected Discourse Type', in M. Coulthard (ed.) *Talking About Text*, Birmingham: English Language Research Discourse Analysis Monographs, 13: 1–26.

Holmes, J. (1984) 'Hedging your bets and sitting on the fence: some evidence for hedges as support structures', *Te Reo* 27: 47–62.

Holmes, J. (1986) 'Functions of *you know* in women's and men's speech', *Language in Society* 15: 1–22.

Holmes, J. (1987) 'Hedging, Fencing and Other Conversational Gambits: An Analysis of Gender Differences in New Zealand Speech', in A. Pauwels (ed.) *Women and Language in Australian and New Zealand Society*, Sydney: Australian Professional Publications, 59–79.

Holmes, J. (1995) *Women, Men and Politeness*, London: Longman.

Holmes, J. (1998) 'Women Talk Too Much', in L. Bauer and P. Trudgill (eds) *Language Myths*, Harmondsworth: Penguin: 41–9.

Holmes, J. (2008) *An Introduction to Sociolinguistics*, 3rd edn, Harlow: Pearson.

Horner, J. R. (2011) 'Clogged systems and toxic assets: News metaphors, neoliberal ideology, and the United States "Wall Street Bailout" of 2008', *Journal of Language and Politics* 10(1): 29–49.

Hudson, Richard A. (1996) *Sociolinguistics*, Cambridge: Cambridge University Press.

Hutchby, I. and Woffit, R. (2008) *Conversation Analysis* 2nd edn, London: Polity.

Irvine, J. and Gal, S. (2000) 'Language Ideology and Linguistic Differentiation', in P. V. Kroskrity (ed.) *Regimes of Language: Ideologies, Polities and Identities*, Santa Fe: School of American Research Press: 35–83.

Jakobson, R. (2000) [1960] 'Linguistics and Poetics', in L. Burke, T. Crowley and A. Girvin (eds) *The Routledge Language and Cultural Theory Reader*, London: Routledge: 334–49.

Jaworski, A. (2011) 'Linguistic landscapes on postcards: Tourist mediation and the sociolinguistics communities of contact', *Sociolinguistics Studies* 4(3): 569–94.

Jenkins, J. (1998) 'Which pronunciation norms and models for English as an International Language?', *ELT journal* 52(2):119–26.

Jenkins, J. (2002) 'A sociolinguistally based, empirically researched pronunciation syllabus for English as an international language', *Applied Linguistics* 23(1): 83–103.

Jenkins, J. (2009) 'English as a lingua franca: Interpretations and attitudes', *World Englishes* 28(2): 200–7.

Johnson, S. and Finlay, F. (1997) 'Do men gossip? An analysis of football talk on television', in S. Johnson and U. Meinhof (eds) *Language and Masculinity*, Oxford: Blackwell: 130–43.

Johnstone, B. (2009) 'Pittsburghese shirts: Commodification and the Enregisterment of an urban dialect', *American Speech* 84(2): 157–75.

Johnstone, B., Andrus, J. and Danielson, A. E. (2006) 'Mobility, indexicality, and the enregisterment of "Pittsburghese"', *Journal of English Linguistics* 32(4): 77–104.

Johnstone, B., Bhasin, N. and Wittofski, D. (2002) '"Dahntahn Pittsburgh": Monophthongal /aw/ and representations of localness in southwestern Pennsylvania', *American Speech* 77: 148–66.

Jones, D. (1980) 'Gossip: Notes on women's oral culture', *Women's Studies International Quarterly* 3(2): 193–8.

Jones, L. (2011) '"The only dykey one": Constructions of (in)authenticity in a lesbian community of practice', *Journal of Homosexuality* 58: 719–41.

Jost, J. T., Federico, C. M. and Napier, J. L. (2009) 'Political ideology: Its structure, functions, and elective affinities', *Annual Review of Psychology* 60: 307–37.

Jucker, A. H. (2003) 'Mass media communication at the beginning of the twenty-first century', *Journal of Historical Pragmatics* 4(1): 129–48.

Kachru, B. B. (1985) 'Standards, Codification, and Sociolinguistic Realism: The English Language in the Outer Circle', in R. Quirk and H. G. Widdowson (eds) *English in the World*, Cambridge: Cambridge University Press: 11–30.

Kachru, B. B. (1991) 'Liberation linguistics and the quirk concern', *English Today* 7(1): 3–13.

Kachru, B. B. (1992) 'World Englishes: Approaches, issues and resources', *Language Teaching* 25(1): 1–14.

Kasanga, L. A. (2012a) 'English in the Democratic Republic of the Congo', *World Englishes* 31(1): 48–69.

Kasanga, L. A. (2012b) 'Mapping the linguistic landscape of a commercial neighbourhood in Central Phnom Penh', *Journal of Multilingual and Multicultural Development* 33(6): 553–67.

Katz, S. and Marshall, B. (2003) 'New sex for old: Lifestyle, consumerism, and the ethics of aging well', *Journal of Aging Studies* 17: 3–16.

Kautsky, R. and Widholm, A. (2008) 'Online methodology: Analysing news flows of online journalism', *Westminster Papers in Communication and Culture* 5(2): 81–97.

Keating, J. (2014) 'North Korea Dog Execution Story Started as a Social Media Joke', *Slate*, 6 January www.slate.com/blogs/the_world_/2014/01/06/north_korea_dog_execution_story_started_as_a_social_media_joke.html [accessed 12 June 2014].

Kemper, S. (1994) 'Elderspeak: Speech accommodations to older adults', *Aging, Neuropsychology, and Cognition: A Journal on Normal and Dysfunctional Development* 1(1): 17–28.

Kennedy, R. L. (1999) 'Who can say "nigger"? And other considerations', *The Journal of Blacks in Higher Education* 26: 86–96.

Khosroshahi, F. (1989) 'Penguins don't care, but women do: A social identity analysis of a Whorfian problem', *Language and Society* 18(4): 505–25.

Kiesling, S. F. (2004) 'Dude', *American Speech* 79(3): 281–305.

Kiesling, S. (2005) 'Variation, stance and style: Word-final −er, high rising tone and ethnicity in Australian English', *English World Wide* 26(1): 1–42.

Kirkpatrick, A. (2007) *World Englishes*, Cambridge: Cambridge University Press.

Knobel, M. and Lankshear, C. (2007) 'Online Memes, Affinities, and Cultural Production', in M. Knobel and C. Lankshear (eds) *A New Literacies Sampler*, New York: Peter Lang: 199–227.

Knox, J. (2007) 'Visual-verbal communication on online newspaper home pages', *Visual Communication* 6(1): 19–53.

Koller, V. (2009) 'Analysing gender and sexual identity in discourse: A critical approach', research paper, Roehampton University, CRELL seminar series, 29 October 2009.

Kress, G. and Hodge, R. (1993) *Language as Ideology*, London: Routledge.

Kress, G. and van Leeuwen, T. (1996) *Reading Images*, London: Routledge.

Kuiper, K. (1991) 'Sporting formulae in New Zealand English: two models of male solidarity' in J. Cheshire (ed.) *English around the World*, Cambridge: Cambridge University Press: 200–9.

Labov, W. (1965) 'On the mechanism of linguistic change', *Georgetown Monographs on Language and Linguistics* 18: 91–114.

Labov, W. (1966) *The Social Stratification of English in New York City*, Washington, DC: Center for Applied Linguistics.

Labov, W. (1972a) *Sociolinguistic Patterns*, Philadelphia: University of Pennsylvania Press.

Labov, W. (1972b) 'Academic Ignorance and Black Intelligence', *The Atlantic* 72(June): 59–67.

Labov, W. (1972c) *Language in the Inner City: Studies in the Black English Vernacular*, Philadelphia: University of Pennsylvania Press.

Labov, W. (1982) 'Objectivity and commitment in linguistic science: The case of the Black English trial in Ann Arbor', *Language in Society* 11: 165–201.

Labov, W. (1989) 'The child as linguistic historian', *Language Variation and Change* 1: 85–94.

Ladegård, H. J. (1998) 'Assessing national stereotypes in language attitude studies: the case of class-consciousness in Denmark', *Journal of Multilingual and Multicultural Development* 19(3): 182–98.

Ladegård, H. J. and Sachdev, I. (2006) 'I like the Americans … but I certainly don't aim for an American accent: Language attitudes, vitality and foreign language learning in Denmark', *Journal of Multilingual and Multicultural Development* 27: 91–108.

Lakoff, G. and Johnson, M. (1980) *Metaphors We Live By*, Chicago: University of Chicago Press.

Lakoff, R. (1975) *Language and Woman's Place*, New York: Harper and Row.

Laserna, C. M., Seih, Y. T. and Pennebaker, J. W. (2014) 'Um … who like says you know filler word use as a function of age, gender, and personality', *Journal of Language and Social Psychology* 33(3): 328–38.

Lawton, C. A., Blakemore, J. E. and Vartanian, L. R. (2003) 'The new meaning of Ms.: Single, but too old for Miss', *Psychology of Women Quarterly* 27: 215–20.

Lazar, M. (2003) 'Semiosis, social change and governance: A critical semiotic analysis of a national campaign', *Social Semiotics* 13(2): 201–21.

Lee, P. (1996) *The Whorf Theory Complex: A Critical Reconstruction*, John Benjamins: Amsterdam.

Lee Eu Fah, E. (n.d) 'Profile of the Singapore Chinese Dialect Groups', *Statistics Singapore Newsletter* www.howardscott.net/4/Swatow_A_Colonial_Heritage/Files/Documentation/Lee%20Eu%20Fah.pdf

Leeman, J. and Modan, G. (2009) 'Commodified language in Chinatown: A contextualized approach to linguistic landscape', *Journal of Sociolinguistics* 13(3): 332–62.

Leimgruber, J. (2012) 'Singapore English: An indexical approach', *World Englishes* 31(1): 1–14.

Lewis, P., Vasagar, J., Williams, R. and Taylor, M. (2010) 'Student Protest over Fees Turns Violent', *The Guardian*, 10 November www.theguardian.com/education/2010/nov/10/student-protest-fees-violent [accessed 12 June 2014].

Liberman, A. (2014) 'Three words of American interest in a prospective new etymological dictionary of English: *ain't*, *alairy* and *alewife*', *American Speech* 89(2): 170–89.

Liberman, M. (2006) 'Sex-Linked Lexical Budgets', *Language Log*, 6 August http://itre.cis.upenn.edu/~myl/languagelog/archives/003420.html [accessed 31 May 2014].

Lippi-Green, R. (1997) *English with an Accent*, London: Routledge

Loftus, E. (1975) 'Leading questions and the eyewitness report', *Cognitive Psychology* 7: 550–72.

LSA (1996) 'The LSA Guidelines for Nonsexist Usage', *LSA Bulletin*, December p. 68.   www.linguisticsociety.org/resource/lsa-guidelines-nonsexist-usage [accessed 12 June 2014].

Lucy, J. (1997) 'Linguistic relativity', *Annual Review of Anthropology* 26: 291–312.

Lucy, J. (2005) 'Through the window of language: Assessing the influence of language diversity on thought', *Theoria* 54: 299–309.

MacFarlane, A. E. and Stuart-Smith, J. (2013) '"One of them sounds sort of Glasgow Uni-ish": Social judgements and fine phonetic variation in Glasgow', *Lingua* 122: 764–78.

Machin, D. and van Leeuwen, T. (2009) 'Toys as discourse: Children's war toys and the war on terror', *Critical Discourse Studies* 6(1): 51–63.

Mallinson, C., Childs, B. and van Herk, G. (2013) *Data Collection in Sociolinguistics: Methods and Applications*, London: Routledge.

Marcus, R. (2014) 'Edward Snowden, the Insufferable Whistleblower', *Washington Post*, 1   January   www.washingtonpost.com/opinions/ruth-marcus-snow

den-the-insufferable-whistleblower/2013/12/31/7649539a-7250-11e3-8b3f-b1666705ca3b_story.html [accessed 12 June 2014].

Marr, T. (2005) 'Language and the capital: A case study of English "language shock" among Chinese students in London', *Language Awareness* 14(4): 239–53.

Martin, L. (1986) '"Eskimo words for snow": A case study in the genesis and decay of an anthropological example', *American Anthropologist* 88: 418–23.

Mather, P-A. (2011) "The social stratification of /r/ in New York City: Labov's department store study revisited", *Journal of English Linguistics* 40(4): 338–56.

Mautner, G. (2007) 'Mining large corpora for social information: The case of elderly', *Language in Society* 36: 51–72.

Mautner, G. (2010) *Language and the market society: Critical reflections on discourse and dominance*, London: Routledge.

Mautner, G. (2012) 'Language, space and the law: A study of directive signs', *International Journal of Speech Language and the Law* 19(2): 189–217.

May, S. (2011) *Language and Minority Rights: Ethnicity, Nationalism and the Politics of Language*, 2nd edn, London: Routledge.

McArthur, T. (1987) 'The English languages?', *English Today* 3: 9–13.

McCarthy, T. (2013) 'NSA Whistleblower Edward Snowden Says US "Treats Dissent as Defection"', *The Guardian*, 1 November, www.theguardian.com/world/2013/nov/01/nsa-whistleblower-edward-snowden-letter-germany [accessed 12 June 2014].

McCulloch, G. (2014) 'A Linguist Explains the Grammar of Doge', *The Toast*, 6 February http://the-toast.net/2014/02/06/linguist-explains-grammar-doge-wow/ [accessed 12 June 2014].

McElhinny, B. (2006) 'Written in sand: Language and landscape in an environmental dispute in Southern Ontario', *Critical Discourse Studies* 3(2): 123–52.

Mendoza-Denton, N. (1996) '"Muy macha": Gender and ideology in gang girls' discourse about makeup', *Ethnos: Journal of Anthropology* 6, 47–63.

Mendoza-Denton, N. (2011) 'The semiotic hitchhiker's guide to creaky voice: Circulation and gendered hardcore in a Chicana/o gang persona', *Journal of Linguistic Anthropology* 21(2): 261–80.

Meyer, D. (2007) 'O2 Prices Force Police to Rethink Vocab', *ZDnet*, 21 February www.zdnet.com/o2-prices-force-police-to-rethink-vocab-3039285997/ [accessed 5 June 2014].

Mills, S. (2008) *Language and Sexism*, Cambridge: Cambridge University Press.

Milroy, L. (1987) *Language and Social Networks*, 2nd edn, Oxford: Basil Blackwell.

Milroy, L. and Gordon, M. (2003) *Sociolinguistics: Method and Interpretation*, Oxford: Blackwell.

Milroy, J. and Milroy, L. (1999) *Authority in Language: Investigating Standard English*, London: Taylor & Francis Ltd.

Moh, C. (2014) 'Venezuelan Ex-Beauty Queen Monica Spear Murdered', *BBC News*, 8 January www.bbc.co.uk/news/world-latin-america-25642041 [accessed 9 January 2014].

Montgomery, M. (2008) *An Introduction to Language and Society*, 3rd edn, London: Routledge.

Motschenbacher, H. (2013) 'Gentlemen before ladies? A corpus-based study of conjunct order in personal binomials', *Journal of English Linguistics* 41(3): 212–42.

Mufwene, S. (2010) 'Globalization, Global English, World Englishes', in N. Coupland (ed.) *Handbook of Language and Globalization*, Chichester: Wiley-Blackwell: 31–55.

Mullany, L. (2007) *Gendered Discourse in the Professional Workplace*, Basingstoke: Palgrave Macmillan.

Murthy, D. (2011) 'Twitter: Microphone for the masses?', *Media, Culture & Society* 33(5): 779–89.

NCTE (2002) 'Guidelines for Gender-Fair Use of Language', NCTE Position Statements on Language www.ncte.org/positions/statements/genderfairuseoflang [accessed 12 June 2014].

Nero, S. (2006) 'Language, identity, and education of Caribbean English speakers', *World Englishes* 25(3/4): 501–11.

Nirmala, M. (2013) 'Waging Propaganda War against Terrorists', *The Straits Times*, 16 December www.straitstimes.com/the-big-story/case-you-missed-it/story/waging-propaganda-war-against-terrorists-20131216?page=96 [accessed 12 June 2014].

NPIA (National Policing Improvement Agency) (2007) *AirwaveSpeak: User Guide*, NPIA: London.

Occupy Movement (2012) 'The "GlobalMay manifesto" of the International Occupy assembly', *The Guardian*, 11 May www.theguardian.com/commentisfree/2012/may/11/occupy-globalmay-manifesto [accessed 18 August 2014].

Ochs, E. and Schieffelin, B. (1994) 'Language Acquisition and Socialization: Three Developmental Stories and Their Implications', in B. G. Blound (ed.) *Language, Culture and Society: A Book of Readings*, 2nd edn, Illinois: Waveland Press: 470–512.

Ochs, E. and Taylor, C. (1992) 'Family narrative as political activity', *Discourse & Society* 3 (3): 301–40.

Ohama, M. L. F., Gotay, C. C., Pagano, I. S., Boles, L. and Craven, D. D. (2000) 'Evaluations of Hawaii creole English and standard English', *Journal of Language and Social Psychology*, 19(3), 357–77.

Orwell, G. (1968 [1946]) 'Politics and the English language', in S. Orwell and I. Angos (eds) *In Front of Your Nose 1945-50* (Vol. 4) T*he Collected Essays, Journalism and Letters of George Orwell*, New York: Harcourt, Brace, Javanovich: 127–40.

Oxford English Dictionary, online www.oed.com

Palmore, E. B. (1999) *Ageism: Negative and Positive*, New York: Springer.

Parfitt, T. (2006) 'Bizarre, Brutal and Self-Obsessed. Now Time's up for Turkmenistan's Dictator', *The Guardian*, 22 December www.guardian.co.uk/world/2006/dec/22/tomparfitt.mainsection [accessed 7 April 2009].

Parkinson, J. and Jaffe, M. (2011) 'What's In a Word? The Debate over "ObamaCare": The Name and the Law', *ABC News* (US), 18 February http://abcnews.go.com/blogs/politics/2011/02/whats-in-a-word-the-debate-over-obamacare-the-name-the-law/ [accessed 12 June 2014].

Parks, J. B. and Roberton, M. A. (2004) 'Attitudes toward women mediate the gender effect on attitudes toward sexist language', *Psychology of Women Quarterly* 28(3): 233–9.

Paton Walsh, N. (2006) 'Turkmenistan Despot Axes Pensions', *The Guardian*, 4 February www.guardian.co.uk/world/2006/feb/04/nickpatonwalsh.mainsection [accessed 7 April 2009].

Patrakar, P. (2013) 'Government to Give Licenses for Rumor Mongering', 9 September, *Faking News*, www.fakingnews.firstpost.com/2013/09/government-to-give-licenses-for-rumor-mongering/ [accessed 26 September 2013].

Pauwels, A. (2001) 'Non-sexist language reform and generic pronouns in Australian English', *English Worldwide* 22(1): 105–19.

Pauwels, A. (2003) 'Linguistic Sexism and Feminist Linguistic Activism', in J. Holmes and M. Meyerhoff (eds) *The Handbook of Language and Gender*, Oxford: Blackwell: 550–70.

Payne, A. (1980) 'Factors Controlling the Acquisition of Philadelphia Dialect by Out-of-State Children', in W. Labov (ed.) *Locating Language in Time and Space*, New York: Academic Press: 143–78.

Peccei, J. (1999) *Child Language*, London: Routledge.

Perry, K. (2014) 'Briton and His Beauty Queen Ex-Wife Killed in Front of Daughter', *The Telegraph*, 8 January www.telegraph.co.uk/news/worldnews/

southamerica/venezuela/10557539/Briton-and-his-beauty-queen-ex-wife-killed-in-front-of-daughter.html [accessed 9 January 2014].

Pettit, J., Couzens, G. and Moore-Bridger, B. (2014) 'Family's Anguish after Beauty Queen and British Ex-Husband Shot Dead in Front of Daughter, 5, in Venezuela', *London Evening Standard*, 7 January www.standard.co.uk/news/london/familys-anguish-after-beauty-queen-and-british-exhusband-shot-dead-in-front-of-daughter-5-in-venezuela-9045101.html [accessed 9 January 2014].

Phillipson, R. (2003) *English-Only Europe?: Challenging Language Policy*, London: Routledge.

Philo, G., Briant, E. and Donald, P. (2013) *Bad News for Refugees*, London: Pluto.

Pichler, P. (2009) *Talking Young Femininities*, Basingstoke: Palgrave Macmillan.

Pichler, P. and E. Eppler (eds) (2009) *Gender and Spoken Interaction*, Basingstoke: Palgrave Macmillan.

Pickles, E. (2013) 'Eric Pickles: Immigrants Must Learn English', *The Telegraph*, 13 November www.telegraph.co.uk/news/uknews/immigration/10445883/Eric-Pickles-Immigrants-must-learn-English.html [accessed 13 June 2014].

Pilkington, J. (1998) '"Don't try and make out that I'm nice!" The different strategies women and men use when gossiping' in J. Coates (ed.) *Language and Gender: A Reader*, Oxford: Blackwell: 254–69.

Piller, I. (2001) 'Identity Constructions in Multilingual Advertising', *Language in Society* 30: 153–186.

Pini, B. and Previte, J. (2013) 'Gender, class and sexuality in contemporary Australia: Representations of the Boganette', *Australian Feminist Studies* 28: 348–63.

Politics.co.uk (2013) 'Godfrey Bloom: Women are Better in the Pantry than the Car', 20 August www.politics.co.uk/news/2013/08/20/godfrey-bloom-women-are-better-in-the-pantry-than-the-car?link=related [accessed 25 June 2014].

Powell, T. (2014) '120 Dogs: Chinese Satirist's Tweet Takes All English News Media for a Ride' http://trevorpowell.com/2014/01/04/120-dogs-chinese-satirists-tweet-takes-all-english-news-media-for-a-ride/4 January [accessed 12 June 2014].

Preston, D. R. (1996) 'Whaddayaknow?: The modes of folk linguistic awareness', *Language Awareness* 5(1): 40–74.

Pullum, G. (1991) 'The Great Eskimo Vocabulary Hoax', in *The Great Eskimo Vocabulary Hoax and Other Irreverent Essays on the Study of Language*, Chicago: University of Chicago Press: 159–74.

Purnell, T. C., Idsardi, W. J. and Baugh, J. (1999) 'Perceptual and phonetic experiments on American English dialect identification', *Journal of Language and Social Psychology* 18(1): 10–30.

Quirk, R. (1990) 'Language varieties and standard language', *English Today* 6(1): 3–10.

Rahman, J. (2008) 'Middle class African Americans: Reactions and attitudes toward African American English', *American Speech* 83(2): 141–76.

Rahman, J. (2012) 'The N word: Its history and use in the African American community', *Journal of English Linguistics* 40(2): 137–71.

Rahman, T. (2009) 'Language ideology, identity and the commodification of language in the call centres of Pakistan', *Language in Society* 38: 233–58.

Rampton, B. (1995) *Crossing: Language and Ethnicity among Adolescents*, London: Longman.

Rampton, B. (1997) 'Language crossing and the redefinition of reality: Implications for research on code-switching community', *Working Papers in Urban Language and Literacies*, paper 5, Kings College www.kcl.ac.uk/schools/sspp/education/research/groups/llg/wpull.html. Also in P. Auer (ed.) (1998) *Code-Switching in Conversation, Language, Interaction and Identity*, London: Routledge: 290–317.

Rampton, B. (2011a) 'Style contrasts, migration and social class', *Journal of Pragmatics* 43: 1236–50.

Rampton, B. (2011b) 'From "Multi-ethnic adolescent heteroglossia" to "Contemporary urban vernaculars"', *Language and Communication* 31: 276–9.

Reah, D. (2002) *The Language of Newspapers* (Intertext), London: Routledge.

Richards, I. A. (1965 [1936]) *The Philosophy of Rhetoric*, Oxford: Oxford University Press.

Richinick, M. (2013) 'Obama Defends Health Care Law – and Delays It', *MSNBC* 26 September www.msnbc.com/morning-joe/obama-defends-health-care-law-and-delays-it [accessed 12 June 2014].

Roberts, J. (2004) 'Child Language Variation', in J. K. Chambers, P. Trudgill and N. Schilling-Estes (eds) *The Handbook of Language Variation and Change*, London: Blackwell: 333–48.

Romaine, S. (1978) 'Postvocalic /r/ in Scottish English: Sound Change in Progress?', in P. Trudgill (ed.) *Sociolinguistic Patterns in British English*, Baltimore, MD: University Park Press: 144–57.

Rose, D. (ed.) (2006) *'They Call Me Naughty Lola': The London Review of Books Personal Ads: A Reader*, London: Profile Books.

Rose, D. (ed.) (2010) *Sexually, I'm More of a Switzerland: More Personal Ads from the London Review of Books*, London: Scribner.

Rudder, C. (2009) 'Exactly What to Say in a First Message', 14 September http://blog.okcupid.com/index.php/online-dating-advice-exactly-what-to-say-in-a-first-message/ [accessed 16th September 2013].

Rutter, T. (2013) '#Barf – How Twitter Can Reduce the Spread of Norovirus', *The Guardian*, 11 December www.theguardian.com/public-leaders-network/2013/dec/11/twitter-reduce-spread-norovirus [accessed 9 January 2014].

Sacks, H., Schegloff, E.A. and Jefferson, G. (1974) 'A simplest systematics for the organisation of turn-taking for conversation', *Language* 50: 696–735.

Safire, W. (2008) 'Toxic Bailout', *The New York Times Magazine*, 3 October 2008. www.nytimes.com/2008/10/05/magazine/05wwln-safire-t.html [accessed 2 June 2 2009].

Sailaja, P. (2009) *Indian English: Dialects of English*, Edinburgh: Edinburgh University Press.

Sailaja, P. (2012) 'Indian English: Features and sociolinguistic aspects', *Language and Linguistics Compass* 6(6): 359–70.

Sakoda, K. and Siegel, J. (2003) *Pidgin Grammar: An Introduction to the Creole English of Hawai'i*, Honolulu: Bess Press.

Sakoda, K. and Tamura, E. H. (2008) 'Kent Sakoda discusses pidgin grammar', *Educational Perspectives* 41: 40–43.

Sankoff, G. (2005) 'Cross-Sectional and Longitudinal Studies in Sociolinguistics', in U. Ammon, N. Dittmar, K. J. Mattheier and P. Trudgill (eds) *An International Handbook of the Science of Language and Society* (Vol. 2), Berlin: Mouton de Gruyter: 1003–13.

Sankoff, D. and Laberge, S. (1978) 'The Linguistic Market and the Statistical Explanation of Variability', in D. Sankoff (ed.) *Linguistic Variation: Models and Methods*, New York: Academic Press: 239–50.

Savage, M., Devine, F., Cunningham, N., Taylor, M., Li, Y., Hjellbrekke, J., Le Roux, B., Friedman, S. and Miles, A. (2013) 'A new model of class? Findings from the BBC's Great British Class Survey Experiment', *Sociology* 47(2): 219–50.

Schilling-Estes, N. (2004) 'Constructing ethnicity in interaction', *Journal of Sociolinguistics* 8(2): 163–95.

Schleef, E. (2008) 'Gender and academic discourse: Global restrictions and local possibilities', *Language in Society* 37(4): 515–38.

Schulz, M. (1975) 'The Semantic Derogation of Women', in B. Thorne and N. Henley (eds) *Language and Sex: Difference and Dominance*, Massachusetts: Newbury House: 64–75.

Schwarz, J. (2003) 'Quantifying Non-Sexist Language: The Case of Ms', in S. Sarangi and T. van Leeuwen (eds) *Applied Linguistics and Communities of Practice*, London: Continuum: 169–83.

Scollon, R. and Scollon, S. (2003) *Discourses in Place: Language in the Material World*, London: Routledge.

Sealey, A. (2000) *Childly Language: Children, Language and the Social World*, Essex: Harlow.

Seidlhofer, B. (2009) 'Common ground and different realities: World Englishes and English as a lingua franca', *World Englishes* 28(2): 236–45.

Shankar, S. (2008) 'Speaking like a model minority: "FOB" styles, gender, and racial meanings among Desi teens in Silicon Valley', *Journal of Linguistic Anthropology* 18(2): 268–9.

Shenk, P. S. (2007) '"I'm Mexican, remember?" Constructing ethnic identities via authentication discourse', *Journal of Sociolinguistics* 11(2): 194–220.

Shon, P. C. H. (2005) '"I'd grab the S-O-B by his hair and yank him out the window": The fraternal order of warnings and threats in police–citizen encounters', *Discourse & Society* 16(6): 829–45.

Siegel, J. (2000) 'Substrate influence in Hawai'i Creole English', *Language in Society* 29: 197–236.

Silver, R. E. (2005) 'The discourse of linguistic capital: Language and economic policy planning in Singapore', *Language Policy* 4(1): 47–66.

Simon-Vandenbergen, A.-M., White, P. R. R. and Aijmer, K. (2007) 'Presupposition and "taking-for-granted" in mass communicated political argument: An illustration from British, Flemish and Swedish political colloquy', in A. Fetzer and G. Lauerbach (eds) *Political Discourse in the Media: Cross-Cultural Perspectives*, Pragmatics and Beyond New Series, Amsterdam: John Benjamins: 31–74.

Simpson, P. (1993) *Language, Ideology and Point of View*, London: Routledge.

Singh, S. (2014) 'Penguin Pulls out Wendy Doniger's Book "The Hindus" from India', *The Times of India*, 12 February www.timesofindia.indiatimes.com [accessed 12 June 2014].

Skutnabb-Kangas, T. and Phillipson, R. (2010) 'The Global Politics of Language: Markets, Maintenance, Marginalization or Murder?' in N. Coupland (ed.) *The Handbook of Language and Globalization*, Oxford: Blackwell: 77–100.

Smitherman, G. (1977) *Talkin and Testifyin: The Language of Black America* (Vol. 51), Detroit: Wayne State University Press.

Sontag, S. (1972) 'The Double Standard of Aging', *The Saturday Review*, 23 September, 29–38.

Spender, D. (1980) *Man Made Language*, London: Routledge.

Starbird, K. and Palen, L. (2010) 'Pass it On? Retweeting in Mass Emergency', *Proceedings of the 7th International ISCRAM Conference*, https://www.cs.colorado.edu/~palen/starbirdpaleniscramretweet.pdf [accessed 12 June 2014].

Stuart-Smith, J., Timmins, C. and Tweedie, F. (2007) '"Talkin" Jockney? Variation and change in Glaswegian accent', *Journal of Sociolinguistics* 11(2): 221–60.

Sutton-Spence, R. and Woll, B. (2004) 'British Sign Language', in A. Davies and C. Elder (eds) *Handbook of Applied Linguistics*, Oxford: Blackwell: 165–86.

Tagliamonte, S. (2005) '*So* who? *Like* how? *Just* what?: Discourse markers in the conversations of Young Canadians', *Journal of Pragmatics*, 37(11), 1896–1915.

Talbot, M. (1992) '"I wish you'd stop interrupting me": Interruptions and asymmetries in speakerrights in equal encounters', *Journal of Pragmatics* 18: 451–66.

Talking Cock (n.d.) Website, www.talkingcock.com [accessed 13 June 2014].

The Occupied Times (2012) 'The Global Occupy Manifesto: A Demand to be Oppressed', June 20 http://theoccupiedtimes.org/?p=5652#sthash.QAnBOz2Z.dpuf [accessed 12 June 2014].

Thelwall, M. and Stuart, D. (2007) 'RUOK? Blogging communication technologies during crises', *Journal of Computer-Mediated Communication* 12: 523–48.

Thomson, K. (2014) 'Edward Snowden, Russian Agent?' *Huffington Post*, 2 January www.huffingtonpost.com/keith-thomson/edward-snowden-russian-ag_b_4531020.html [accessed 12th June 2014].

Thornborrow, J. (2001) 'Authenticating talk: Building public identities in audience participation broadcasting', *Discourse Studies* 3(4): 459–79.

Thurlow, C. (2001) 'Talkin' 'bout my communication: Communication awareness in mid-adolescence', *Language Awareness* 10(2/3): 213–31.

Thurlow, C. with Brown, A. (2003) 'Generation txt? The sociolinguistics of young people's text-messaging', *Discourse analysis online* 1(1) http://extra.shu.ac.uk/daol/articles/v1/n1/a3/thurlow2002003-paper.html [accessed 11 November 2014].

Thurlow, C. (2006) 'From statistical panic to moral panic: The metadiscursive construction and popular exaggeration of new media language in the print media', *Journal of Computer Mediated Communication* 11(3): 667–701.

Tolson, A. (2010) 'A new authenticity? Communicative practices on YouTube', *Critical Discourse Studies* 7(4): 277–89.

Topping, A. (2013) 'Boris Johnson criticised for suggesting women go to university to find husbands', *The Guardian*, 8 July www.theguardian.com/politics/2013/jul/08/boris-johnson-women-university-husband?view=mobile [accessed 12 June 2014].

Triska, Z. (2012) 'Annoying Words: The Word "Literally" Is Literally Overused', *Huffington Post*, 12 March www.huffingtonpost.com/zoe-triska/rachel-zoe-doesnt-know-what-literally-means_b_1332462.html [accessed 4 June 2014].

Troyer, R. (2012) 'English in the Thai linguistic netscape', *World Englishes* 31(1): 93–112.

Trudgill, P. (1972) 'Sex, covert prestige and linguistic change in the urban British English of Norwich', *Language in Society* 1(2): 179–95.

Trudgill, P. (1974) *The Social Differentiation of English in Norwich*, Cambridge: Cambridge University Press.

Trudgill, P. and Hannah, J. (2002) *International English*, 4th edn, London: Routledge.

Tyler, I. (2008) '"Chav mum chav scum": Class disgust in contemporary Britain', *Feminist Media Studies* 8(1): 17–34.

Underhill, R. (1988) 'Like is, like, focus', *American Speech* 63(3): 234–46.

United Nations (1979) CEDAW, Convention on the Elimination of Discrimination Against Women www.un.org/womenwatch/daw/cedaw/text/econvention.htm [accessed 12 June 2014].

van Dijk, T. (1983) 'Discourse analysis: Its development and application to the structure of news', *Journal of Communication* 33(2): 20–43.

van Dijk, T. A. (1993) *Elite Discourse and Racism*, Newbury Park, London: Sage.

van Dijk, T. (1999) 'Discourse and the Denial of Racism', in A. Jaworski and N. Coupland (eds) *The Discourse Reader*, London: Routledge: 541–8.

van Dijk, T. (2004) 'Racist Discourse', in E. Cashmere (ed.) *Routledge Encyclopaedia of Race and Ethnic Studies*, London: Routledge: 351–5.

van Dijk, T. A. (2006) 'Discourse and manipulation', *Discourse & Society* 17(3): 359–83.

van Leeuwen, T. (2004) *Introducing Social Semiotics*, London: Routledge.

Vosamana, S. (2012) 'Gossiping is a Crime', *Fiji Times*, 16 March www.fijitimes.com/story.aspx?id=196121 [accessed 26 September].

Wagner, S. E. (2008) 'Linguistic change and stabilization in the transition from adolescence to adulthood'. Unpublished PhD dissertation, University of Pennsylvania.

Walker, D. (2004) 'Can Cartoons Animate Voters?' *BBC News*, 17 March http://news.bbc.co.uk/1/hi/magazine/3513658.stm [accessed 12 June 2014].

Warren, J. (1999) 'Wogspeak: Transformations of Australian English', *Journal of Australian Studies* 23(62): 85–94.

Washington Post (2014) 'Former Miss Venezuela Monica Spear is slain', 8 January www.washingtonpost.com/world/former-miss-venezuela-monica-spear-is-slain/2014/01/08/6c314d52-788d-11e3-af7f-13bf0e9965f6_gallery.html [accessed 9 January 2014].

Wassink, A. B. (1999) 'Historic low prestige and seeds of change: Attitudes toward Jamaican creole', *Language in Society* 28(1): 57–92.

Wassink, A. B. and Dyer, J. (2004) 'Language ideology and the transmission of phonological change changing indexicality in two situations of language contact', *Journal of English Linguistics* 32(1): 3–30.

Wee, L. (2005) 'Intra-language discrimination and linguistic human rights: The case of Singlish', *Applied Linguistics* 26(1): 48–69.

Whorf, B. L. (1954) 'The Relation of Habitual Thought and Behaviour to Language', in S. I. Hayakawa (ed.) *Language, Meaning and Maturity: Selections from Etc., a Review of General Semantics*, 1943–1953, New York: Harper: 197–215.

Wierzbicka, A. (2005) 'There are no "color universals" but there are universals of visual semantics', *Anthropological Linguistics* 47(2): 217–44.

Williams, A. and Thurlow, C. (eds) (2005) *Talking Adolescence: Perspectives on Communication in the Teenage Years* (Vol. 3), New York: Peter Lang.

Williams, F., Whitehead, J. L. and Miller, L. (1972) 'Relations between language attitudes and teacher expectancy', *American Educational Research Journal* 9(2): 263–77.

Winawer, J., Witthoft, N., Frank, M. C., Wu, L., Wade, A. R. and Boroditsky, L. (2007) 'Russian blues reveal effects of language on color discrimination', *PNAS* 104(19): 7780–5, May 8 www.pnas.org_cgi_doi_10.1073_pnas.0701644104 [accessed 19 April 2010].

Wittgenstein, L. (1963) *Tractatus Logico-Philosophicus*, D. F.Pears and B. F. McGuinness, (trans.), London: Routledge and Kegan Paul.

Wolfram, W. (1969) *A Sociolinguistic Description of Detroit Negro Speech*, Washington, DC: Center for Applied Linguistics.

Wolfram, W. (1998) 'Language ideology and dialect', *Journal of English Linguistics* 26(2): 108–21.

Wolfram, W. (2009) 'African American English', in B. B. Kachru, Y. Kachru and C. L. Nelson (eds) *The Handbook of World Englishes*, Malden, MA: Blackwell: 328–46.

Wolfram, W. and Schilling-Estes, N. (1998) *American English: Dialect and Variation*, Oxford: Wiley Blackwell.

Woods, N. (1989) 'Talking shop: Sex and status as determinants of floor apportionment in a work setting', C. Jennifer and D. Cameron (eds) *Women in Their Speech Communities*. London: Longman: 141–57.

Woods, M. (2007) 'Unnatural acts: Nuclear language, proliferation and order', *Journal of Language and Politics* 6(1): 91–128.

Wray, A. and Bloomer, A. (2012) *Projects in Linguistics and Language Studies*, 3rd edn, London: Routledge.

Wray, A., Evans, B., Coupland, N. and Bishop, H. (2003) 'Singing in Welsh, becoming Welsh: "Turfing" a "grass roots" identity', *Language Awareness* 2(1): 49–71.

Ylänne, V. (ed.) (2012) *Representing Ageing: Images and Identities*, Basingstoke: Palgrave Macmillan.

Ylänne-McEwan, V. (1999) '"Young at heart": Discourse of age identity in travel agency interaction', *Aging and Society* 19(4): 417–40.

Zhang, Qi (2013) 'The attitudes of Hong Kong students towards Hong Kong English and Mandarin-accented English', *English Today* 29(2) (Jun): 9–16.

Zhang, Y. B., Harwood, J., Williams, A., Ylänne-McEwan, V., Wadleigh, P. M. and Thimm, C. (2007) 'The portrayal of older adults in advertising: A cross national review', *Journal of Language and Social Psychology* 25(3): 264–82.

Zimmer, B., Solomon, J. and Carson, C. E. (2014) 'Among the New Words', *American Speech* 89(1): 89–110.

Index

accent 5, 18, 187; neutral 214
active voice 35, 36
actor deletion *see* agent deletion
adolescents 143–5, 148–9,
    153–5, 160–6, 187–90, 191–3;
    and computer mediated
    communication 164–6; use of
    'like' 162–4; use of multiple
    negation 161–2
advertising 45, 218–19; dating
    169–71; and media 65–7, 81,
    89, 92; and politics 43
affective tags 117
African American English 139–41,
    142, 143, 148
age 157–76; grading 163
ageism 167, 175–6
agency 60, 101, 106, 136
agent deletion 37–8, 48
AirWave Talk 34
Althusser, Louis 17–18
ARGUMENT IS WAR 32–3, 55
Aristotle 45
asymmetry, lexical 110–11; media
    64
asynchronous communication
    77–8
Australian English 5, 137–9,
    180–1, 199–200; Aboriginal
    English 151–3
authenticity 146–8, 155, 182,
    200

backchannel 119–20
because: new use of 6
Bell, Allan 72–4, 133

Blommaert, Jan 97–8, 217–18,
    229
bottom up discourse 87–9, 92–3,
    95, 101, 105–7
boundary: signs 91–2
Bourdieu, Pierre 15, 17, 194, 213
Boyce, Tammy 74–7
building codes: of language 4, 6, 8,
    10–11, 28

call centres 214
Canada 162–3, 214
child directed language 159–60,
    172
children's language 159–60
Chomsky, Noam 4, 64–6, 72
code-switching 146–7, 153–4
collocation 48, 110, 114; of 'elderly'
    167–8
colour 30–1; women's use of terms
    116
communicative competence 4, 12,
    22, 160, 164
competence 4, 22
competitive communication 122–3
computer-mediated communication
    164–5; *see also* Twitter; internet
conative 12, 13, 17
consumer/customer relationship
    32, 57–9, 173–4, 214
contrasts: rhetorical effect 46, 48,
    51, 70–1, 135–6
conversational floor 120, 122–3
cooperative communication
    119–20
Coupland, Justine 169–71

Coupland, Nikolas 172
courtesy campaign: Singapore 99–101
covert prestige 141, 179, 187, 194
creaky voice 144–5
creole 150–1, 173–4, 211–12
cultural capital 194–5, 196, 217; see also symbolic capital

de Saussure, Ferdinand 2, 21–5, 35
deaf community 196
deictic: in signs 90–1
denotation 12
descriptive: vs prescriptive 7–8
dialect 5, 140, 150–2, 182, 206; see also variety
dictionary 6–8, 10, 69
discourse 52–7, 69–70, 77, 87–9, 90–2, 100; in linguistic landscape 218–19; lesbian 129–30; racist 135–6
discourse marker 162–4, 209–10
Dixon, Robert 27–8
dude 126–8
Dyirbal 27–8
dysphemism 52

Eckert, Penelope 158, 160–1, 162, 191–3, 193–4
EFL (English as a Foreign Language) 200–1; see also global Englishes
Eisikovits, Edina 161–2
elder directed communication see elderspeak
elderspeak 171–2
English: standard 8–10, 188, 189, 195, 203–4, 217
epistemic 117, 235
ESL (English as a Second Language) 200–1, 202–6, 206–7
ethnicity 132–56
ethnographic 143, 153
ethnolect 137–41, 141–6, 149–53

ethos 45, 64
euphemism 51–2
expanding circle English 199–201, 204–5, 219
experts: and news 74–7, 103

Fairclough, Norman 2, 15, 31, 64
foreground 13, 35, 37, 48

gangs: girls 143–5
geek 7
gender 108–30; definition 108–9; expectations of 109, 116, 127–8; and power 123–6; representation of 110–11, 115–16
gender norms 116–17; men 120–3, 127–8; women 117–20, 126
generic he 111–12
geosemiotics 90; see also linguistic landscapes
given information 89
Glasgow, UK 187–8
global Englishes 198–9; linguistic markets 213; see also World Englishes
global warming 61–2
gossip 14–15, 118–22, 123
grammar 4; Dyirbal 27; prescriptive 8–9; see also English, standard

hailing 17–18
Hartley, John 59–62
hashtag 83–4
hegemonic 16, 141, 181, 214
heterosexuality 126–8, 129–30, 169
high rising terminal 137–9
higher education 57–9, 67–8; social capital of 193–4
Holmes, Janet 117
homosexuality 104, 127, 128–30
hypermedia 72

identity 134; adolescent 161, 194; and age 170, 174; and

ethnicity 136–7, 139, 141–5, 148–9, 150; lesbian 129–30; local 182; Singapore 206, 209, 217; turfing 149

Ideological State Apparatus 17

ideology 16–17, 31–2, 36; and class 178–9; and ethnicity 134; and gender 118; interpellation 17; media 64–7; politics 43; signs 99–101; toys 54–5; war 51–3; see also language ideology

imperative 12

index 90–2, 148–9, 180–1, 209, 218

Indian English 203, 210–11

in-group 136–7, 146

inner circle English 199–202, 205, 207–8, 213

internet 102–7; news 77–82; video 60

interpellation 17–18

interruptions 120, 123; in Australian Aboriginal English 151–2

intertextuality 50–1, 106

Jakobson, Roman 11–13

Jenkins, Jennifer 201, 205–6, 206–7

Johnson, Mark 32–3

journalism: ambient 104–5; citizen 82–4; see also news

Jucker, Andreas 63, 77–8

Kachru, Braj 199–200, 203–5

Lakoff, George 32–3

Lakoff, Robin 116–17

langage 22

language 1–13; as a system 22–3; see also building codes

language attitudes 14, 18, 140; and class 178, 179–80; and computer-mediated communication 164–5; global Englishes 201, 204–6, 213

language ideology see language attitudes; linguistic subordination; prescription

Lazar, Michelle 99–101

lexical asymmetry 110–11, 118

lexicographer 8

life stage 158; adolescent 160–6; early 159–60; middle 166; later 167–75

like: as discourse marker 162–4

lingua franca, core 206–7; English as 206–7

linguistic determinism 28–9, 38

linguistic diversity 26–8

linguistic landscapes 86–107, 218–19; online 102–7, 218–19

linguistic relativism 28–9

linguistic subordination 123–4, 133, 140

Lippi-Green, Rosina 205

literacy 83, 105–7, 165

literally: figurative use of 9–10

logos 45

London Review of Books 171

Lucy, John 29

Lumbee English 141–3

Manufacture of Consent 64–5

marked 16, 48; ethnicity 133–4; gender 123, 128; terms 110–12, 114

masculinity 54–5, 120–2, 187

mass media 64–5, 66, 74–7

Mautner, Gerlinde 56–7, 91–2, 167–8, 169, 176

meme 105–7

men's talk 120–3, 124–6, 126–8

metalingual 12–13

metalinguistic 178

metaphor 10, 50–1, 55–7; conceptual 32–3, 55–7, 57–9, 115

middle age see life stage

minimal response 119–20

MMR (Measles, Mumps and Rubella) 74–7

modals 117

morphology 2, 4, 53
Mufwene, Salikoko 201, 215–16
multilingualism: and nation state 134–5; on signs 96–7
multimodality 82

narrative 68, 70, 102
nation state 134
netspeak 9, 164; *see also* computer-mediated communication
new information 49, 89
news: and experts 74–7; citizen journalism 82–4; fake 14–15; fast and slow 73–4; hard and soft 73, 81; and ideology 64–8; mass media 64; online 77–82, 218–19; structure of 70–2, 79–82; Twitter 82–4; values 72–4, 81, 85
newsworthiness *see* news
nominalization 53
nuclear language 51–3

Obamacare 68–9
Occupy Movement 45–51
Ochs, Elinor 160
older people *see* life stage
other/othering 133–4, 135–6, 180–2
outer circle English 199–201, 204–5, 209–11
out-group 136–7, 146
overlaps 123; *see also* interruptions
overt prestige 141

paradigmatic 35
parallelism 46–8
parole 22–3, 25
passive voice 35–7, 48–9, 89
pathos 45
Peccei, Jean 159
performance 4, 22; of identity 109, 128–30, 141–2, 148, 178, 194
personal advertisements *see* advertising, dating
personification 56–7

persuasion 45–51
phatic 12, 120
phonetics and phonology 2, 148, 161, 166, 212
pidgin 211–12
poetic function 12–13
police 34
political correctness 38–40
politics 42–4, 59–61; toys 54–5; war 51–3
pragmatic presupposition *see* presupposition
prescription 7–8, 9–11, 208
presupposition 49–50, 57
public space 86–7, 91–2; graffiti in 101–2
public transport 90–1, 92, 99–101
Pullum, Geoff 26

racism *see* racist discourse
racist discourse 135–7
reclaiming terms 69, 115, 136–7
referential 12
repetition 47–8, 51, 62
representation 21–40, 54; of class 180–2; of elderly 168–70, 175; of ethnicity 135; of experts 74–7; and media 65–6, 68; of women 110–12
rhoticity 142–3, 183, 187–8

Sapir, Edward 26–7, 28–30
Sapir-Whorf hypothesis 26–7, 28–30
Schieffelin, Bambi 160
Scollon, Ron 90–3
Scollon, Suzi Wong 90–3
Sealey, Alison 159, 172
second linguistic relativity 217–18
semantic derogation 115–16
semantic presupposition *see* presupposition
semantic unity 69–71
semantics 2, 24–5
semiotic landscape *see* linguistic landscapes
semiotics 86, 87, 96

sex 108–9, 110–12; and age 161; and class 186
sexism 48, 112–15, 115–16
shared floor 119–20
sign 20, 21–2, 22, 24–5, 26; physical 5; *see also* linguistic landscapes
sign language 3–4, 196
signified *see* sign
signifier *see* sign
silence: in conversation 122–3, 126, 151–2; as a verb 151–2
silly citizenship 59–62, 102
Simpson, Paul 31–2, 36–7
simultaneous talk 123
Singapore 70, 216; courtesy campaign 99–101; English 205–6, 208–10, 217
Singlish, *see* Singapore, English
slut 25–6, 115
Snowden, Edward 2, 65–6
social capital 194–6, 213; *see also* symbolic capital
social class 177–8, 194–5, 207; attitudes to 179–83; and clothing 182; and community of practice 191–3; and deafness 195; linguistic variation 183–9; and power 196; and social networks 190–1
social construction *see* identity
sociolinguistic competence *see* communicative competence
space: construction of 29–30, 90–3, 96–7, 102
Speak Good English campaign Singapore 205–6
spinster 110, 115
stereotypes, age 167, 169, 171, 172–3; class 181
structuralist theory 22
student: as customer 57–9; protests (UK) 67–8
Sydney, Australia 137–8, 161–2
symbolic capital 193–4, 196; *see also* cultural capital; social capital

symbolic power 15–16
synchronous communication *see* asynchronous communication
syntagmatic 35
syntax 2, 4, 5

tag questions 117–18
teenagers *see* adolescents
terrorist 66, 70, 135–6
three part list 46–7
Thurlow, Crispin 164–6
titles 111, 112–3
top down discourse 87–9, 91, 92, 93, 95, 96, 97
toys 54–5
transgressive discourse: and signs 90, 92, 101–2, 106
transitive verbs 36
transitivity analysis 36–8
Twitter 82–4, 104

unmarked *see* marked
us/them 46, 54, 70–1, 134, 135–6, 146, 180
user generated content 83, 104

van Dijk, Teun 69, 135–6
variety: language 5–6
verbosity: of women 124–6
vocative 12

war 32–3, 51–3, 54–5; 'on terror' 70–1
Wee, Lionel 205, 206
Welsh 87–8, 97, 149
Whorf, Benjamin 26, 28–9
'wogspeak' 137–9
women's talk 116–20, 124–6, 128–30
World Englishes 199–202, 203–5, 206–7
World Wide Web 64, 102–7; *see also* internet

Ylänne, Virpi 167, 173–4
YouTube 60, 102–4